Developing Skills for Economic Transformation and Social Harmony in China

DIRECTIONS IN DEVELOPMENT
Human Development

Developing Skills for Economic Transformation and Social Harmony in China

A Study of Yunnan Province

Xiaoyan Liang and Shuang Chen

THE WORLD BANK
Washington, D.C.

© 2014 International Bank for Reconstruction and Development/The World Bank
1818 H Street NW, Washington, DC 20433
Telephone: 202-473-1000; Internet: www.worldbank.org

Some rights reserved

1 2 3 4 16 15 14 13

This work is a product of the staff of The World Bank with external contributions. Note that The World Bank does not necessarily own each component of the content included in the work. The World Bank therefore does not warrant that the use of the content contained in the work will not infringe on the rights of third parties. The risk of claims resulting from such infringement rests solely with you.

The findings, interpretations, and conclusions expressed in this work do not necessarily reflect the views of The World Bank, its Board of Executive Directors, or the governments they represent. The World Bank does not guarantee the accuracy of the data included in this work. The boundaries, colors, denominations, and other information shown on any map in this work do not imply any judgment on the part of The World Bank concerning the legal status of any territory or the endorsement or acceptance of such boundaries.

Nothing herein shall constitute or be considered to be a limitation upon or waiver of the privileges and immunities of The World Bank, all of which are specifically reserved.

Rights and Permissions

This work is available under the Creative Commons Attribution 3.0 Unported license (CC BY 3.0) http://creativecommons.org/licenses/by/3.0. Under the Creative Commons Attribution license, you are free to copy, distribute, transmit, and adapt this work, including for commercial purposes, under the following conditions:

Attribution—Please cite the work as follows: Liang, Xiaoyan, and Shuang Chen. 2013. *Developing Skills for Economic Transformation and Social Harmony in China: A Study of Yunnan Province*. Washington, DC: World Bank. doi:10.1596/978-1-4648-0079-5. License: Creative Commons Attribution CC BY 3.0

Translations—If you create a translation of this work, please add the following disclaimer along with the attribution: *This translation was not created by The World Bank and should not be considered an official World Bank translation. The World Bank shall not be liable for any content or error in this translation.*

All queries on rights and licenses should be addressed to the World Bank Publications, The World Bank, 1818 H Street NW, Washington, DC 20433, USA; fax: 202-522-2625; e-mail: pubrights@worldbank.org.

ISBN (paper): 978-1-4648-0079-5
ISBN (electronic): 978-1-4648-0080-1
DOI: 10.1596/978-1-4648-0079-5

Cover photo: Qiong Liu/Yunnan Transportation Technician College, Kunming, Yunnan, China. Further permission required for reuse.

Library of Congress Cataloging-in-Publication data has been requested.

Contents

Preface	*xiii*
Acknowledgments	*xv*
About the Authors	*xvii*
Abbreviations	*xix*

	Overview	1
	Skills Challenges: Demand, Gaps, and Mismatches	2
	Education and Training	3
	Conclusions and Policy Implications	8
Chapter 1	**Introduction**	13
	Context of Yunnan	14
	Definition and Measurement of Skills	16
	Conceptual Framework	17
	Notes	19
	Bibliography	19
Chapter 2	**Skills Challenges: Demand, Gaps, and Mismatches**	21
	Labor Market Trends in China and Yunnan	21
	Skills Composition of the Current Workforce	25
	Trends in Returns to Education	34
	Wage Returns to Skills	40
	Demand for Skills: Evidence from STEP Employer Survey	41
	Skills Gaps and Mismatches	45
	Drivers of Future Demand for Skills	49
	Summary	54
	Notes	55
	Bibliography	55
Chapter 3	**Overview of Yunnan's Education and Training System**	57
	Formal Education System	57
	Non-Formal Training	59
	Bibliography	63

Chapter 4	**Strengthening Technical and Vocational Education and Training**	**65**
	Legal and Policy Framework	65
	Governance and Management	66
	School–Industry Links	68
	Quality Assurance	71
	Curriculum Reform	79
	Employment and Pathways	81
	Financing Formal TVET	84
	Summary	95
	Bibliography	99
Chapter 5	**Non-Formal Training**	**101**
	Rural Work Force and Surplus Labor Transfer	101
	Rural-to-Urban Migration and Employment: Policy Evolution	103
	Demand for and Supply of Rural Worker Training	104
	Managing and Financing Rural Worker Training Programs	105
	Content and Delivery of Rural Labor Training	107
	Impact of Rural Training: Evidence from Honghe Prefecture	108
	Summary and Policy Implications	110
	Note	112
	Bibliography	113
Chapter 6	**Work-Based Training in Urban Yunnan**	**115**
	Demand for and Supply of Work-Based Training in Urban Yunnan	115
	Policy Framework	116
	Participation in Work-Based Training	117
	Financial Input in Work-Based Training	119
	Training Implementation in SMEs	123
	Summary and Policy Implications	124
	Bibliography	127
Chapter 7	**Developing Cognitive Skills in Schools: Lessons from PISA Shanghai 2009**	**129**
	PISA and Skills	129
	PISA Shanghai 2009	130
	Comparing School Characteristics	134
	School Characteristics and Student Performance	135
	Lessons from Shanghai	140
	Notes	143
	Bibliography	144

Chapter 8	Conclusions and Policy Implications	145
	Implications for Cross-Subsector Issues	147
	Implications for Subsector-Specific Issues	150
Appendix A	Returns to Education and Skills	153
	References	164
Appendix B	Education and Training System in Yunnan	165
	Bibliography	169
Appendix C	Honghe Rural Labor Training Impact Evaluation	171
	Technical Notes on Propensity Score Matching	173
	Bibliography	174
Appendix D	PISA Shanghai	175
	References	179

Boxes

2.1	Yunnan Non-Public Enterprise Survey, 2008	30
2.2	CHIP 1988, 1995, 2002, and RUMiC 2007	36
2.3	STEP Employer Survey 2012	42
3.1	Government Subsidies for Non-Formal Training in Yunnan	62
4.1	Overcoming Fragmented Governance of TVET: Xinjiang and Shanghai	68
4.2	APINDO, the Employer Association of Indonesia	69
4.3	Ningbo's Regulation for Promoting TVET School–Industry Collaboration	71
4.4	Vocational Education Groups in Yunnan	72
4.5	Turkey: Involving Industry and Training Providers in the Development of the National Qualification Framework (NQF)	77
4.6	Hong Kong SAR, China's Qualification Framework	78
4.7	Main Results and Outputs of the Implementation of TVET Curriculum Reform in China	80
5.1	Yunnan's Policies on Rural Worker Training, 2004–08	104
5.2	The Honghe Rural Household Survey and Analytic Sample	109
5.3	Consolidating Funds for Non-Formal Training	112
6.1	The Korean Employment Insurance System (EIS)	125
6.2	Singapore's Skills Development Fund (SDF)	126
6.3	Providing Institutional and Technical Assistance to SMEs: Korea's SME Training Consortium	127
7.1	Definitions of the PISA Domains	130
7.2	PISA Shanghai 2009	134

Figures

1.1	Contribution of Tertiary, Secondary, and Primary Sector to GDP Growth in Yunnan, 1957–2010	15

1.2	Conceptual Framework for the Study of Skills Demand and Supply in Yunnan	18
2.1	Composition of Employed Persons at Year-End by Sector in Yunnan and China, 1980–2010	22
2.2	Quarterly Number of Job Vacancies by Sector, Yunnan, 2010–11	23
2.3	Workers in Urban Areas by Ownership, Yunnan	24
2.4	Trends in Real Wages (Index 1994 = 100) of China and Yunnan	25
2.5	Real Wages (Index 1994 = 100) by Types of Ownership	26
2.6	Labor Productivity of Selected Countries	27
2.7	Labor Productivity of Yunnan Compared to Selected Provinces	27
2.8	Education Composition of the Employed, Yunnan and China, 2001–10	28
2.9	Proportion of Total Employed with Upper Secondary or Tertiary Education in China by Province, 2010	29
2.10	Education Composition of Male and Female Workers in Yunnan, 2010	29
2.11	Educational Attainment by Human Resources Type, 2008	32
2.12	Education Composition in Non-Public Enterprises by Industry, 2008	33
2.13	Share of Certified Workers by Type and Level, 2008	33
2.14	Share of Certified Workers at Medium and Senior Level in Non-Public Enterprises, 2008	34
2.15	Percent Change in Wages Relative to Middle School Graduates, Yunnan and China, 1998–2012	38
2.16	Changes in Marginal Returns to Education in the 1990s in Latin America	39
2.17	Number of Workers 12 Months Ago, Currently, and Expected in 12 Months	42
2.18	Percent of Firms Reporting Various Job-Related Skills as Important to Employee Retention	43
2.19	Percent of Firms Reporting Various Personality Traits as Important to Employee Retention	44
2.20	Percent of Firms Reporting Various Factors as Important to Employee Retention	45
2.21	Firms Facing Factors Constraining Growth in Yunnan and China, 2005	46
2.22	Rankings of Labor Factors Impeding Business Operation and Growth	46
2.23	Percent of Employees Considered Qualified for Their Jobs	47
2.24	Quarterly Job Vacancies and Applications in Yunnan, 2010–11	47
2.25	Percent of Firms Encountering Problems Hiring Employees at Various Levels	48
2.26	Real GDP and Number of People Employed in Yunnan, Real and Projected, 1957–2015	51
2.27	Real GDP and Employment by Sector, 1957–2008	52

3.1	Structure of the Formal Education System, Yunnan	58
3.2	Advancement Rates Across Cities and Prefectures	60
4.1	Horizontal Arrangements of TVET, Yunnan	67
4.2	Vertical Arrangements of TVET, Yunnan	67
4.3	Pathways Taken by Secondary TVET Graduates in Yunnan, 2008	82
4.4	Public Spending on Education as a Share of Total Government Spending, 2010	86
4.5	International Comparison of Yunnan's Public Expenditure on Education, 2009	87
4.6	Budgetary Recurrent Expenditure per Student by Level of Education in Yunnan, 2010	89
4.7	Budgetary Recurrent Expenditure per Student on Secondary TVET, 2009	89
4.8	Budgetary Recurrent Expenditure per Student in Yunnan, 2009	90
4.9	Total Budgetary and Nonbudgetary Expenditure by Level of Schooling in Yunnan, 2009	91
4.10	Household Income and Educational Expenditure in Yunnan, 2010	92
4.11	Perceptions of Financial Burden Posed by Education Expenditures in Yunnan, 2010	93
4.12	Gross Enrollment Ratio in Yunnan at Upper Secondary Level by City and Prefecture, 2010	94
4.13	Student-Teacher Ratio Compared to Recurrent Expenditure per Student in Yunnan, 2010	96
4.14	Operating Conditions of Secondary TVET Institutions in Yunnan, 2010	97
5.1	Number of Workers in Rural Areas and Share of Total Employment in Yunnan, 1978–2010	102
5.2	Demand for and Supply of Rural Labor Training	105
6.1	Demand for and Supply of Work-Based Training in Urban Yunnan	116
6.2	Percentage of Employees Receiving Training, China and Various Cities, Histogram and k-Density Plot	118
6.3	Provision and Duration of Training on the Premises of the Workplace, Kunming	120
6.4	Percent of Workers Receiving Employer-Organized Formal Training Outside the Workplace	121
6.5	Percent of Wage Bill and Compensation Fund Spent by Firms on Outside Training Providers	122
6.6	Average Amount Spent per Employee on External Training Providers	122
B6.1.1	Evolution of Vocational Training Funding Schemes in Korea	125
B6.1.2	Transformation of Korea's Vocational Training System	126
7.1	University Participation at Age 21 by PISA Reading Proficiency at Age 15 in Canada, 2009	131

7.2	PISA Reading Performance of Shanghai and OECD Countries, 2009	132
7.3	Proportion of Resilient Achievers and Disadvantaged Low Achievers	133
7.4	Per Student Expenditure at the Pre-Primary Level, Yunnan	143
7.5	Enrollment Rates in Pre-Primary Schools, Yunnan	143

Tables

2.1	Total Number of Staff and Workers at Year-End in Yunnan by Industry, 2007 and 2010	23
2.2	Number of People Employed in Non-Public Enterprises, by Industry and Occupation, 2008	31
2.3	Rates of Return to Schooling, Yunnan and China, 1988–2012	37
2.4	Percent of Firms Encountering Hiring Problems, Type A Occupations	49
2.5	Percent of Firms Encountering Hiring Problems, Type B Occupations	49
2.6	Selected Goals Specified in Yunnan's 12th Five-Year Plan	50
2.7	Projected Demand for Skills in Yunnan, 2010–20	53
3.1	Impressions of the TVET and General Education Systems, Yunnan	61
4.1	Extent of School-Enterprise Collaboration, Kunming	70
4.2	Standards for the Setup of Secondary and Tertiary TVET Institutions, Yunnan	73
4.3	Selected Teacher Qualifications and Standards for Secondary and Tertiary TVET Institutions	74
4.4	Provinces Meeting the Establishment Standards for Secondary TVET by Region, 2009	75
4.5	Provinces Meeting the Establishment Standards for Tertiary TVET by Region, 2009	76
4.6	Comparison of ISCO-08 and China's Occupational Classifications by Major Groups	76
4.7	Year-End Employment Rates in Yunnan, 2010	83
4.8	Private Provision of Education in Yunnan, 2010	91
4.9	Comparison of Enrollment Rates and Advancement Rates in Yunnan and China, 2010	93
4.10	Selected Standards for Secondary TVET Institutions in Yunnan, 2010	94
4.11	Selected Standards for Tertiary TVET Institutions in Yunnan, 2010	95
5.1	Major Training Programs for Rural Workers in Yunnan	106
5.2	Content and Provision of Rural Worker Training Programs in Yunnan	107

B5.2.1	Training in Rural Honghe	109
5.3	Estimated Effects of Training on Net Income per Person, 2007 and 2008	110
7.1	Mean PISA Scores, Shanghai and OECD, 2009	131
7.2	PISA Scores of Schools in Shanghai and OECD Average	134
7.3	Characteristics and Performance of Middle Schools	136
7.4	Characteristics and Performance of General High Schools	138
7.5	Characteristics and Performance of Vocational Schools	140
A.1	Estimates of Rates of Return to Education in Urban China	154
A.2	Estimates of Rates of Return to Education in Urban Yunnan	156
A.3	Description of the Weighted Analytic Sample from STEP Household Survey, Kunming, 2012	158
A.4	Estimates of Rates of Return to Education, Kunming, 2012	158
A.5	Rates of Return to Education by Gender, Ownership, and Ethnicity	159
A.6	Definitions of Variables Used in the Analysis, STEP Household Survey 2012	160
A.7	Estimates of Wage Returns to Cognitive and Technical Skills, Kunming, 2012	162
A.8	Estimates of Wage Returns to Non-Cognitive Skills, Kunming, 2012	163
B.1	Number of Students Admitted, Enrolled, and Graduated in Yunnan, 2010	165
B.2	Training Duration, Certification Rates, and Employment Rates by Training Providers in Yunnan, 2009	165
B.3	Formal Technical and Vocational Education and Training Provision in Yunnan, 2010	166
B.4	Sources of Financing for Education in Yunnan and China, 2009	166
B.5	Recurrent Budgetary Expenditures per Student by Level of Education, 2010	167
B.6	Total and Rural Budgetary Expenditure per Student in Yunnan, 2009	167
B.7	Per Student Expenditure in Yunnan and China, 2009	168
C.1	Tracing Households with and without Training in 2006	172
C.2	Selected Characteristics of Households with and without Training	173
D.1	PISA Shanghai 2009 Sample Description	175
D.2	Variables and Definitions Used in the PISA Analysis	176
D.3	Comparison of Student Backgrounds by Type of School	177
D.4	Comparison of Student Backgrounds in Model and Experimental High Schools and General High Schools	177
D.5	Comparison of School Characteristics	178
D.6	Comparison of School-Level Characteristics of Model and Experimental vs. General High Schools	179

Preface

The World Bank has a long history of investing in China's technical and vocational education and training (TVET), dating back to the 1963 Higher Education Project, which benefited selected tertiary TVET programs in project schools. The initial World Bank projects for TVET in China were designed mostly on the national level, supporting selected institutions in multiple provinces. Examples of such projects include the Vocational Education Project I, the Vocational Education Project II, the Labor Market Development Project, and the Migrant Training Project.

Starting in 2006, based on strong analytical work and increased demand from various provinces, the World Bank began a direct policy dialogue with interested provinces, and in turn started supporting provincial level projects in TVET. These include the Guangdong Technical and Vocational Education Project and the Liaoning and Shandong Technical and Vocational Education Project, both of which are currently under implementation. Progress to date indicates that sub-national lending tends to result in more focused and efficient policy dialogue and project implementation, especially when a good national policy framework is in place and provincial "good practices" are sought. In particular, the World Bank is able to fill an important gap by introducing international experience and innovation in school-based reforms, spreading such reforms within and outside the project provinces, supporting learning activities to capture lessons from reforms, and informing government policies and investments in the sector.

In 2010, through the Ministry of Finance and the National Development and Reform Commission, the World Bank received a project proposal from the Yunnan Department of Education for a US$50 million loan to support the development of TVET in the province. Both the provincial counterparts and the World Bank team felt the need to first develop a common knowledge base to help design the lending operation. As a result, the Yunnan Department of Education requested that the World Bank conduct a background study for the Yunnan Technical and Vocational Education and Training Project. As a result of consultation with their counterparts and within the World Bank, the scope of the study was broadened beyond a review of the formal TVET system to include skills-demand analysis and a review of the work-based and non-formal training systems.

The study is aimed at facilitating policy development leading to a demand-driven, high-quality, and equitable education and training system conducive to lifelong learning. The experience of Yunnan also sheds light on skills development in China, as the analysis in this report situates Yunnan in the broader national context. The intended audience includes policy makers in the Ministries of Education, Human Resources and Social Security, Agriculture, and Finance, and the Poverty Alleviation Office and National Development and Reform Commission. The report would also be of interest to researchers and development workers interested in understanding skills development in China.

Acknowledgments

The design and preparation of the study was led by the task team leader, Xiaoyan Liang (Senior Education Specialist, East Asia and Pacific, Human Development Sector [EAP HD], Education Sector [ES] Unit), under the guidance of Xiaoqing Yu (Director, EAP HD) and Luis Benveniste (Sector Manager, EAP HD, ES Unit). The report was co-authored by Xiaoyan Liang and Shuang Chen (consultant), with significant contributions from a few researchers who partnered with us to carry out background studies:

Prof. Xingxu Li of the Yunnan University of Finance and Economics conducted the initial analysis and background study on the Honghe Rural Training Impact Evaluation. He has also given us access to Yunnan's 2008 Survey of Nonstate Enterprises. Under the leadership of Prof. Li, the Yunnan University of Finance and Economics was contracted to implement the STEP (Skills Toward Employment and Productivity) Household Survey and the STEP Employer Survey. Their excellent work in the field has provided this report with the most up-to-date and first-hand data.

The Shanghai Academy of Educational Services, under the leadership of Director Shuchao Ma, Vice-Director Yang Guo, and Mr. Chen Zhang, conducted a review of the implementation and outcomes of the TVET (technical and vocational education and training) curriculum reforms in Guangdong, Liaoning, Shandong, Yunnan, and Shanghai. The Academy also provided us with data on the financing, standards, and status of TVET.

Prof. Linlin Pu, Prof. Xing Dong, and Dr. Fang Lu from the Yunnan National University were the principal investigators for the World Bank's Systems Approach for Better Education Results–Workforce Development (SABER-WfD) benchmarking study. Their input in the data collection instrument has provided critical information for analyzing Yunnan's TVET system.

Dr. Zhenyi Guo conducted a background study on work-based training and rural labor training and allowed us to use her related research as an input for the work-based training chapter.

Mr. Bo Yun, Mr. Haijun Liu, and Ms. Yaqin Li, from the Yunnan Academy of Educational Sciences, prepared a background report on the status of TVET in Yunnan.

Further, the report benefitted from upstream review by Prof. Simpson Poon from the Technological and Higher Education Institute of Hong Kong and the

Hong Kong Vocational Training Council, and by Prof. Sung Joon Paik from the Korea Development Institute School of Public Policy and Management. Within the World Bank, peer reviewers, including Jee-peng Tan (Advisor), Mamta Murti (Advisor), and Andreas Blom (Lead Education Specialist, Africa Region), provided valuable comments. Former EAP Sector Manager Eduardo Bustillo Velez also provided constructive feedback. Emanuela Di Gropello (Sector Leader, Africa, Human Development) advised the team on the initial conceptual framework. Dewen Wang (Social Protection Economist, EAP HD Sector, SP Unit) offered valuable input on non-formal training and training funds. Harry Patrinos (Sector Manager, Human Development [HD] Network, Education Team) gave comments on the initial analysis of the PISA (Programme for International Student Assessment) data.

The study benefitted from a multidonor trust fund for the data collection and analysis of the STEP Household and Employer Surveys. The HD Network's Education and Social Protection teams, led by Maria Laura Sanchez-Puerta and Alexandria Valerio, provided excellent technical assistance and other support both to the Bank team and the local implementers.

Finally, the study would not have been possible without the support and collaboration from the officials in the Yunnan Provincial Department of Education, who demonstrated ample commitment and professionalism. Officials and colleagues in the Yunnan Department of Human Resources and Social Security, Poverty Alleviation Office, and Provincial Research Institute also provided valuable inputs.

About the Authors

Xiaoyan Liang is a senior education specialist in the World Bank's East Asia and Pacific Region Human Development Department. Ms. Liang formally joined the World Bank's Young Professionals Program in 1998, after having obtained a doctor of education degree from Harvard University. Since then she has led policy dialogue and managed education programs in many countries in Africa, Latin America, and East Asia Regions. Ms. Liang has wide-ranging research and operational expertise and interests including early childhood education, technical and vocational education and skills development, higher education, science and technology, education finance, and teacher education. Currently, Ms. Liang is leading the World Bank's China education program, which focuses on skills development and early childhood education.

Shuang Chen is a former consultant with the World Bank. She currently works as a junior program officer for the International Household Survey Network/Accelerated Data Program at OECD/PARIS21. She holds a master's degree in international educational administration and policy analysis and a bachelor's degree in mathematics with honors in education from Stanford University.

Abbreviations

ATC	average treatment effect on the controls
ATE	average treatment effect
ATT	average treatment effect on the treated
CHIP	China Household Income Project
EIS	employment insurance system
ESCS	economic, social and cultural status
GDP	gross domestic product
GER	gross enrollment ratio
HEI	Higher Education Institution
HRSS	Human Resources and Social Security
ICA	Investment Climate Assessment
ISCO	International Standard Classification of Occupations
ITACs	Industry Training Advisory Committees
NDRC	National Development and Reform Commission
NQF	National Qualification Framework
OECD	Organisation for Economic Co-operation and Development
PISA	Programme for International Student Assessment
PPP	purchasing power parity
R&D	research and development
RPL	recognition of prior learning
RUMiC	Longitudinal Survey on Rural Urban Migration in China
SAR	Special Administrative Region
SCS	specification of competency standards
SDF	Skill Development Fund
SMEs	small and medium-sized enterprises
SOEs	state-owned enterprises
STEP	Skills Toward Employment and Productivity
TVET	Technical and Vocational Education and Training
UNDP	United Nations Development Programme

Overview

China has achieved impressive growth over the last three decades and has now become the second-largest economy in the world. To sustain its growth, China is transitioning from an investment-led, high-carbon growth model to a consumption-led, green growth model, less reliant on low-cost manufacturing and more on technology and innovation. Skills development has been a key factor enabling China's unprecedented growth and will continue to play a vital role in sustaining its ongoing economic transformation and pursuit of a harmonious society.

Located on the southwestern border of China, Yunnan is a medium-sized Chinese province with abundant natural resources and high levels of ethnic diversity. Although Yunnan is still one of the poorest provinces in China, it has experienced rapid economic growth rates over the last decade and is expected to maintain an annual growth rate of 10 percent or higher. The recent national Bridgehead Strategy has further positioned Yunnan as a strategic gateway in the Southwest region, providing tremendous new opportunities for its development. Is Yunnan ready to meet the skills challenges posed by rapid economic growth? What critical skills are needed for workers to help achieve Yunnan's economic and social transformation? Is Yunnan's current education and training system capable of supplying sufficient and relevant skills demanded by the economic and social transformation?

This report consists of three parts. The first part, *Skills Challenges: Demand, Gaps, and Mismatch*, examines the sources of the mismatch of supply and demand for skilled labor in Yunnan. The second part, *Education and Training*, sets out the challenges facing Yunnan as it seeks to strengthen the Technical and Vocational Training and Education (TVET) system, improve access to education and the quality of educational outputs, encourage more robust work-based and rural training, and invest additional resources in general education. Finally, in *Conclusions and Policy Implications*, the report lays out specific policy proposals that cross both sector lines and address sector-specific issues.

Skills Challenges: Demand, Gaps, and Mismatches

Yunnan is primarily an agricultural economy and rural society. Currently over 60 percent of workers are still engaged in the agricultural sector, compared to the national average of 37 percent. Over the last decade, however, the share of employment in the secondary and tertiary sectors has been on the rise. The tertiary sector has seen the fastest growth in employment. Within the secondary sector, employment in mining and construction has also maintained strong growth. Further, after three decades of opening up and attendant economic development, the non-public sector now generates almost half of total urban employment, as the share of employment in state-owned enterprises and collectives has dropped significantly.

The labor force in Yunnan generally possesses low levels of education and skills. The majority of the workers have completed only nine years of compulsory education or less. Skills certification rates are also low among professional and technical workers and operative frontline workers. In non-public enterprises, only about 24 percent of the professional and technical workers and 12 percent of operative frontline workers have obtained skills certification or professional ranking. Consequently, Yunnan workers have on average lower wages and productivity than the national average.

Even with rapid large-scale education expansion and reform, average rates of return to education have risen from 3 percent in 1988 to 7 percent in 2002. The most dramatic increase has occurred at the tertiary level. Bachelor's degree holders earned 79 percent more than middle school graduates in 2002, and the gap is even larger among workers in urban Kunming as of 2012. Gaps in returns have been widening between tertiary and secondary education and between Bachelor's degrees and associate degrees. The trend is similar to patterns found across China, indicating strong and growing demand for workers with tertiary education. Although returns to secondary TVET were historically higher than those to general high school, at the upper secondary level our data suggest that the gaps are narrowing in recent years, implying that the secondary high school degree and TVET degree are less distinguished in Yunnan's labor market.

Selected cognitive, technical, and non-cognitive skills are associated with higher wages even after controlling for educational attainment. In particular, workers who perform at higher levels of reading and writing tend to have higher earnings. Their jobs tend to be more cognitively challenging and autonomous. Computer and foreign language skills are associated with higher wages across and within occupations and sectors. In addition, workers who are more creative and open to new challenges also earn significantly more even after controlling for their technical and cognitive skills and educational attainment.

From the employers' perspective, high-skilled professionals, technicians, and operative workers are in high demand. In deciding which employees to retain after a probation period, employers consider non-cognitive skills such as "communication skills" and "leadership skills" along with job-specific technical skills to be the most important.

The latest policy developments, as laid out in Yunnan's 12th Five-Year Plan, are expected to further drive the demand for skills. Projected economic growth, together with the structural adjustment within and across sectors, will create more demand for workers in the secondary and tertiary sectors. More importantly, the successful implementation of the Bridgehead Strategy, which would help Yunnan further accelerate its growth and open up to neighboring countries and provinces, relies on an abundant supply of highly skilled professionals and technical workers.

Faced with an increasing demand for skills, especially for professional and technical workers and operative frontline workers, the stock of skills among Yunnan's current labor force appears insufficient. Skills gaps have become more apparent. Throughout 2010 and 2011, only 35–45 percent of the job openings in Yunnan were filled, and only 50–55 percent of job applicants were hired. The vast majority of firms surveyed in Kunming considered "difficulties with finding experienced workers" and the "technical and vocational education and training of workers" to be the most problematic labor factors inhibiting business growth. The lack of required skills has been the most commonly cited problem in hiring for both highly skilled professionals and technical occupations, as well as operative frontline positions. In addition, the mismatch of wage expectations poses a major issue for firms hiring high-skilled managers, professionals, and technicians. For construction workers and operative frontline jobs, lack of applicants is an issue.

Education and Training

Yunnan has a more than sufficient supply of labor, yet the large population does not possess a high stock of skills. As the shortage of high-skilled workers becomes more apparent, Yunnan also faces a surplus of low-skilled laborers, especially among the 65 percent of its population still residing in rural areas. An imbalance in the demand and supply of skills exists in almost all country contexts. It is imperative to develop an education and training system that is responsive to the ever-changing demand from the economy and society at large.

This report identifies challenges associated with the need to improve the four major areas of the education and training system: (1) the formal TVET system; (2) non-formal training; (3) work-based training; and (4) general school education.

Challenges to Strengthening the Formal TVET System

Governance and Management: The legal framework for the TVET sector in Yunnan adheres closely to Chinese national laws and regulations. A relatively complete set of legal instruments ensures education and training rights for all citizens and provides direction for governance and management, quality assurance arrangements, financing of TVET, and collaborating with enterprises.

The Ministries of Education and Human Resources and Social Security are the two departments substantially in charge of the management of all TVET, with the former responsible for all secondary and tertiary educational institutions and the latter responsible for vocational training institutions. The Ministry of Education considers itself the overall leader for coordinating system reform in TVET. Interdepartmental TVET Coordination Committees have been established at the national level and in a few provinces in an effort to overcome fragmentation. In reality, these committees are advisory with little executive power, and membership is restricted to government officials. Industry and social groups have little formal representation in the management of the TVET system or in the running of public TVET schools.

School–Industry Links

The involvement of industry in the governance and management of TVET institutions would provide school leaders with crucial support in developing programs to provide the skills that enterprises need. With industry participation, students could gain relevant workplace skills before graduation. Currently, at the school level, collaboration with industry is often ad hoc and dependent on personal connections. Collaboration tends to be limited to recruiting graduates or providing internships and training. Efforts to establish formal school–industry links through school–industry collaboration advisory committees and sector-specific advisory committees have recently started to emerge with support from the national model TVET school project and development partners such as the World Bank. Very few enterprises, however, are involved in the development of training programs.

Curriculum Reform

In recent years, schools have become more aware of the need to develop programs that are aligned with the demands of the labor market and society and have started to update their curriculums accordingly. A lack of up-to-date and industry-led competency-based standards at the system level, however, hampers curriculum reform at the school level. The development by individual schools with their own set of standards for teaching may be a practical solution in the short term. However, in the long run, Yunnan would be better served by a systematic province-wide approach to developing competency-based standards with input from industry that schools can use as the basis for curriculum development. Lack of resources at the school level has further impeded the successful implementation of curriculum reform. Schools are constrained by teacher capacity, high student-teacher ratios, and outdated facilities and equipment.

Quality Assurance

There is no independent accreditation agency for training providers. Administrative departments of the Ministries of Education and Human Resources and Social Security have recently updated the standards for establishing TVET institutions on both the secondary and tertiary levels to reflect the government's most recent talent development plans. Although the standards are comprehensive and specific to each type of institution, they reflect educational "inputs," including physical space, equipment per student, student-teacher ratios, and the proportion of instructors who obtain the double qualification of teacher qualifications and technical skills certificates, rather than the "outputs" of specific skills training and certifications. In reality, some institutions, particularly secondary TVET institutions located in rural areas, continue to have difficulty meeting the standards.

Skills Certification
An increasing number of students are required to obtain skills certifications in addition to their academic diplomas. The occupational classification and competency standards for each occupation, however, have not kept up with the evolving demands of the market. Evidence shows that existing skills certificates do not carry much weight among employers; indeed, the most recent quarterly job vacancy data show that only about 20 percent of job openings in Yunnan require a skills certification. Only a minority of existing workers in Yunnan have obtained certification.

Financing
Yunnan's level of total public spending on education is high compared to other provinces and even to some developed countries. Yunnan allocates over 6 percent of its gross domestic product and over 19 percent of total government spending to education as compared to less than 4 percent and about 16 percent, respectively, nationwide. Yet, owing to the large number of students in its educational system and low level of economic development, expenditure per student in Yunnan is lower than the national average at every level of education. Overall resources appear insufficient.

There are huge disparities in education financing between rural and urban Yunnan. As education finance is decentralized to local governments, including TVET at the secondary level, schools in poor rural areas struggle to cover both personnel and operating costs. Particularly hard hit are rural vocational high schools in Yunnan. Province-wide, rural vocational high schools average a per pupil expenditure of Y2,333, which is less than two-thirds of the provincial average of Y3,960. Special funds for TVET from provincial and national governments are awarded to provide incentives and motivation to improve quality and innovation. However, these funds tend to be allocated based on the quality of the proposals submitted, which results in resource-rich schools benefiting disproportionately more than resource-poor schools. Although competitively awarded funds can be effective in promoting quality improvement in the long term, it is important to consider equity-based financing in the short term to bring all schools to a minimum level of inputs and standards. The rural vocational high schools across China and Yunnan will need renewed policy direction and favorable financing from the provincial and central governments in order to close the resource gap and enable all to participate on a level playing field with the rest of the country.

Private provision of TVET in Yunnan is emerging with 12 percent of secondary TVET students and 25 percent of tertiary TVET students enrolling in private institutions. Yunnan can explore expanding the private provision of training, particularly at the tertiary level, that is, beyond its current level to mobilize additional resources and to have a healthy dose of "competition" in the system. Across both public and private institutions, the level of private spending on TVET in Yunnan remains lower than the national average. In this context, private support could be more strongly mobilized.

Challenges to Improving Access and Quality of Non-Formal Training

Non-formal education and training constitutes a significant safety net and provides second chances for those who have left the formal TVET system. In Yunnan's context, a significant number of unskilled rural surplus laborers, accounting for a third of its rural population, need to be trained and transferred to the secondary or tertiary sectors. Those who remain in the farming sector must upgrade their skills to boost agricultural productivity.

Both the central and provincial governments have introduced a number of training and employment schemes targeted at rural surplus labor. Our quantitative evaluation using propensity score matching has illustrated the positive and statistically significant effect of those training programs: Rural households who participated in training in 2006 earned 26 percent more income per person in 2007 and 11 percent more income per person in 2008 than if they did not participate. On average, having household members attend training increases the net income per person in 2007 and 2008 by over 20 percent.

Our analysis has shown the economic returns of rural labor training—in particular highlighting that, although training is given to individual household members, the effect of training seems to spill over to the net income of the entire family. However, implementation of rural labor training faces a number of challenges.

First, financial input in rural labor training appears insufficient, directly affecting the quality of training delivery. For example, due to the relatively short duration of most training programs, the skills acquired through training are rather limited. Guidance training, the main form of rural worker training, covers only basic work- and living-related orientation for rural workers before migration. Only a quarter of all the training programs actually equip participants with practical skills.

Second, participation rates in rural training are low. Many rural laborers do not have the minimum education level (usually completion of middle school) required by certain training programs. Some are unaware of the value of training, and some are concerned that the training might take too much of their time away from their paid agricultural activities. Households in ethnic minority villages are also less likely to participate.

Third, given the low educational attainment of the rural training participants, training materials should be tailored to their specific needs and should bridge the gaps between their lack of preliminary knowledge and necessary skills.

Finally, because multiple agencies are involved in the management, financing, and delivery of non-formal training, there is a lack of coordinated policy and implementation. Regular monitoring and evaluation of the programs is also missing.

Challenges to Incentivizing and Supporting Firms to Provide Work-Based Training

Enterprises play an important role in training and upgrading the skills of their employees. Globally available evidence demonstrates that investment in work-based training is correlated with higher firm productivity. Before the economic reform, work-based training was provided by the government in state-owned enterprises. The government's role now, however, is more that of a regulator than a provider. Most recently, the Chinese government stipulated that enterprises devote 1.5–2.5 percent of their total wage bill to employee training. However, compliance with the law and the details of its implementation are left very much in the hands of the enterprises themselves. As a result, how and the extent to which work-based training is provided varies greatly.

Although survey results indicate that more than 90 percent of the firms in Yunnan and in China overall have provided training, the majority of enterprises in Yunnan have provided training to fewer than 10 percent of their employees. Most training is conducted in-house by firm managers, technical personnel, or peers, or through on-the-job learning. Very few firms have paid external trainers to conduct training.

Small and medium-sized enterprises find it particularly difficult to comply with the requirement that 1.5–2.5 percent of payroll be spent on training. Financial constraints aside, the capacity and willingness to provide employee training are major issues. It is thus important for the government to assess the particular needs of these enterprises and employ different incentive and subsidizing mechanisms, instead of relying solely on compulsory requirements.

The relevance and quality of training are also called into question. Strategic planning for upgrading skills, particularly among small and medium-sized enterprises, is lacking. Thus, technical assistance, in addition to financial assistance, is needed to enable firms to conduct training-needs assessments and develop training plans. A monitoring and evaluation system also needs to be in place for quality assurance.

Challenges to Investing in General Education for the Development of Cognitive Skills

Cognitive skills form the core part of skill sets required by the economy and society as a whole. Drawing on 2009 data from the Shanghai Programme for International Student Assessment (PISA), we investigated what school-level characteristics correlate with higher cognitive skills among 15-year-olds, including mathematical, reading, and science skills, as measured by PISA. We then examined Yunnan's school systems in light of lessons learned from Shanghai.

Shanghai's experience shows that school resources matter. School resources include instructional resources and facilities, as well as the extracurricular activities available to students. They also include abundant teacher resources, high rates of good teacher qualifications, and supportive student-teacher relations. Shanghai's experience also suggests that teacher involvement in decision making about a school's resource allocation and curriculum might be beneficial for both general high schools and vocational schools.

Lessons from Shanghai also show the benefits of pre-primary education on students' subsequent cognitive skill development. Children who have attended pre-primary schools for at least one year perform significantly better across all subjects on PISA. Currently, however, participation in pre-primary education is limited in Yunnan and varies greatly across cities and prefectures. Investing in and popularizing pre-primary education in Yunnan might be a cost-effective way to develop cognitive skills in early youth.

Conclusions and Policy Implications

The Chinese TVET system is vast and complicated. Every reform effort, such as curriculum development and teacher training, has enormous resource implications. Accordingly, developing and implementing a set of centralized policies poses enormous challenges, especially for a resource-constrained province like Yunnan. The analyses in the report reveal certain policy gaps and challenges that have hampered Yunnan's education and training system from operating at its full potential. In light of global trends, the report offers a broad set of policy recommendations.

A number of policy areas such as governance and coordination, industry participation, quality assurance, financing, and monitoring and evaluation cut across sectors and pertain not just to the formal TVET system, but also to non-formal education, and even to work-based training. Specific recommendations for non-formal training, work-based training, especially for small and medium enterprises, and pre-primary education follow.

Implications for Cross-Subsector Issues
Governance and Coordination

The effective functioning of all TVET subsectors could be improved by greater coordination among the relevant stakeholders in government, education, and industry.

In the short- and medium-term, it is feasible to develop and strengthen the role of existing coordination mechanisms, such as the creation of Interdepartmental TVET Coordination Committees, in areas such as policy development, planning, and service delivery at both the provincial and local levels. The operations of Yunnan's committee could be regularized and the committee's functioning improved.

In the long term, Yunnan might consider consolidating policy making, planning, financing, and service delivery of TVET into a central government agency, such as a new Skills Development Authority, or, alternatively, into one of the existing ministries. This would eliminate the distinction between schools governed by the Ministry of Education and those governed by the Ministry of Human Resources and Social Security, as Shanghai has already done for its secondary TVET institutions.

Consolidated governance and management may be even more pertinent for non-formal training, which currently appears to be even more fragmented and less structured. The strongly vested interests of various stakeholders in this sector may mean that consolidation will be a long-term effort.

Industry Participation

Industry and employer involvement can play a key role in ensuring that the educational and training system, especially at the TVET level, is responsive to the demand side of the skills equation. Emerging industry participation has yet to be systematically incorporated into the governance structure of any of the education and training sectors. Industry involvement should be institutionalized and expanded to include a diverse range of issues related to skills development, including setting skills development priorities, developing competency standards for skills certification, allocating resources, and making policies regarding work-based training. In many countries, employer- or industry-based bodies participate at different levels, providing advice, taking part in setting development strategies, voicing the needs and demands of industry, and even exerting decision-making power.

At the school level, Yunnan could introduce a legal framework and implementation guidelines to promote school–industry collaboration. The framework and regulations should establish the rights and obligations of employers, schools, teachers, students, and all relevant stakeholders in the school–industry partnership.

Similar principles are applicable to non-formal education and work-based training. For example, industry and employers could be further involved in managing work-based training funds, designing training programs, and assessing training participants.

Quality Assurance

Under an effective qualifications framework, skills certifications are demanded by employers and sought by students and employees. Certifications are accepted measures of competency and substantive learning. A well-developed framework could address both accreditation of providers and certification of learners.

The existing qualifications framework needs to be updated with standards and competencies that reflect the demands of the labor market. Competency standards for occupations and skills certification should be based on input from industry, employers, education and training providers, and other stakeholders. An effective qualifications framework can also facilitate recognition of non-formal learning, integrating different kinds of non-formal education and training, and improving their quality and efficiency. The qualifications framework should respect all forms of learning, that is, learners should be assessed on the basis of competencies rather than credentials, and the framework should not disadvantage one type of learning against another.

At the operational level, there are various important parameters for Yunnan to consider as it develops its qualifications framework. For example, to what extent will Yunnan rely on the existing national framework in developing one more specific to its provincial context? How will the coordinating entity be chosen, and how will industry input be systematically incorporated into the development of the framework and each of the underlying standards? To what extent should the framework take into consideration regional and even international standards? It might be most feasible to develop a framework first in key industries with mature, organized private sectors before extending it to all sectors and occupations. Good examples can be found in Turkey, Australia, New Zealand, Hong Kong SAR, China, Singapore, and the European Union. Ultimately, what is most important is the development of a consensus specific to Yunnan regarding the scope and depth of the framework and operational details.

Financing TVET

School resources appear insufficient in the current system, especially for secondary TVET, even though public expenditures are high when measured as a percentage of Yunnan's provincial gross domestic product and total government spending. Yunnan could explore ways to increase private expenditures in TVET and, at the same time, use its existing public resources more efficiently.

Returns to private financing of upper secondary and tertiary education are high, however, and continue to increase. Yunnan could mobilize more private resources to increase the level of investment in education and training, leading to even greater returns. Yunnan should be able to increase the relatively low level of private financing and provision in the current system, letting high-income households share the cost of education and training, while further diversifying and freeing up other sources of revenue for education and training. The Yunnan government's recent announcement of regulations and establishment standards for private TVET institutions is an important first step.

At the same time, more public resources could be directed toward alleviating the huge disparities that exist in secondary TVET between rural and urban areas and between schools. Special funds for TVET tend to disproportionally benefit already stronger schools. Public finance should be targeted at helping TVET schools in disadvantaged localities, low-income families, and poor-performing schools with more resource constraints.

Finally, Yunnan could consider introducing demand-side financing mechanisms such as vouchers to improve the efficiency of public spending and quality of training.

Monitoring and Evaluation

Monitoring and evaluation provide feedback on the extent to which policies have been implemented across the system, what outcomes have been achieved, and what interventions have been effective or ineffective in achieving these outcomes. The very fact that the monitoring system exists and works creates an incentive for local authorities and schools to implement required policies and adhere to standards. Evaluation findings can be further used to promote good practices within the system and, in turn, replicate them on a wider scale.

Although this analysis identifies certain policy gaps in Yunnan's skills development system and proposes broad policy suggestions, to a large extent many of the challenges and issues arise not from a lack of central policies but from a lack of consistent and full implementation of those policies, particularly in rural and disadvantaged areas. This suggests the need to invest further in monitoring and evaluation of existing policies and programs. Commissioned special studies and ad hoc impact evaluations currently exist, but conducting routine monitoring and evaluation in a more systematic manner and with more sophisticated methodologies would be helpful.

In addition, the use of pilot and experimental programs and analysis of their results are critical to ensuring the long-term health of the education and training system. China has been learning from other TVET systems around the world, but its unique social, cultural, and economic context make the adoption of any imported good practice a challenge. Even within China, practices differ among provinces. Policies and practices that are effective in Shanghai will not easily be transplanted to Yunnan. Developing a unique Yunnan-style TVET system is the best and only policy choice. In this context, the willingness to experiment and evaluate is key.

Implications for Subsector-Specific Issues
Non-Formal Training

China's industrial sector growth and economic development strategies have led to the need to retrain large numbers of rural workers outside of the formal educational system for transfer to the secondary and tertiary sectors. In Yunnan, the rural surplus labor amounts to a third of the total rural labor force. Yunnan's rural working-age population averages only seven years of education, and more than 85 percent of rural workers have received no training. Those who remain in the agricultural sector also need training both in higher-value-added agricultural activities and in technology to improve their productivity. Non-formal training is a critical means of implementing the necessary rural training.

Yunnan faces challenges in improving the content, delivery of, and access to non-formal training. The design and implementation of non-formal training need to be better informed by a needs assessment and demand analysis. Forms of delivery and the content of training should be tailored to the specific needs and circumstances of training participants, such as rural laborers with relatively low levels of education and literacy, and the employers in the industrial sectors in which they may ultimately work. An improved qualifications framework would provide a mechanism that would enable non-formal training programs to lead to skills certification. Participation in non-formal training is hampered by barriers such as the requirement of a minimum education level, a lack of awareness of the value of such training, and the quality and relevance of the training itself. Encouraging both enterprises and learners to value skills certifications, and adding flexibility that accounts for prior work and life experience, can help overcome these barriers.

Public, private, and industry sources of funding for non-formal training could be consolidated into a single fund. A set of transparent funding criteria for the disbursement of training funds would be necessary. To assure quality of training, the funding criteria should be outcome-based rather than input-based. Training vouchers would be another option, creating a competitive market for non-formal training while giving participants more choices.

Incentives and Technical Assistance for Work-Based Training

China's ambitious economic goals require a well-educated and highly-skilled labor force. Work-based training will be the means by which enterprises improve the skills and performance of their existing employees.

Employers are currently required to dedicate 1.5–2.5 percent of their total wage bill to training, and Yunnan must ensure the effective implementation of this requirement. Other mechanisms that provide more incentives and quality assurance for work-based training should also be considered. South Korea's Employment Insurance Scheme is a good example that might be emulated in Yunnan.

In addition to financial assistance, the government should provide technical and institutional assistance to facilitate the provision of work-based training, especially by small and medium-sized enterprises. Technical assistance is particularly required in the areas of needs assessment, training design and implementation, and monitoring and evaluation. Institutional support might include organizing groups of small and medium-sized enterprises to reduce the cost of training design and delivery. Government can also systematically help firms build partnerships with training providers.

Pre-Primary Education

Yunnan could invest more heavily in and popularize pre-primary education. Ample research demonstrates that early childhood development programs, such as nutrition and health services, parenting interventions, and center-based programs can improve children's physical and cognitive development, as well as social and emotional wellbeing. Data from the Shanghai PISA and other cross-national evidence show the benefits of early childhood education for children's later cognitive development. Currently, government investment and enrollment rates in pre-primary schools and early childhood development programs in Yunnan are low. Investing in pre-primary education might be a relatively cost-effective way to improve the skill levels of a young generation.

CHAPTER 1

Introduction

China is one of the world's fastest growing economies with an average annual growth rate of 9 percent over the last three decades. By 2010, China had surpassed Japan to become the second largest economy in the world by gross domestic product (GDP), as measured in purchasing power parity (PPP) terms. As of 2008, fewer than 30 percent of the population lived on less than US$2 a day (the official definition of poverty), an almost 40 percent reduction in the poverty rate within a decade. However, as of 2010, China—even as the world's second largest economy—ranks significantly low in GDP per capita, at about US$4,393.

According to the 12th Chinese National Economic and Social Development Five-Year Plan (2011–15, the 12th Five-Year Plan), China's annual GDP growth will slow, but will still remain above a rate of 7 percent. The Chinese government is keenly aware that it is critical to sustain economic growth and social development. Indeed, the government is aware that it will also be necessary to successfully shift economic growth from low- to high- value-added labor, and from investment-led to consumption-led industries. This would ideally be accomplished within a framework of inclusive growth and environmental sustainability. Improving the quality and productivity of its labor force is explicitly put forth as an enabling factor to the success of the 12th Five-Year Plan.

The education and skills of the workforce have played a key role in enabling China's unprecedented economic and social development over the last three decades. China has made phenomenal improvements in the quantity and quality of its human resources since the 1980s. Within just a few decades, China has universalized nine-year compulsory education, developed general and vocational secondary education, and rapidly expanded higher education. The gross enrollment ratio has increased at the lower secondary level from 52 to 98 percent, at the upper secondary level from 29 to 78 percent, and at the tertiary level from under 3 percent to more than 23 percent. At the same time, the overall quality of China's labor force has improved significantly. Out of a population of 1.3 billion, China's economically active population totaled 0.78 billion in 2010. Of the 761 million total employed, 114 million are considered high-skilled "talents."

The average years of schooling of the labor force has now reached nine years, while new labor market entrants have on average 12 years of schooling.

However, when compared to the more developed countries, China remains a human resource–poor country. At the tertiary level, the gross enrollment ratio of 26 percent remains below the world average of 30 percent. China has only about 40 research and development personnel per 10,000 laborers, as compared to 110 in the United Kingdom, 115 in the Russian Federation, and 137 in Japan. According to the Academic Ranking of World Universities 2010, only 6.8 percent of the world's top 500 universities are in China, as compared to 30 percent in the United States. None of the Chinese universities are in the top 100. For example, Peking University and Tsinghua University ranked 151st and 200th, respectively.[1]

The majority of China's labor force is unskilled or low skilled. Nearly half the workers have attained only the nine-year compulsory education, 24 percent have completed only primary education, and more than 3 percent remain illiterate. Among technical workers, only a quarter qualified as high-skilled workers with skills certifications.[2] Furthermore, among China's 253 million rural workers, including 159 million migrant workers, only about 23 percent have attained a high school education or above, and as many as 69 percent of the rural workers have not received any type of training (National Bureau of Statistics of China 2008).

Context of Yunnan

Located on the southwestern border of China, Yunnan is a medium-sized province with abundant natural resources, including minerals, forests, animals, and plants. Yunnan has a population of 46 million, 30 million of whom reside in rural and 16 million in urban areas. Nearly 84 percent of Yunnan's land mass is rural areas and mountainous. Yunnan further distinguishes itself with its ethnic diversity: one-third of its population, or 15 million people, belong to 26 different non-Han ethnic groups.

The total GDP of Yunnan has increased from Y8.4 billion in 1980 to Y722 billion in 2010, registering an annual growth rate of over 10 percent. However, compared to the rest of China, particularly the coastal provinces, Yunnan's economy is still underdeveloped. Its GDP per capita in 2010 was Y15,752, only slightly more than half the national average of Y29,992. The annual net income per capita of Yunnan's rural population was only Y3,952 (US$623) in 2010. About 22 percent of its population, or 10 million people, still live under the national poverty line of Y2,300, making Yunnan the third poorest province in China after Gansu and Guizhou. At the end of 2011, Yunnan had 73 national-level poverty counties, the highest number among all provinces.

Like the rest of China, the structure of Yunnan's economy has been undergoing a fundamental transformation. In 1980, 43 percent of Yunnan's GDP came from the primary sector. By 2010, the contribution of the primary sector was only 15 percent, with the other 85 percent coming from the secondary and tertiary sectors (figure 1.1).

Figure 1.1 Contribution of Tertiary, Secondary, and Primary Sector to GDP Growth in Yunnan, 1957–2010

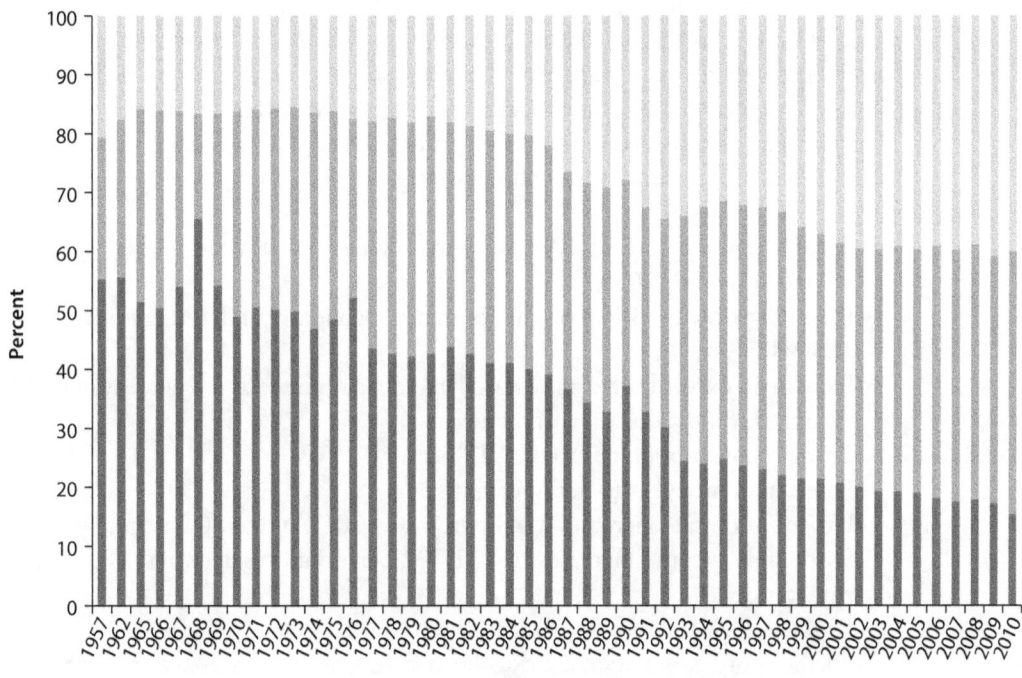

Source: Yunnan Statistical Yearbook 2011.

As urbanization continues and development patterns shift, the demand for skills will also change, and the resulting skill bottlenecks are likely to constrain growth. Although more than 60 percent of Yunnan's labor force is still engaged in the primary sector, the demand for skilled labor in the secondary and tertiary sectors, especially Yunnan's pillar sectors such as mining, energy, biotechnology, and tourism, continues to increase. Skills gaps are emerging. At the same time, employers have been increasingly faced with problems such as insufficient numbers of applicants, irrelevant skills, and unmatched expectations, suggesting skills mismatches.

The educational attainment of Yunnan's labor force has been rising over the past decade. The proportion of workers who are illiterate dropped from 20 percent in 2000 to only 11 percent in 2010, while the share of workers with high school degrees and above increased from more than 6 percent to more than 9 percent. Yet the average educational attainment of workers in Yunnan has consistently lagged behind the national average. By the end of 2010, Yunnan still had a higher share of illiterate workers (11 percent vs. 3 percent nationwide), a higher share of workers with only a primary education (47 percent vs. 24 percent nationwide), and a lower share of workers with high school education or above (14 percent vs. 24 percent nationwide).

Looking ahead, fueled by global forces and government economic development policies, China's future growth will involve radical transformations: an economy that will be increasingly led by consumption rather than investment, a move from high-energy to low-carbon energy sources, and greater reliance on innovation over low-cost manufacturing. Aligned with those principles, Yunnan has also laid out its economic development strategy as articulated in its 12th Five-Year Plan. It includes the following targets:

- A GDP growth rate of 10 percent or higher with a goal of total GDP of Y1,163 billion by 2015;
- Percentage composition of the primary, secondary, and tertiary sectors of 15:43:42;
- Increase in expenditures on research and development to 1.4 percent of GDP;
- Average level of education of nine years;
- Energy consumption reduced by 12 percent;
- Forestation increases to 5.45 percent;
- Urbanization rate increases to 44 percent by 2015 and to 50 percent by 2020;
- Disposable income increases to Y31,722 per urban resident and Y8,081 per rural resident.

Furthermore, the national Bridgehead Strategy has positioned Yunnan as a strategic gateway in the southwest of the country. The ambitious development goals and the resulting government investment not only present tremendous opportunities, but also pose major skills challenges for Yunnan.

The objectives of this study are to provide an in-depth analysis of the current and future demand for skills, identify skills gaps and sources of mismatches, and review the formal and non-formal education and training systems. For example, what levels and composition of skills are in demand? Are the current skills of the labor force adequate to meet the skills demand? What roles can education and training play in bridging the skills gaps and addressing the skills mismatches? We attempt to address these questions in this report.

Definition and Measurement of Skills

Definitions of the term "skill" vary greatly in the current literature. For the purposes of this report, skills are categorized and defined as the following:

- *Generic skills.* Cognitive skills include subject-specific knowledge, such as literacy and numeracy, as well as non-subject-specific skills, such as critical and creative thinking, and problem solving. Non-cognitive skills include characteristics not included under cognitive skills, for example, behavioral skills such as perseverance, self-discipline, teamwork, and the ability to negotiate conflict and manage risks.

- *Technical and vocational skills.* A mix of knowledge and skills used to perform specific jobs that rely on clearly defined tasks. For the purposes of this report, we define them as job-specific skills as opposed to generic skills that are transferable across jobs.

The measurement of skills used in the various datasets and in this report includes:

- *Educational attainment.* Educational attainment comprises widely available measures, which could potentially indicate a broad range of skills—generic and technical, cognitive and non-cognitive—at different levels.
- *Skills certification.* Rates of skills certification among graduates and employees, as well as the levels of certification, are important measures of technical and vocational skills.
- *Skills Toward Employment and Productivity (STEP) Survey.* The household and employer surveys of STEP provide direct measures of cognitive, non-cognitive, and technical skills through tests. The survey also links individual skills with labor market outcomes (Sanchez-Puerta et al. 2012).
- *Programme for International Student Assessment (PISA)* provides measures of generic, non-subject-based, cognitive skills acquired by 15-year-olds in the domains of reading, mathematics, and science literacy (OECD 2009).

Conceptual Framework

This study employs a demand-supply framework, as illustrated in figure 1.2. It starts with a demand-side analysis in chapter 2, examining historical trends in demand for skills, revealing the types of skills in demand, and projecting future demand for skills driven by economic growth and policy development. Chapter 2 also highlights the emerging skills shortages and mismatches in Yunnan. The rest of the report focuses on the access, quality, and relevance of Yunnan's education and training system and how effective it is in supplying the skills in demand.

Skills development takes place in formal programs that lead to recognized diplomas and qualifications. It also takes place through non-formal training, which tends to be less structured, and of shorter duration, and often does not lead to a formal certification. It is important to note that the line between formal and non-formal training is increasingly blurred in the Chinese context: Formal educational institutions are increasingly being contracted to provide non-formal training, while students and employees have increasing opportunities to qualify for formal certifications based on a series of short-term, non-formal training courses.

An overview of Yunnan's formal and non-formal education and training system is presented in chapter 3. Chapter 4 focuses on the formal Technical and Vocational Education and Training (TVET) system, examining its governance,

Figure 1.2 Conceptual Framework for the Study of Skills Demand and Supply in Yunnan

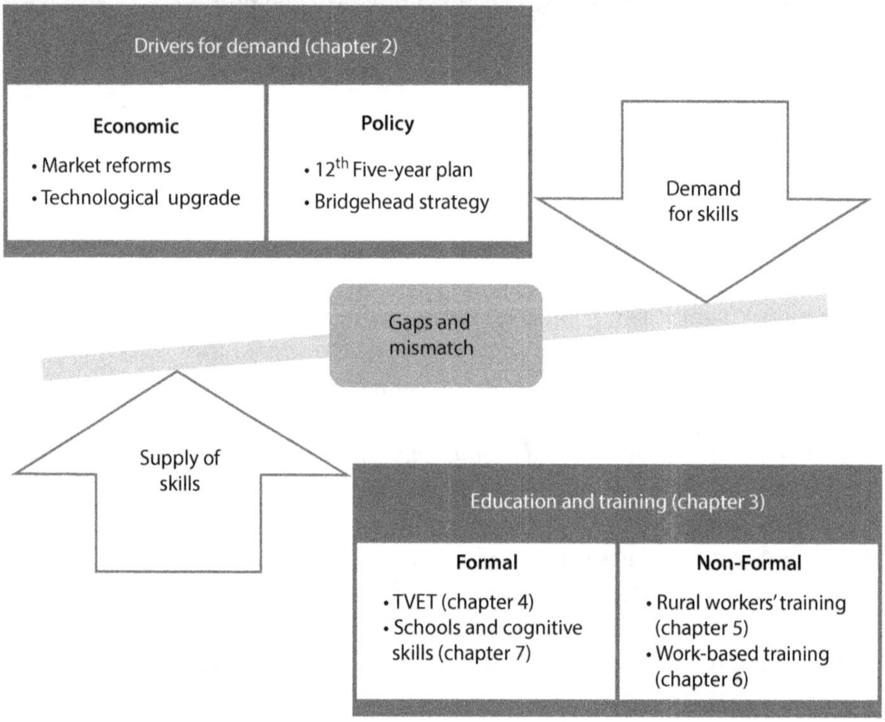

- Drivers for demand (chapter 2)
  - **Economic**
    - Market reforms
    - Technological upgrade
  - **Policy**
    - 12th Five-year plan
    - Bridgehead strategy

→ Demand for skills

Gaps and mismatch

← Supply of skills

- Education and training (chapter 3)
  - **Formal**
    - TVET (chapter 4)
    - Schools and cognitive skills (chapter 7)
  - **Non-Formal**
    - Rural workers' training (chapter 5)
    - Work-based training (chapter 6)

Note: TVET = Technical and Vocational Education and Training.

industry participation, curriculum reforms, quality assurance, and finances. Analysis of the formal education and training system focuses mainly on secondary and tertiary TVET. Due to the limited scope of the report, we are unable to conduct an in-depth analysis of Yunnan's basic education system or the academic tracks of higher education.

Chapters 5 and 6 address two major training programs outside the formal education system: non-formal training for rural workers and work-based training for urban workers, both of strategic importance. Finally, Chapter 7 draws on lessons from the Shanghai PISA to demonstrate the role of schools in developing the cognitive skills of 15-year-olds. The report concludes with a summary of findings and a set of policy recommendations for meeting the skills challenges and improving the education and training system.

Admittedly, education and training are only part of the equation for a balanced skills development system. The recent World Bank initiative, Stepping Up the Skills for More Jobs and Higher Productivity (World Bank 2010), broadly defines a skills development system to include five steps: (1) getting children off to the right start; (2) ensuring that all students learn; (3) building job-relevant skills; (4) encouraging entrepreneurship and innovation; and (5) facilitating labor mobility and job matching.

In view of the broad scope of a skills development system, this report focuses primarily on steps (2) and (3). The report does not venture into labor market policies such as *hukou* (household registration), minimum wages and pensions, which are also integral parts of a skills supply and demand system.

Notes

1. Rankings vary by the methodologies used. For example, the Times Higher Education World University Rankings (2011–12) ranked Peking University and Tsinghua University 49th and 71st, respectively. The U.S. News & World Report ranked the two universities 44th and 48th, respectively, for the same year.
2. China's vocational certifications are granted at five levels: Level 1 (senior technicians), Level 2 (technicians), Level 3 (senior-skilled workers), Level 4 (medium-skilled workers), and Level 5 (junior-skilled workers).

Bibliography

National Bureau of Statistics of China. 2008. http://www.stats.gov.cn/tjfx/dfxx/t20080220_402463674.htm.

OECD (Organisation for Economic Co-operation and Development). 2009. *PISA 2009 Assessment Framework*. Paris: OECD.

Sanchez-Puerta, M. L., A. Valerio, G. Pierre, and S. Urzua. 2012. "STEP Skills Measurement Surveys Methodology Note Draft." World Bank, Washington, DC.

World Bank. 2010. *Stepping Up the Skills for More Jobs and Higher Productivity*. Washington, DC: World Bank.

Yunnan Bureau of Statistics. 2011. *Yunnan Statistical Yearbook*. Beijing: China Statistics Press.

CHAPTER 2

Skills Challenges: Demand, Gaps, and Mismatches

This chapter reviews the skills challenges in Yunnan using a demand-supply framework. Data for both the provincial and national levels allow us to compare Yunnan against national trends and situate the results within a broader context. The chapter begins with an overview of the employment trends and skills composition of the current labor force. Increasing demand for skilled labor is implied by the rising educational attainment of the labor force, along with the increasing wage returns to education in the job market. Data from household and employer surveys shed further light on the specific cognitive, non-cognitive, and technical skills in demand from both employee and employer perspectives. Our analysis also indicates emerging skills shortages and identifies skills mismatches by examining problems encountered by firms in hiring new employees. Recent developments in national and provincial policies are expected to pose further skills challenges, as Yunnan is presented with immense opportunities for economic growth, structural change, and greater openness through the Bridgehead Strategy.

Labor Market Trends in China and Yunnan

By the end of 2011, employment in Yunnan totaled over 27 million. The agricultural sector still dominates Yunnan's total employment with nearly 17 million workers, although its share has been declining steadily since the early 1990s. Compared to the national averages, Yunnan has historically had a higher share of employment in the primary sector, and a lower share in the secondary and tertiary sectors (figure 2.1). Across China, the share of primary sector employment has dropped by 32 percent percentage points from 1980 (69 percent) to 2010 (37 percent), while the share of tertiary sector employment has more than doubled from 13 percent to 34 percent within the last three decades. The composition of the primary, secondary, and tertiary sectors in 2010 was 37 percent, 29 percent, and 35 percent nationwide, respectively, in contrast to Yunnan's composition of 60 percent, 13 percent, and 27 percent, respectively.

Figure 2.1 Composition of Employed Persons at Year-End by Sector in Yunnan and China, 1980–2010

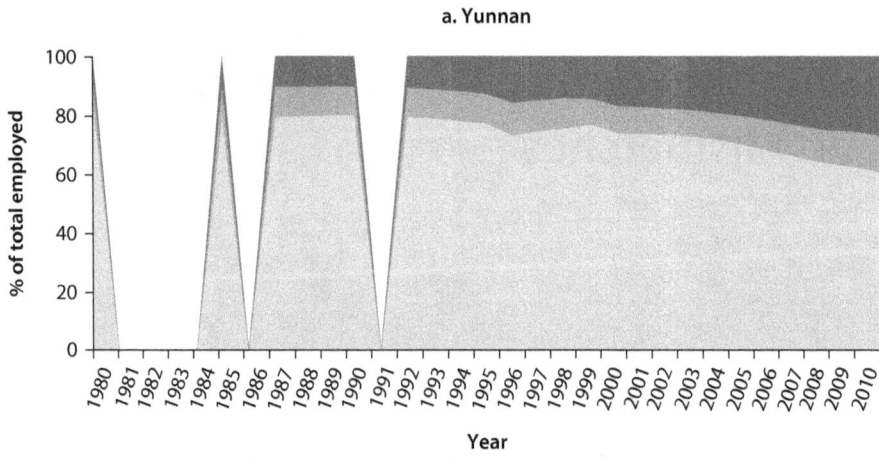

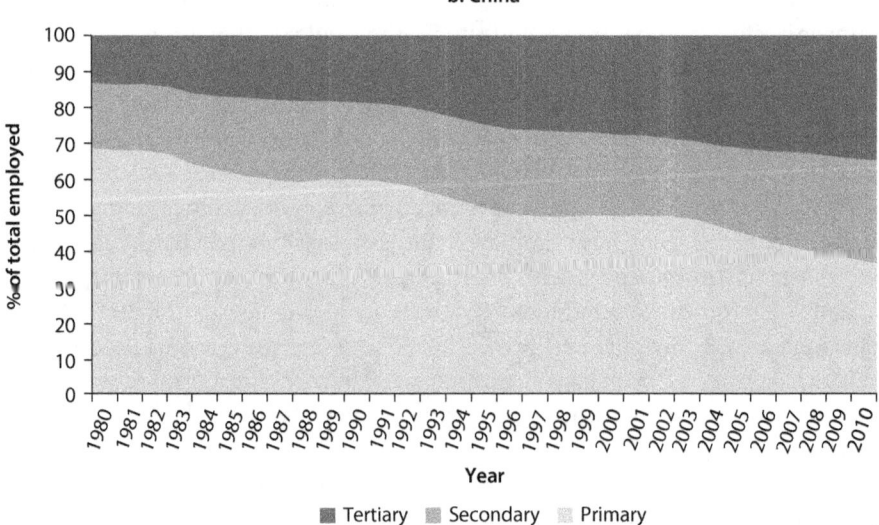

Source: Yunnan Statistical Yearbook 2011.

Growth in employment in Yunnan in recent years has been driven mostly by demand from the tertiary sector. Quarterly job vacancy data show that the tertiary sector had the largest number of job openings throughout 2010 and 2011, followed by the secondary sector (figure 2.2). In 2011 alone, Yunnan's tertiary sector generated 453,298 job openings.

Within the tertiary sector, the largest increases in employment occurred in relatively smaller-sized sectors (table 2.1): for example, between 2007 and 2010, employment in leasing/trade/business services increased by 49 percent, followed by services to households/other services (36 percent) and real estate (32 percent). In terms of the absolute number of workers, education and public

Figure 2.2 Quarterly Number of Job Vacancies by Sector, Yunnan, 2010–11

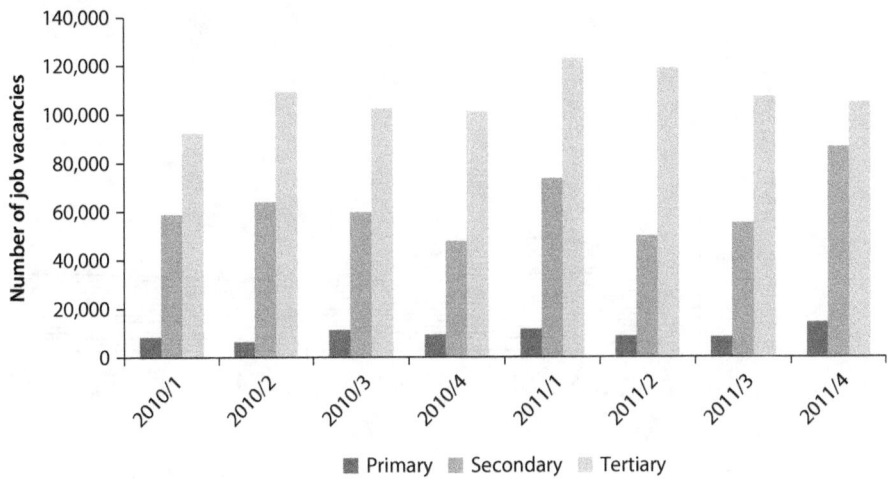

Source: HRSS 2010a, 2011.

Table 2.1 Total Number of Staff and Workers at Year-End in Yunnan by Industry, 2007 and 2010

Sector	Industry	2007	2010	Total growth (%)
		(10,000 persons)		
Primary	Farming, forestry, animal husbandry, and fishery	15.1	13.1	−13.1
Secondary	Mining	11.9	14.4	20.9
	Manufacturing	53.0	55.1	3.9
	Production and supply of electricity, gas, and water	7.5	8.2	9.4
	Construction	29.9	34.2	14.5
Tertiary	Transportation, storage, and post	12.0	12.6	4.8
	Information transmission, computers service, and software service	2.9	2.9	0.0
	Wholesale and retail trades	13.3	14.9	11.5
	Hotels and catering services	5.6	5.6	0.0
	Finance	7.0	8.1	16.7
	Real estate	2.9	3.8	31.6
	Leasing trade and business service	4.7	6.9	49.0
	Scientific research, technology service, and geological prospecting	5.4	6.0	9.4
	Water conservancy, administration of environment, and public facilities	4.2	4.5	7.1
	Services to households and other services	0.6	0.8	36.4
	Education	47.9	50.5	5.4
	Health care, social security, and social welfare	13.1	14.7	12.5
	Culture, sports, and entertainment	3.4	3.4	2.4
	Public administration and social organization	40.4	44.0	8.8

Source: Yunnan Statistical Yearbook 2010, 2011.

Figure 2.3 Workers in Urban Areas by Ownership, Yunnan

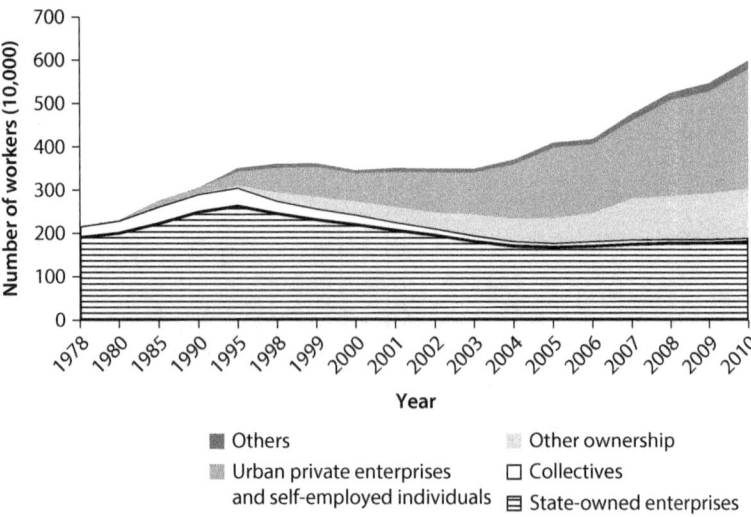

Source: Yunnan Statistical Yearbook 2011.

administration/social organization together employed over 0.99 million workers in 2010. *The secondary sector, with its large work force, has also seen continued growth in employment.* For example, employment in mining and construction expanded by 21 percent and 14.5 percent, respectively, between 2007 and 2010.

Measured by ownership of employer, Yunnan's employment composition has shifted away from the dominance of state-owned enterprises (SOEs) as the nonpublic sector increasingly generates employment (figure 2.3). At the beginning of China's economic reforms in 1978, SOEs dominated employment in Yunnan with an 88 percent share. Three decades later, the share of SOEs has dropped to 30 percent, while the non-public sector (including self-employment) constitutes 46 percent of the total employment in urban Yunnan (with nearly 4 million workers).

Along with gross domestic product (GDP) and employment, real wages in China and Yunnan have seen tremendous growth since the early 1990s (figure 2.4). Across China, real wages have increased fivefold. Real wages of workers in SOEs surpass those in other types of enterprises, and the disparities have been growing.

The growth in real wages has been uneven across ownership types and regions. In Yunnan, real wages have increased fourfold between 1994 and 2010, but the gaps between China and Yunnan have been widening over the same period (figure 2.4). In particular, the growth seems to be driven solely by SOEs and urban collectives in Yunnan, as real wages in other types of enterprises have been almost unchanged between 1994 and 2010. In 2010, real wages of workers in SOEs and urban collectives are more than four times those in other types of enterprises in Yunnan (figure 2.5).

Figure 2.4 Trends in Real Wages (Index 1994 = 100) of China and Yunnan

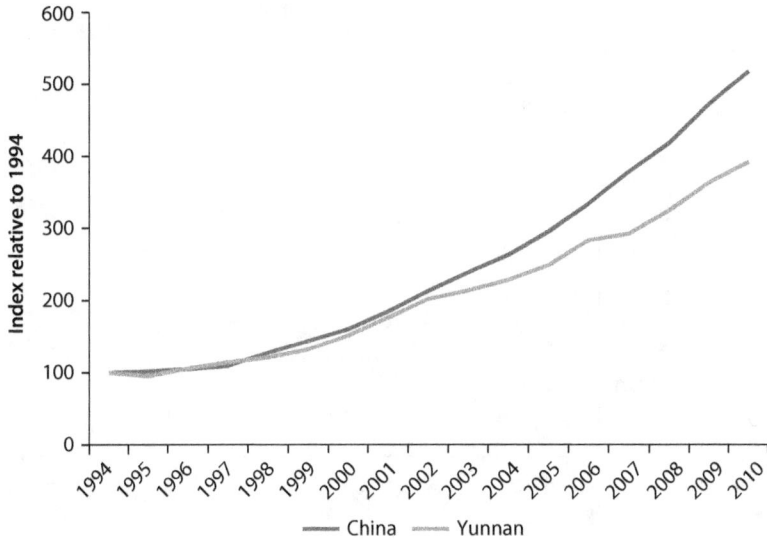

Sources: China Statistical Yearbook 2011; Yunnan Statistical Yearbook 2011.

During the same period, China's labor productivity, defined by GDP per person employed, has more than quadrupled. Much of the gains in labor productivity were driven by manufacturing and expansion of competition (World Bank 2012). However, despite the huge gains over the last two decades, the level of labor productivity of China remains lower compared to other middle-income and high-income countries in East Asia, such as Japan, the Republic of Korea, Thailand, and Malaysia (figure 2.6). The gap is even larger when compared to the average of Organisation for Economic Co-operation and Development (OECD) member countries. Significant regional disparities in productivity also exist within China (figure 2.7). For example, the productivity of the Eastern region is more than twice that of the Western region. The productivity of workers in Yunnan increased by 76 percent between 2004 and 2009, but it remains at one of the lowest levels in China. Even within the Western provinces, the productivity of Yunnan's labor force in 2009 was the second lowest, after the Guizhou province.

Skills Composition of the Current Workforce

The educational attainment of the labor force in Yunnan has been increasing over the last decade. As shown in figure 2.8, the proportion of workers who are illiterate has dropped from 20 percent in 2000 to 11 percent in 2010. Over the same period, the share of workers with a high school degree or above has increased from 6.5 percent to 9.3 percent, and the share of workers with tertiary education has increased from 1.4 percent to 3.2 percent.

Figure 2.5 Real Wages (Index 1994 = 100) by Types of Ownership

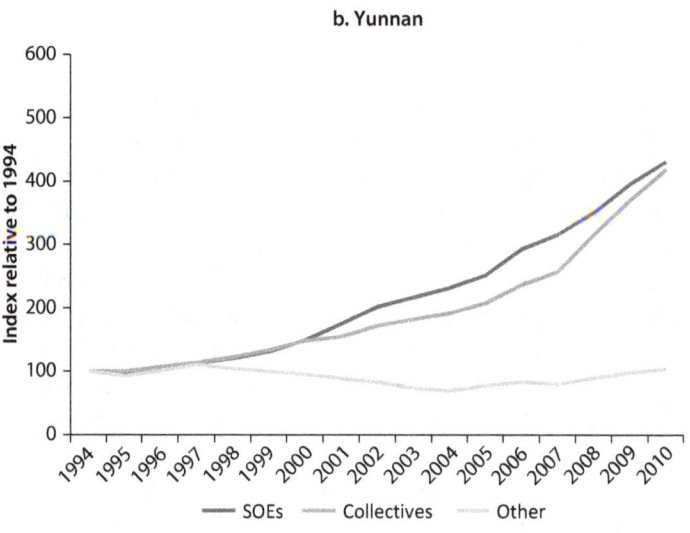

Sources: China Statistical Yearbook 2011; Yunnan Statistical Yearbook 2011.

Despite the increase in educational attainment over the past decade, the vast majority of Yunnan's current workforce is still composed of workers with only a basic education or less. As of 2010, 33 percent of workers in Yunnan had completed only compulsory education, and 47 percent had only a primary school education. Yunnan has a much higher share of illiterate workers (11 percent) than the national average (3 percent). Moreover, skilled workers with a high school education and above constitute only about 14 percent of Yunnan's labor force, the third lowest in China, after Tibet and Guizhou (figure 2.9).

Figure 2.6 Labor Productivity of Selected Countries

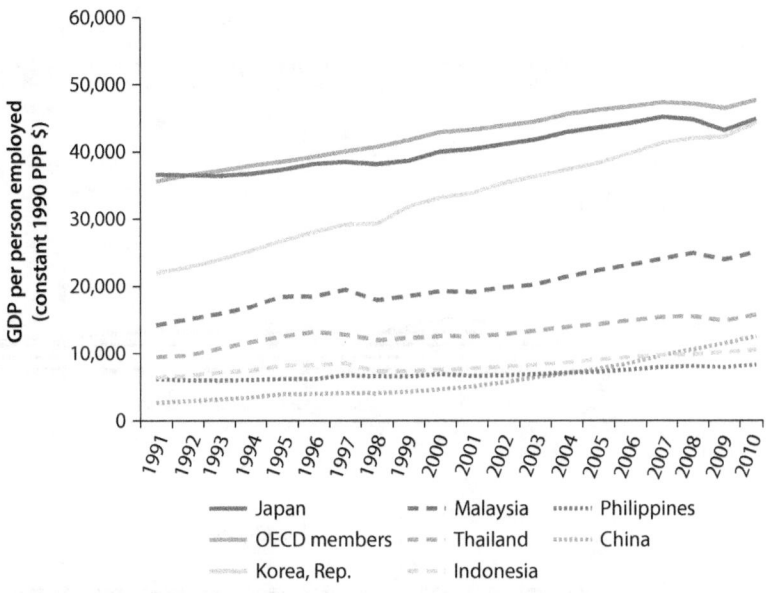

Source: World Development Indicators.

Figure 2.7 Labor Productivity of Yunnan Compared to Selected Provinces

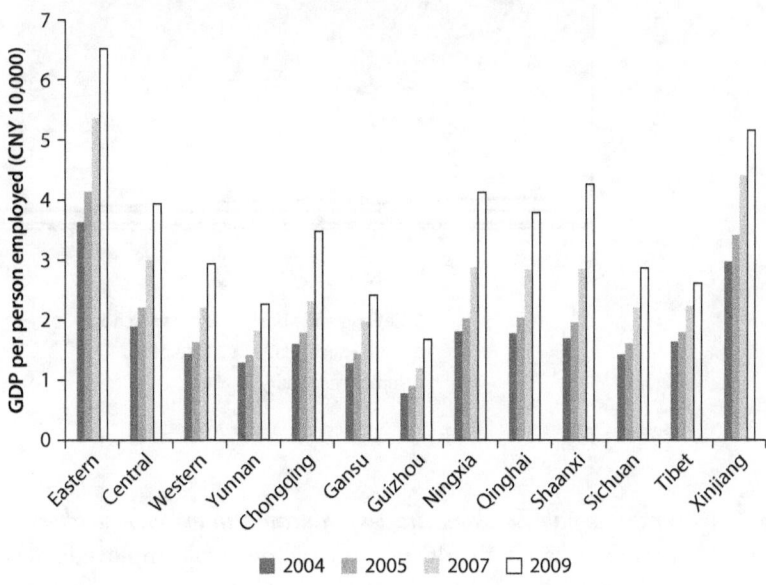

Source: World Bank 2012.

Figure 2.8 Education Composition of the Employed, Yunnan and China, 2001–10

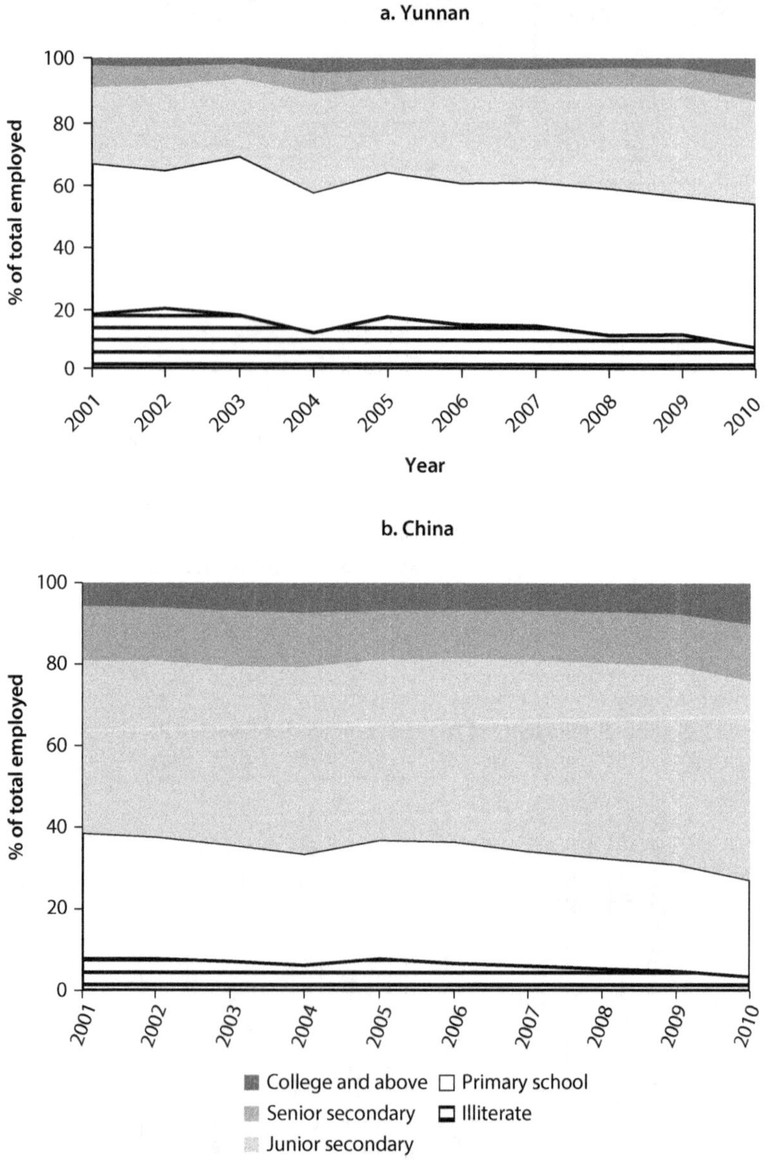

a. Yunnan

b. China

■ College and above   □ Primary school
▒ Senior secondary   ▢ Illiterate
▒ Junior secondary

Sources: China Statistical Yearbook; Yunnan Statistical Yearbook 2002–11.

On average, female workers are less educated than male workers in Yunnan. Female workers account for 46 percent of the total employed in Yunnan. As shown in figure 2.10, a larger proportion of female workers are illiterate (10 percent vs. 4 percent of male workers) or have only a primary education (50 percent vs. 44 percent of male workers). Among high-skilled workers, however, the gender gaps are narrower: 12 percent of female workers have an upper secondary education or above, compared to 15 percent of male workers.

Figure 2.9 Proportion of Total Employed with Upper Secondary or Tertiary Education in China by Province, 2010

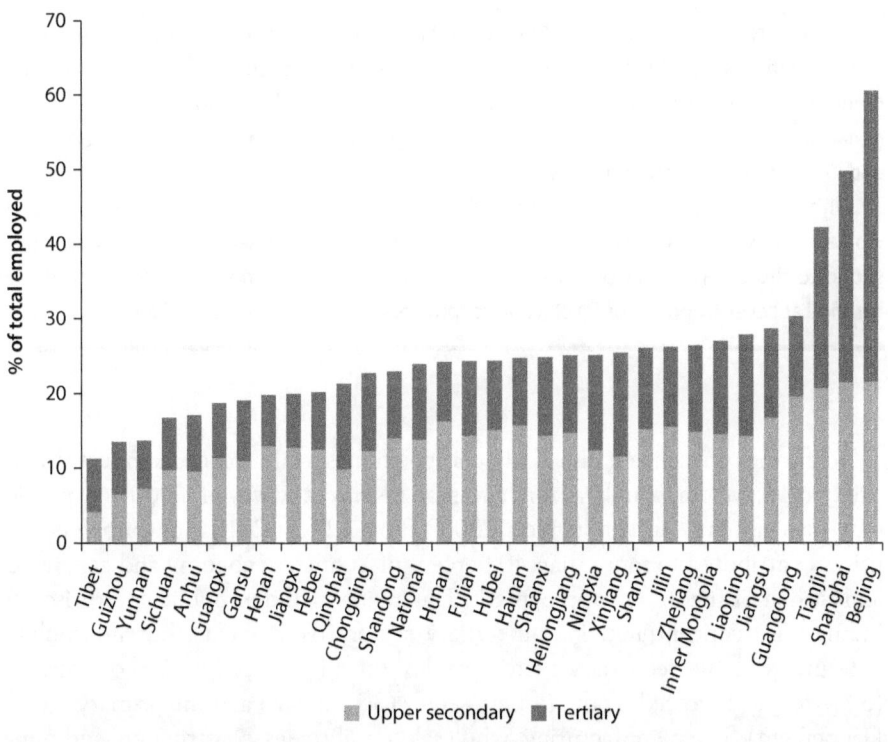

Source: China Labor Statistical Yearbook 2011.

Figure 2.10 Education Composition of Male and Female Workers in Yunnan, 2010

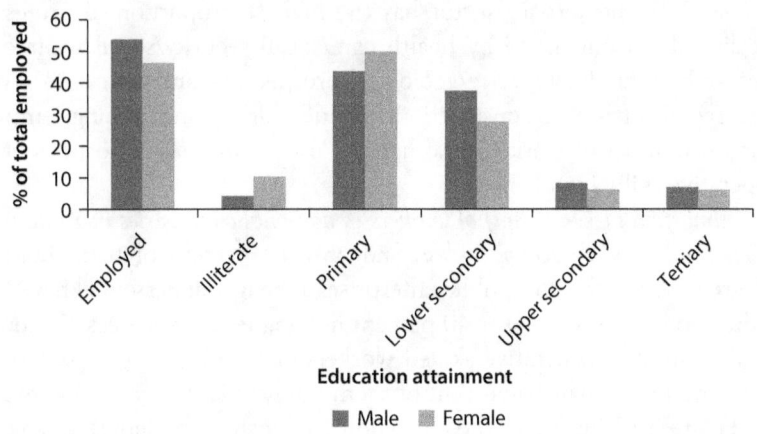

Source: China Labor Statistical Yearbook 2011.

Box 2.1 Yunnan Non-Public Enterprise Survey, 2008

The Yunnan Non-public Enterprise Survey used in this report was conducted in 2008 by the Yunnan Statistical Bureau. The survey selected 46,208 enterprises across Yunnan using stratified random sampling by industry and size. Workers are categorized by occupation into: (1) managerial personnel (经营管理人员); (2) professional and technical personnel (专业技术人员); and (3) frontline/operative skilled workers (技能人员).

Within each occupation, workers are further divided into senior-, medium-, and junior-level workers. For workers who have obtained vocational certification, senior-level workers correspond to those certified at Levels 1 through 3, medium-level workers correspond to those certified at Level 4, and junior-level workers correspond to those certified at Level 5.

To further investigate the skills composition specific to each industry and occupation, we draw on data from a human resources survey of 3,000 non-public enterprises in Yunnan conducted in 2008 (box 2.1). In 2010, non-public enterprises contributed to more than 40 percent of Yunnan's economy and generated almost half of the urban employment. The majority of non-public enterprises in Yunnan are concentrated in the tertiary sector (61 percent), but non-public enterprises in the secondary sector employ the highest proportion of workers (52 percent), followed by the tertiary sector (36 percent) and the primary sector (13 percent). The manufacturing, wholesale/retail trades, construction, and mining industries employ the largest number of workers (figure 2.6).

Human resources in Yunnan's non-public enterprises are composed mostly of frontline/operative skilled workers (29 percent), followed by professional and technical personnel (18 percent) and managerial personnel (17 percent). Across sectors (table 2.2), the tertiary sector has the highest proportion of professional and technical personnel, led by health care/social security/social welfare, scientific research/technology service/geological prospecting, and education. The secondary sector, including construction, manufacturing, and mining, employing the largest number of workers, also has one of the highest proportions of frontline/operative skilled workers.

Almost half (49 percent) of workers in non-public industries in Yunnan have completed only middle school or less, and only 18 percent of them hold a tertiary degree. Within the non-public enterprises, managerial personnel have the highest education levels, with over 40 percent holding tertiary degrees. By contrast, over half of frontline/operative skilled workers have only a middle school degree or less, and fewer than 10 percent of them hold tertiary degrees (figure 2.11).

Figure 2.12 illustrates the education composition by industry, ranked by proportion of workers with tertiary degrees. The finance industry has the highest share of educated workers (72 percent with tertiary degrees and 97 percent with high school degrees or above), followed by scientific research/technology service/

Table 2.2 Number of People Employed in Non-Public Enterprises, by Industry and Occupation, 2008

Industry	Managerial personnel	Professional and technical personnel	Frontline skilled workers
Farming, forestry, animal husbandry, and fishery	8,667	5,303	15,462
Mining	27,786	19,232	53,023
Manufacturing	84,295	84,117	206,503
Production and supply of electricity, gas, and water	3,108	4,660	3,572
Construction	43,352	89,575	112,762
Transportation, storage, and post	8,665	6,678	19,705
Information transmission, computer services, and software services	3,700	3,633	2,469
Wholesale and retail trades	63,448	43,193	44,353
Hotels and catering services	12,011	6,430	17,841
Finance	1,436	1,625	1,157
Real estate	14,694	14,436	11,295
Leasing trade and business services	12,716	16,443	11,713
Scientific research, technology services, and geological prospecting	3,325	7,777	1,863
Water conservancy, administration of environment, and public facilities	1,617	1,970	1,903
Services to households and other services	3,924	4,034	5,145
Education	4,644	10,954	5,439
Health care, social security, and social welfare	1,530	8,185	1,373
Culture, sports, and entertainment	2,517	1,589	2,442

Source: Yunnan Non-public Enterprise Survey 2008.

geological prospecting (63 percent with tertiary degrees and 90 percent with high school degrees or above). By contrast, industries in the primary and secondary sectors, such as mining, farming/forestry/animal husbandry/fishing, manufacturing, and construction, have the highest proportion of workers with only a middle school education or below.

In addition to education composition, certification rates are low among professional and technical personnel and frontline/operative skilled workers (figure 2.13). Overall, roughly 24 percent of professional and technical personnel and 12 percent of frontline/operative skilled workers have obtained professional or vocational certification. Among those certified, the majority are junior-level workers. Only about 2 percent of professional and technical personnel and 2 percent of frontline/operative skilled workers at the senior level are certified.

Figure 2.14 depicts the share of medium- and senior-level professional and technical and frontline/operative workers who have skills certification or professional rankings. Among the five industries that employ the highest proportion of professional and technical personnel, education and scientific research/

Figure 2.11 Educational Attainment by Human Resources Type, 2008

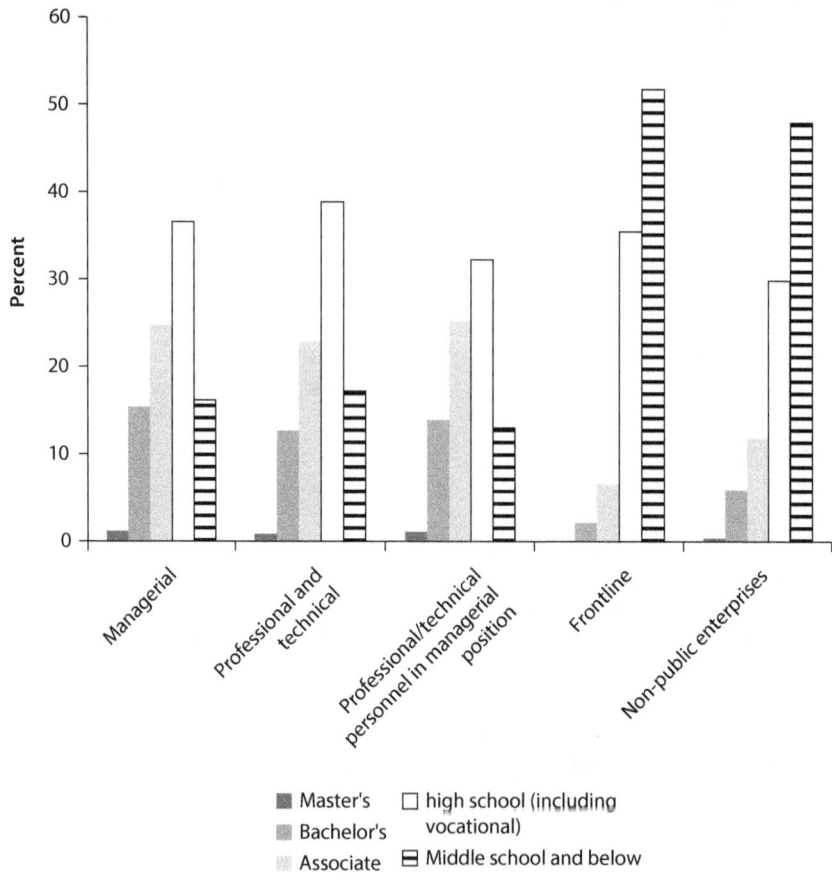

Source: Yunnan Non-public Enterprise Survey 2008.

technology service/geological prospecting also have a relatively high proportion of medium- and senior-level technicians and professionals who are certified. In comparison, production and supply of electricity, gas, and water has one of the highest proportions of professional and technical workers, but fewer than 5 percent of them are certified.

Certification rates are even lower among frontline/operative skilled laborers. In particular, although the agricultural sector employs one of the highest proportions of frontline/operative skilled workers, fewer than 0.3 percent of its medium- and senior-level frontline/operative workers are certified. Likewise, within the secondary sector, mining consists of 28 percent frontline/operative skilled workers, but fewer than 0.3 percent of its frontline/operative skilled workers at the medium or senior level are certified. In both manufacturing and construction, which employ a large number of people and a high proportion of frontline/operative skilled laborers, only 6–7 percent of the medium- or senior-level employees are certified.

Skills Challenges: Demand, Gaps, and Mismatches

Figure 2.12 Education Composition in Non-Public Enterprises by Industry, 2008

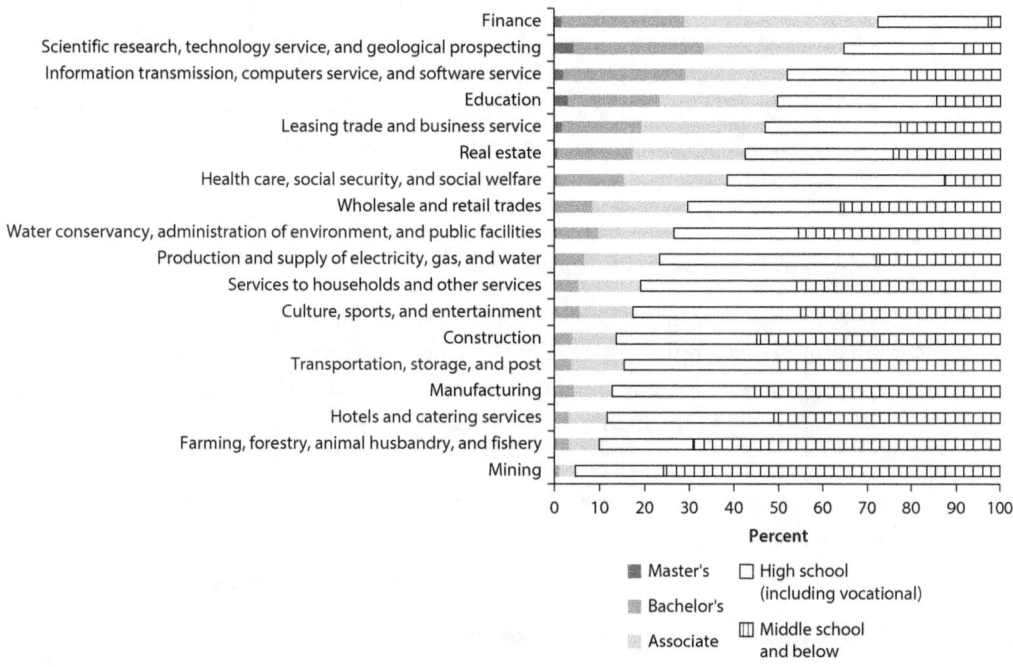

Source: Yunnan Non-public Enterprise Survey 2008.

Figure 2.13 Share of Certified Workers by Type and Level, 2008

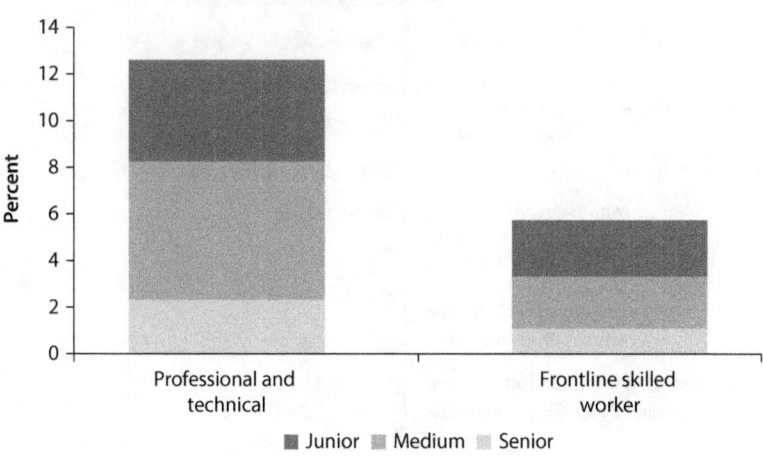

Source: Yunnan Non-public Enterprise Survey 2008.

Low certification rates reflect, in part, the relatively low skill levels of workers. However, they also call into question the effectiveness and relevance of the skills certification system in Yunnan. Employers do not seem to demand that their employees be certified. The low recognition of skills certification among employers not only calls into question the validity and relevance of skills certificates, but also reduces the incentives for employees to acquire certified skills or for employers to provide skills training.

Trends in Returns to Education

At the same time that the educational attainment of the population and labor force has been improving rapidly, demand for education and skills continues to rise as evidenced by dramatic increases in the past decade in the returns to education, especially at the high school level and beyond. Using household survey data

Figure 2.14 Share of Certified Workers at Medium and Senior Level in Non-Public Enterprises, 2008

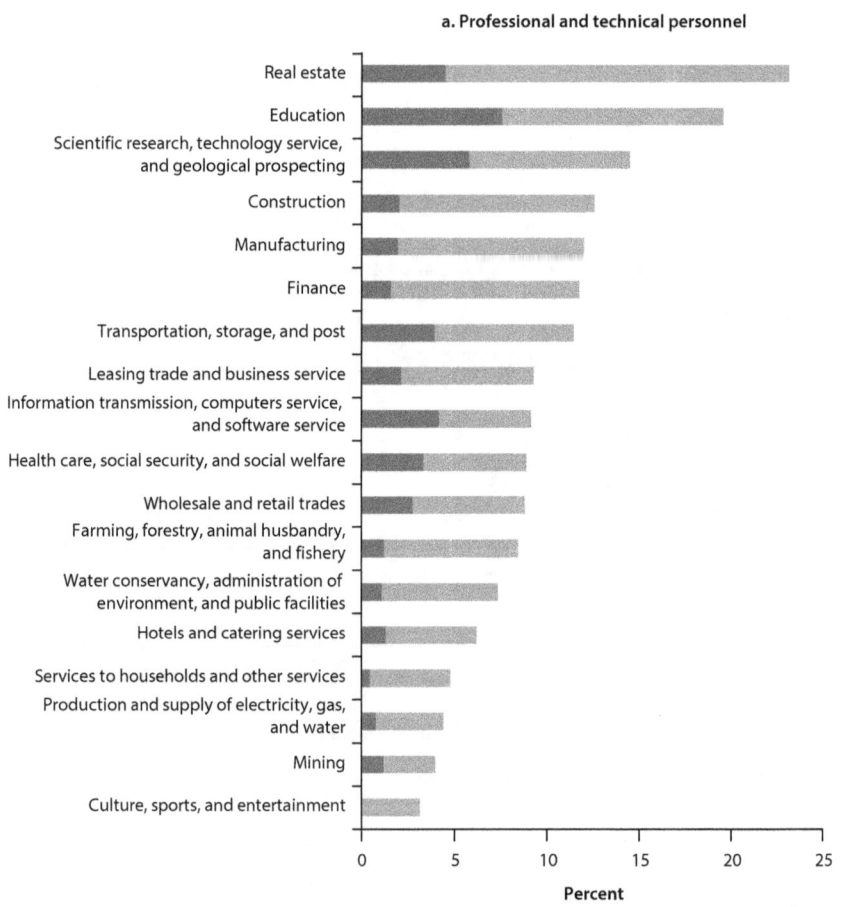

figure continues next page

Figure 2.14 Share of Certified Workers at Medium and Senior Level in Non-Public Enterprises, 2008 *(continued)*

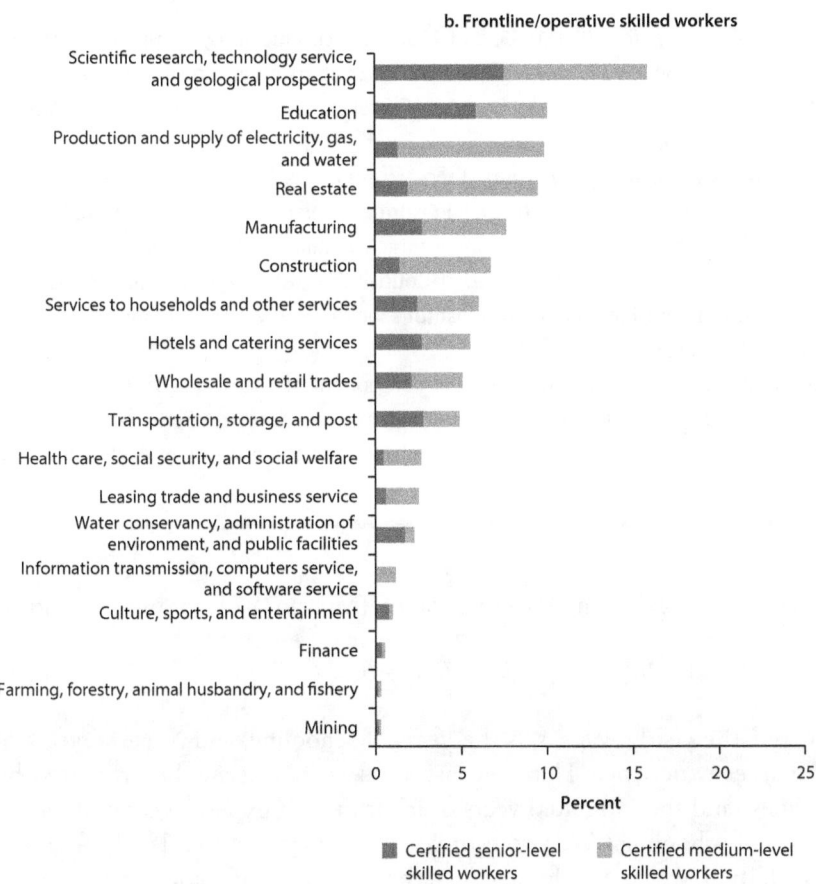

Source: Yunnan Non-public Enterprise Survey 2008.

from 1988 to 2012, we estimate the private returns to schooling in Yunnan and China and examine how they have changed over time from the late 1980s through the 2000s.

Data for 1988, 1995, and 2002 were drawn from the Chinese Household Income Project (CHIP) (box 2.2). For more recent years, we use data from the Longitudinal Survey on Rural Urban Migration in China (RUMiC) 2007 to examine national trends. Yunnan was not included in the RUMiC 2007 sample. To complete our analysis, we draw from the most recent STEP Household Survey 2012, which sampled 2,000 individuals from 2,000 households in urban Kunming, the capital city of Yunnan (Sanchez-Puerta et al. 2012). A description of the analytic sample from the STEP Household Survey is available in appendix A. It is important to note that the weighted sample only represents the urban population in Kunming. Although not representative of the entire province, workers in the urban Kunming sample have higher education levels and are concentrated in the service sector.

Box 2.2 CHIP 1988, 1995, 2002, and RUMiC 2007

The three CHIP surveys for 1988, 1995, and 2002 were conducted by researchers from the Chinese Academy of Social Sciences together with associated Chinese and international scholars, with the assistance of the National Bureau of Statistics (Keith and Zhao 1993; Li *et al*. 2008; Riskin, Renwei, and Shi 2001).

RUMiC 2007 was initiated by a group of researchers at the Australian National University, the University of Queensland, and the Beijing Normal University and was supported by the Institute for the Study of Labor, which provides the Scientific Use Files. Financial support for RUMiC was provided by the Australian Research Council, the Australian Agency for International Development, the Ford Foundation, the Institute for the Study of Labor, and the Chinese Foundation of Social Sciences.

This study draws on the urban household component of each wave of the survey and restricts the samples to workers with positive yearly earnings. Owners of private or individual enterprises are not included. Yunnan was sampled in the three waves of CHIP, but not in RUMiC 2007.

We employ the following Mincer equation (Mincer 1974) for our calculation:

$$\ln Y_i = \beta_0 + \beta_1 s_i + \beta_2 X_i + \beta_3 X_i^2 + \varepsilon_i \qquad (2.1)$$

where Y_i is the yearly wage, s_i is the years of schooling, and X_i is the years of labor market experience. Here, we use total years of schooling reported by individuals[1] and the estimated years of labor market experience based on age and years of schooling.[2] We also estimate the returns to each level of schooling. In addition, we control for gender, ethnicity,[3] type of company ownership, city, and industry. Table 2.3 presents the estimated results from the OLS regressions.

Rates of return to an additional year of education have been increasing throughout the 1990s in both Yunnan and China. Liu, Park, and Zhao (2010) attributed the rising returns to education throughout the 1990s to skill-biased technical progress, specifically, changes in available technologies and institutional changes associated with the economic transition and maturation of China's urban labor market. Another important contributing factor is the changes in industrial wage rents, reflecting the growing specialization of more-educated workers in higher rent industries relative to less-educated workers.

Although national data suggest dramatic increases in returns to education during two periods of time, 1992–94, and 1994–99 (Zhang et al. 2005), significant changes in returns to education in Yunnan do not seem to emerge until the latter half of the 1990s. Based on our data in Yunnan, the change is most pronounced during the period between 1995 and 2002, when the rate of return to an additional year of education increased by 3.18 percentage points. During the 2000s, nationwide data suggest a slight decrease in the average rates

Table 2.3 Rates of Return to Schooling, Yunnan and China, 1988–2012

		1988	1995	2002	2007	2012[a]
Per additional year (%)	Yunnan	3.37	3.99	7.17	—	8.02
	China	3.24	4.32	7.05	6.10	—
Percentage increase in wages relative to middle school (%)						
High school	Yunnan	4.73	9.16	19.01	—	19.84
	China	7.33	10.37	12.30	11.74	—
Secondary Technical and Vocational Education and Training (TVET)	Yunnan	14.68	18.65	25.11	—	24.86
	China	12.41	23.49	29.69	32.31	—
Tertiary, associate degree	Yunnan	22.38	23.74	53.73	—	57.93
	China	18.77	32.71	52.50	57.62	—
Bachelor's and above	Yunnan	30.34	37.71	79.32	—	112.55
	China	30.08	43.48	77.54	96.60	—
N	Yunnan	893	1,082	833	—	1,026
	China	6,788	11,137	9,147	5,695	—

Source: Authors' calculation using CHIP 1988, 1995, 2002; RUMiC 2007; and STEP Household Survey 2012. Full models presented in appendix A.
Note: — = not available.
a. STEP Household Survey 2012 was sampled only in Kunming.

of returns to an additional year of education, most likely due to the decreased returns to education below high school. Data from urban Kunming suggest that the rates of returns to an additional year of education remain at around 8 percent in 2012.

Table 2.3 also lists the returns by education level expressed as a percentage change in wages relative to those of middle school graduates. *There are positive and significant returns to every level of education beyond middle school, and the rates of return increase with the level of education.* Returns to secondary Technical and Vocational Education and Training (TVET) appear to be higher than returns to general high school both in Yunnan and nationwide.

In figure 2.15, we graphed our results to better illustrate the changes in returns to different levels of schooling over time. Between 1988 and 2002, although returns to schooling have been increasing rapidly at every level of education beyond the compulsory level, the most dramatic increase is seen on the tertiary level. The increase in returns to tertiary-level education in Yunnan has been even more dramatic than the increase in the national average. In 1995, individuals in Yunnan with tertiary associate degrees earned 24 percent more than middle school graduates. Less than a decade later, in 2002, the difference had become as large as 54 percent. Even more, for workers with Bachelor's degrees and above, the wage difference above middle school graduates increased from 38 percent in 1995 to 79 percent in 2002. In 2010, earnings of Bachelor's degree holders and above in urban Kunming were more than double those of middle school graduates.

As the returns to tertiary degrees dramatically increase, the gap between returns to tertiary education and secondary education have been widening. Since 2002, returns to tertiary education, especially Bachelor's degrees, continued to

Figure 2.15 Percent Change in Wages Relative to Middle School Graduates, Yunnan and China, 1998–2012

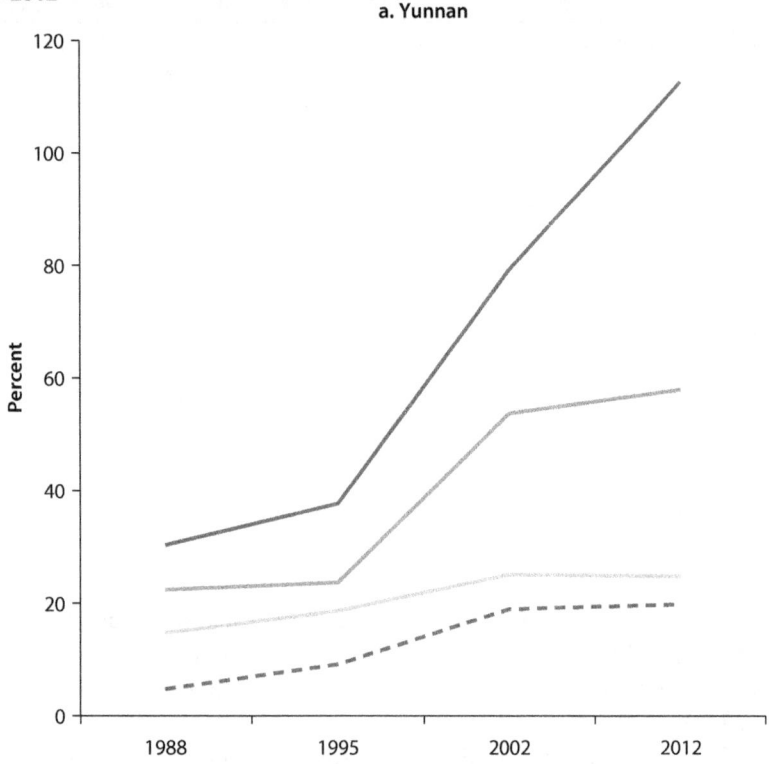

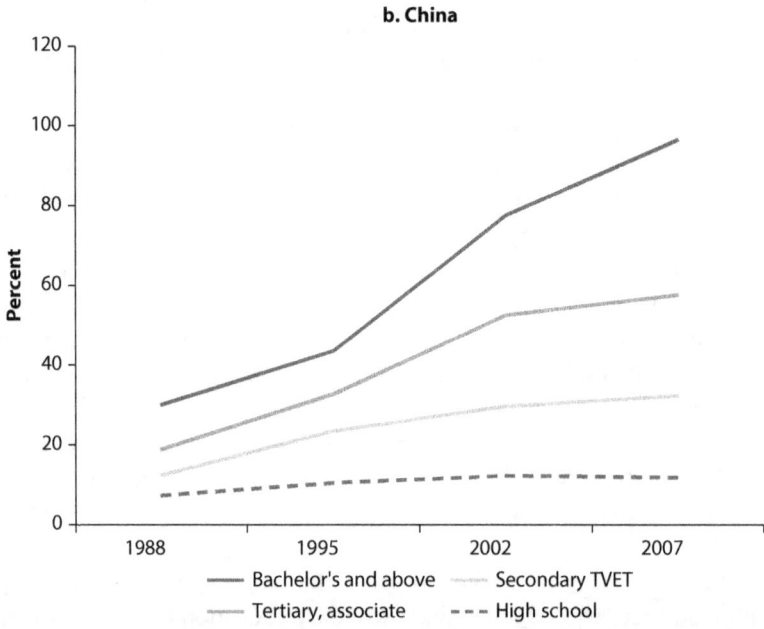

Source: Authors' calculations using CHIP 1988, 1995, 2002; RUMiC 2007; and STEP Household Survey 2012.

increase, while returns to general high school graduates seem to have stabilized. At the same time, the gap between returns to tertiary associate degrees and Bachelor's degrees has also been increasing. National data suggest that, between 2002 and 2007, the gap continued to widen: Returns to Bachelor's degrees increased by over 19 percent, while returns to secondary TVET and tertiary associate degrees exhibited only slight increases as compared to the previous decade. These changes reflect the increasingly stronger demand for workers with tertiary education relative to those with secondary education; within the tertiary level, Bachelor's degrees are rewarded in the job market at increasingly higher rates over associate degrees.

The increasing returns to tertiary education are not a pattern unique to Yunnan; similar trends have been found in other medium- and low-income countries during the 1990s (see, for example, Behrman, Birdsall, and Szekely 2003; Blom, Holm-Nielsen, and Verner 2001; Fiszbein, Patrinos, and Giovagnoli 2007; Riboud, Savchenko, and Tan 2007).

Figure 2.16 shows the patterns in Latin America in the 1990s (Behrman, Birdsall, and Szekely 2003). Colclough, Kingdon, and Patrinos (2010) suggest that the causes of such patterns lie mainly on the supply side: Educational expansion at the basic level leads to rising qualifications required for particular jobs, making it increasingly difficult to find jobs without an education beyond the basic level. On the demand side, increased

Figure 2.16 Changes in Marginal Returns to Education in the 1990s in Latin America

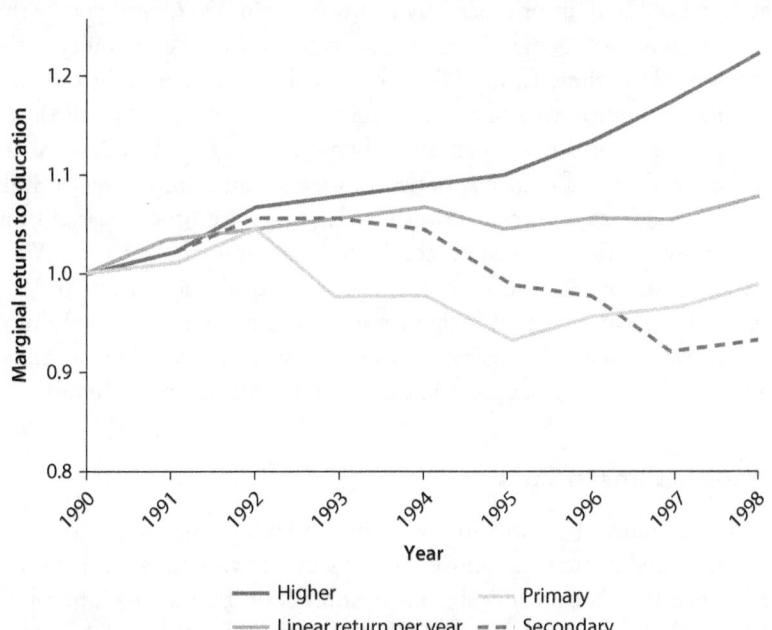

Source: Behrman, Birdsall, and Szekely 2003.

openness to trade and foreign investment might also have driven up demand for high-skilled workers.

On the one hand, these trends send a strong signal that government should continue to expand the upper secondary and tertiary levels of education. On the other hand, the high private returns to higher levels of education also imply that, for relatively poor provinces such as Yunnan, public financing of upper secondary and tertiary education should focus more on equity and supporting low-income students, while letting high-income families share the private costs.

At the upper secondary level, both in Yunnan and nationwide, the returns to secondary TVET appear to be higher than the returns to a general high school education. Nationwide, the gap between returns to general high school education and secondary TVET has been widening over time, with returns to high school slightly increasing between 1995 and 2002, and eventually decreasing between 2002 and 2007. *In contrast to the national trend, in Yunnan, returns to a general high school education exhibit a steeper increase between 1995 and 2002 than returns to secondary TVET, narrowing the gap between the two.* Our data from Kunming suggest that, in 2012, holders of secondary TVET diplomas only earn about 5 percent more than holders of high school diplomas. The narrowing gap between secondary TVET and general high school in Kunming seems to suggest that secondary high school degrees and TVET degrees are becoming less differentiated in terms of their returns in Yunnan's labor market.

We also tested whether rates of return to an additional year of education vary by gender, ethnicity, or enterprise ownership. The results are presented in appendix A. Nationwide, women have higher returns to education, and the difference is statistically significant. The difference was most pronounced in 2002, at 3 percent, and dropped slightly to 1 percent in 2007. Workers of ethnic minority groups do not seem to have returns to education that are much different from those of Han ethnicity. In 2007, we are able to categorize firm ownership, and we find that employees of SOEs, government agencies, and public institutions all have lower returns to education than employees of entities that are not publicly owned, and the difference is statistically significant. Employees of SOEs seem to have as much as 4 percent lower returns to education compared to non-public enterprises. Although we also conducted the same analysis using Yunnan's subsample, most of these differences are not statistically significant. In 1995, women seemed to have 2 percent higher returns to education. In urban Kunming, working in government administration also generates 3 percent higher returns for each additional year of education than working for other types of employers.

Wage Returns to Skills

Trends in rates of returns imply an increasing demand for workers with upper secondary education and above. In this section, we estimate returns to cognitive, non-cognitive, and technical skills beyond education as measured by the STEP household survey. Definitions of all measures used in the analysis and full estimation results are presented in appendix A.

Among cognitive skills, reading and writing skills are associated with higher wages. Workers who read at work earn on average 8–12 percent more than those who do not read. Furthermore, the difference remains positive and significant after we control for education levels, occupations, and sectors. Workers whose work involved writing more than 25 pages earn about 19–23 percent more than those who do not write at work. In comparison, more advanced levels of numeracy skills are not associated with higher wages, except that people who need to perform simple tasks such as measuring and calculating prices earn 11 percent more than those who do not do any math at work, holding education levels constant. However, the association is no longer significant once we control for occupations, suggesting that the demand for basic numeracy skills might be specific to occupation. In addition, higher-wage jobs appear to be more cognitively challenging as workers who have to spend at least 30 minutes thinking at work every day earn 20–25 percent more than those whose jobs barely involve any thinking, and the difference is significant even after controlling for education levels, occupations, and sectors.

A number of technical skills appear to be associated with higher wages across and within industries and occupations. For example, jobs that involve computer use pay 9–17 percent more than those which do not—even after controlling for education levels, sectors, and occupations. Higher paying jobs also appear to offer workers more freedom and autonomy. Fluency in a foreign language is associated with about 11 percent higher wages. The difference is no longer significant once we control for non-cognitive skills. Interestingly, jobs that involve more contact with people outside of co-workers, such as firm clients, seem to pay less.

We also estimated the returns to non-cognitive skills, and the results are presented in appendix A. Most of the non-cognitive skills do not seem to be significantly associated with wages, except for openness, which measures creativity and how open people are to new experiences. Openness seems to be correlated with higher education levels, but even after controlling for education levels, sector, industry, and cognitive and technical skills, higher measures of openness remain significantly associated with higher wages.

Demand for Skills: Evidence from STEP Employer Survey

Analysis of the STEP Household survey data from Kunming suggests that jobs that involve more reading, writing, and thinking pay better. It also suggests that technical skills such as computer use and foreign languages are demanded across occupations and sectors, in addition to level of education. Moreover, people rated to be more open also earn higher wages in our analysis. In this section, we examine the demand for skills from the employers' perspective. Which occupations are in high demand? What cognitive, non-cognitive, and technical skills are most sought after?

According to the STEP Employer Survey (box 2.3), the demand for workers in every type of occupation has been growing, but the fastest growth in demand is for technicians, professionals, and managers.

Box 2.3 STEP Employer Survey 2012

The STEP Employer Survey was conducted in Kunming, Yunnan, in 2012. The survey selected 300 non-public enterprises in Kunming using stratified random sampling based on industry and firm size. The survey contains such information as the firms' background information, hiring and recruiting practices, employers' perception of vocational and general education, and compensation.

The survey helps identify the cognitive, non-cognitive and technical skills most used and sought after by employers in each occupational category. Ten occupational categories are grouped into type A, which demands more skills (managers, professionals, technicians/associate professionals), and type B (clerical support workers, service workers, sales workers, skilled agricultural/forestry/fishery workers, construction/craft and related trades workers, plant and machine operators/assemblers, and elementary occupations).

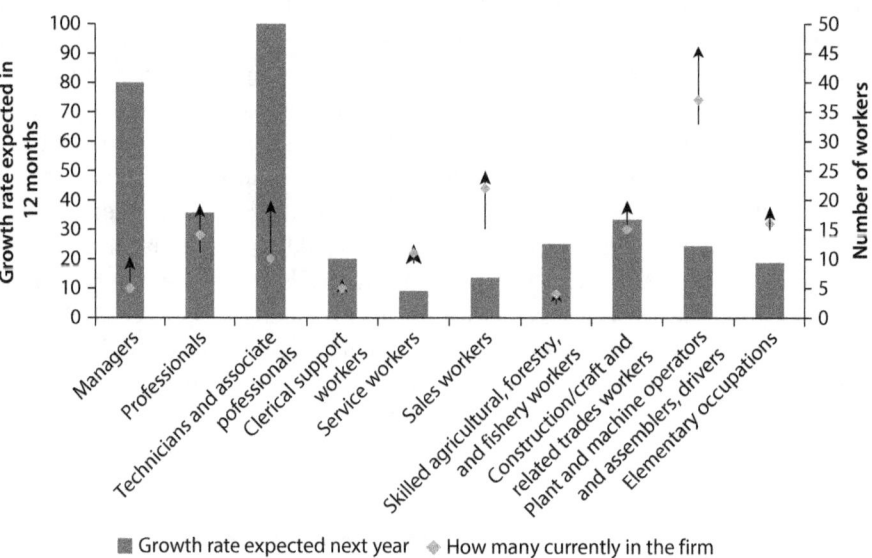

Figure 2.17 Number of Workers 12 Months Ago, Currently, and Expected in 12 Months

Source: STEP Employer Survey 2012.
Note: The starting point of each arrow represents the average number of workers in each category 12 months before the survey; the endpoint represents the average number of workers expected within 12 months after the survey. The purple dots mark the average number of workers during the time of the survey, and the blue bars represent the expected growth rate.

In figure 2.17, the starting point of each arrow represents the average number of workers in each category 12 months before, while the endpoint represents the average number of workers expected within 12 months after the survey. The orange dots mark the average number of workers during the time of the survey, and the blue bars represent the expected growth rate. Among all occupations, the number of technicians/associate professionals is expected to double in

Skills Challenges: Demand, Gaps, and Mismatches

12 months' time, the highest growth rate. The number of managers is also expected to grow by 40 percent. Kunming currently has the highest number of plant and machine operators/assemblers/drivers, and the number is expected to continue to grow by over 20 percent. In addition, the number of construction/craft and related trades workers is also expected to grow by over 30 percent in 12 months' time.

The STEP Employer Survey also shows the specific skills in demand for different types of occupations. Figure 2.18 illustrates the job-related skills considered most important by firms deciding which new employees to retain after a probation period. For type A occupations, 34 percent of the firms consider

Figure 2.18 Percent of Firms Reporting Various Job-Related Skills as Important to Employee Retention
Percent

a. Type A occupations

Skill	Percent
Leadership skills	35.56
Job-specific technical skills	27.16
Communication skills	16.84
Ability to read and write in a foreign language	5.82
Literacy	5.02
Numeracy	4.24
Creative and critical thinking	2.40
Problem solving skills	1.90
Teamwork skills	1.51
Ability to work independently	0.94
Time management skills	0.60

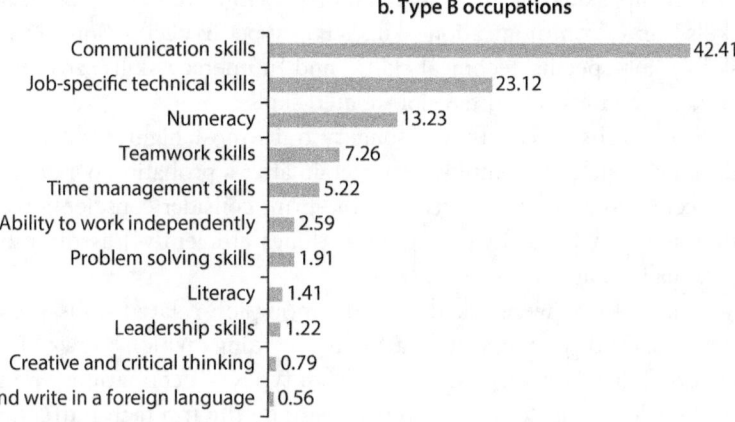

b. Type B occupations

Skill	Percent
Communication skills	42.41
Job-specific technical skills	23.12
Numeracy	13.23
Teamwork skills	7.26
Time management skills	5.22
Ability to work independently	2.59
Problem solving skills	1.91
Literacy	1.41
Leadership skills	1.22
Creative and critical thinking	0.79
Ability to read and write in a foreign language	0.56

Source: STEP Employer Survey 2012.
Note: Type A occupations include managers, professionals, technicians/associate professionals; type B occupations include clerical support workers, service workers, sales workers, skilled agricultural/forestry/fishery workers, construction/craft and related trades workers, plant and machine operators/assemblers, and elementary occupations.

Figure 2.19 Percent of Firms Reporting Various Personality Traits as Important to Employee Retention

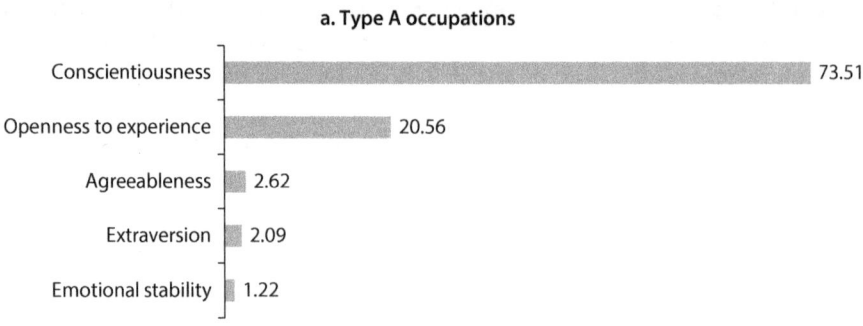

Source: STEP Employer Survey 2012.
Note: Type A occupations include managers, professionals, technicians/associate professionals; type B occupations include clerical support workers, service workers, sales workers, skilled agricultural/forestry/fishery workers, construction/craft and related trades workers, plant and machine operators/assemblers, and elementary occupations.

"leadership skills" as the most important, followed by "job-specific technical skills," and "communication skills." For type B occupations, "communication skills", "job-specific technical skills," and "numeracy skills" are most commonly cited as the most important job-related skills.

Figure 2.19 reveals the personality traits most highly valued by firms when deciding which new employees to retain after a probation period. For both types of occupations, over 70 percent of the firms consider conscientiousness ("Does a thorough job, is hard working, does things efficiently") as the most important personality trait.

Finally, firms were asked to rank among job-related skills, personal characteristics, and personality traits in deciding which new hires to retain (figure 2.20). Not surprisingly, for both types of occupations, the vast majority of the firms consider job-related skills to be the top factor affecting their decision to retain new hires after a probation period. Personality traits are considered more important than personal characteristics such as appearance, age, and gender.

Figure 2.20 Percent of Firms Reporting Various Factors as Important to Employee Retention

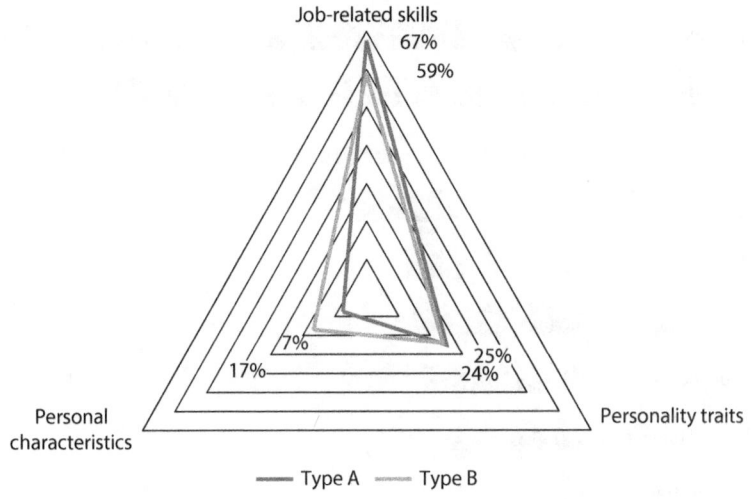

Source: STEP Employer Survey 2012.
Note: Type A occupations include managers, professionals, technicians/associate professionals; type B occupations include clerical support workers, service workers, sales workers, skilled agricultural/forestry/fishery workers, construction/craft and related trades workers, plant and machine operators/assemblers, and elementary occupations.

Skills Gaps and Mismatches

Compared to other parts of China, a skills shortage was not yet a major factor impeding Yunnan's growth in the mid-2000s. Thirteen percent of the enterprises surveyed by the World Bank's Investment Climate Assessment (2005) in Yunnan indicated worker skills and education level as the most or second most severe factors constraining growth, placing it 7th among the 14 factors listed on the survey. As shown in figure 2.21, the top constraints faced by the firms are electricity, access to finance, and transport. In comparison, when we take into account all 120 cities across China, as many as 28 percent of the firms surveyed list worker skills and education level as the most severe constraint, the second most common of all factors.

Yunnan undertook economic reforms at a relatively later date than the rest of China, especially in the coastal areas. Thus, the survey likely reveals that the challenges faced by Yunnan are different from those faced by major cities in other parts of China: Infrastructure and access to finance were the most pressing concerns for firms' growth in Yunnan in 2005.

The most recent employer survey conducted in Kunming in 2012 suggests that the situation has changed: *Labor factors are now considered the most pressing in constraining operations and growth.* Among various labor factors, "finding workers with previous experience" and "[TVET] of workers" are the two most severe factors impeding the operation and growth of business, as indicated by figure 2.22. In comparison, the general education of workers and availability of labor are considered less problematic.

Figure 2.21 Firms Facing Factors Constraining Growth in Yunnan and China, 2005

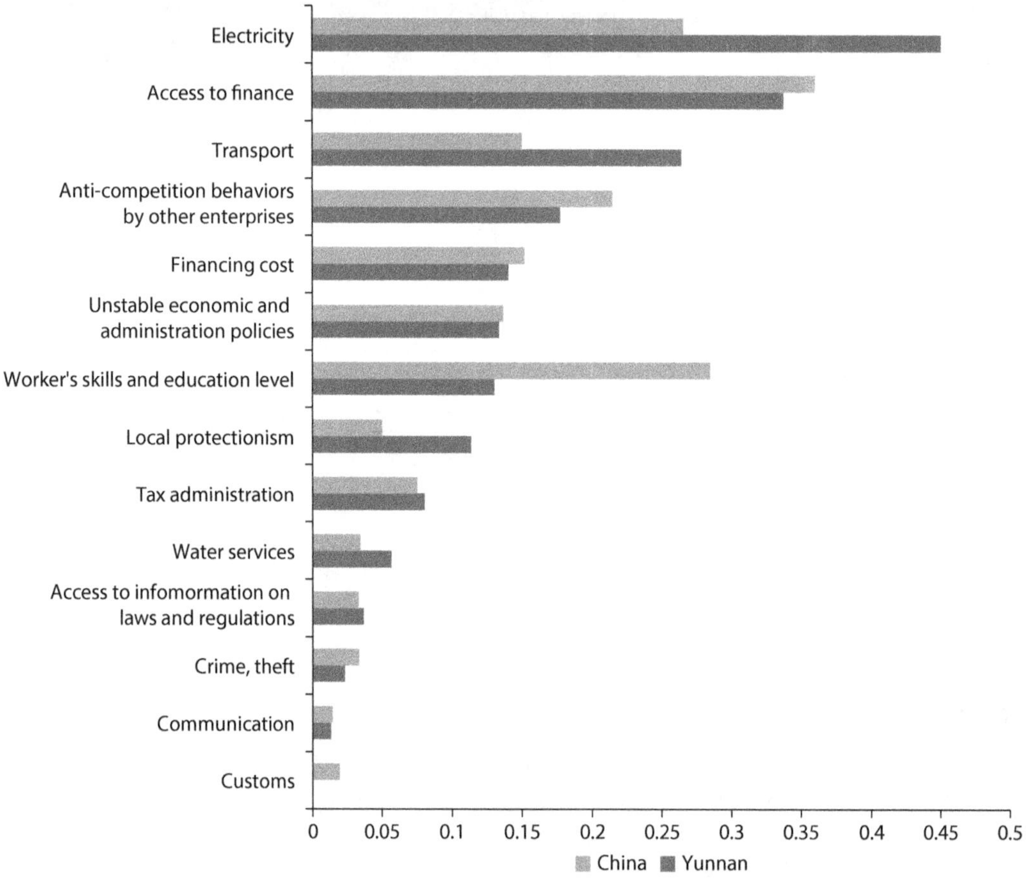

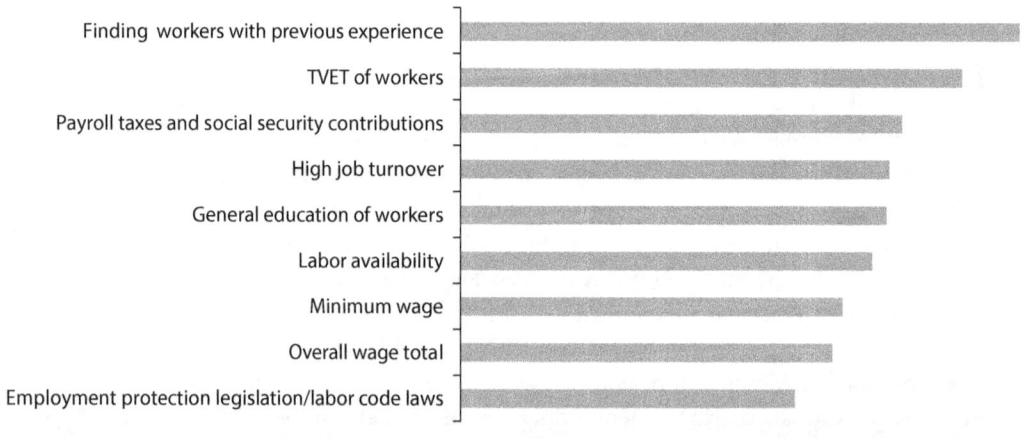

Source: World Bank 2005.
Note: The figure shows the percentage of firms that consider the factor as the most or second most severe factor constraining growth.

Figure 2.22 Rankings of Labor Factors Impeding Business Operation and Growth

Source: STEP Employer Survey 2012.

Skills Challenges: Demand, Gaps, and Mismatches

Moreover, on average, firms in Kunming considered only around 82–84 percent of their employees qualified for the job. Illustrated by the histogram in figure 2.23, fewer than 45 percent of the firms considered over 90 percent of their employees qualified for their jobs. Nearly 10 percent of the firms considered 30 percent or fewer of their managers, professionals, and technicians qualified.

Potential skills gaps and mismatches are further indicated by the job vacancy data. Throughout 2010 and 2011, although the total number of job openings in Yunnan exceeded the pool of applicants, only around 50–55 percent of the applicants were hired, filling 35–45 percent of the total openings (figure 2.24).

Figure 2.23 Percent of Employees Considered Qualified for Their Jobs

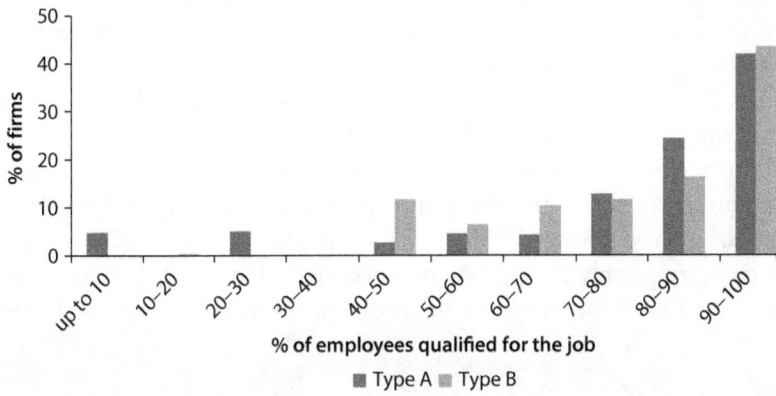

Source: STEP Employer Survey 2012.
Note: Type A occupations include managers, professionals, technicians/associate professionals; type B occupations include clerical support workers, service workers, sales workers, skilled agricultural/forestry/fishery workers, construction/craft and related trades workers, plant and machine operators/assemblers, and elementary occupations.

Figure 2.24 Quarterly Job Vacancies and Applications in Yunnan, 2010–11

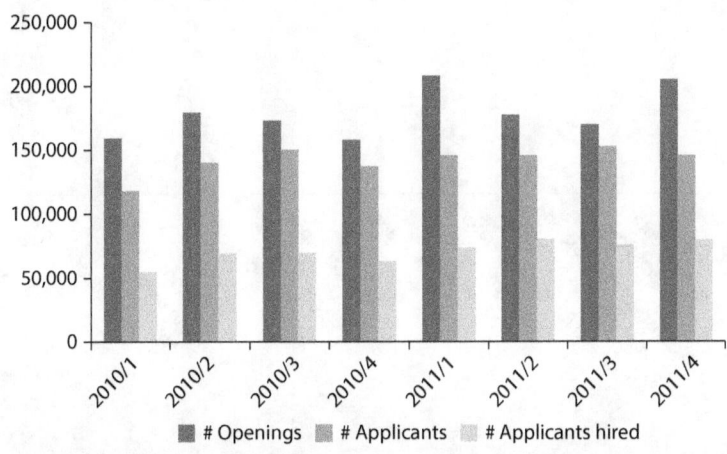

Source: HRSS 2010a, 2011.

To further characterize the potential skills gaps and mismatches, we draw on insights into firm hiring of new employees as revealed by the STEP Employer Survey. According to the survey, for firms in Kunming, it takes on average 34 days to fill a manager/professional/technician position, that is, much longer than the 16 days needed to fill a less-skilled type B position. On average, each job opening receives 14–16 applications. Moreover, more than 9 percent of the firms have used contractors for skill shortages in type A positions, and more than 17 percent have used contractors for type B positions.

More firms have encountered problems hiring professional and technical workers than hiring workers in lower-skilled occupations (figure 2.25). Among firms that have tried to hire in the past year, 89 percent have encountered problems hiring sales workers, 74 percent hiring professionals, and 72 percent hiring technicians/associate professionals. In comparison, only 1.4 percent and 30 percent of the firms have encountered problems in trying to hire skilled agricultural/forestry/fishery workers and elementary occupation workers, respectively.

Tables 2.4 and 2.5 show the specific problems encountered in hiring. *Across type A occupations, the lack of skills and mismatches of expected wages are the two most common problems encountered.* Lack of skills is identified as an issue by 73–81 percent of the firms hiring professionals and technicians/associate professionals. For type B occupations, "applicants lacked required skills" is again one of the most commonly cited problems encountered in hiring. In particular, over 91 percent of the firms reported the problem when hiring plant and machine

Figure 2.25 Percent of Firms Encountering Problems Hiring Employees at Various Levels

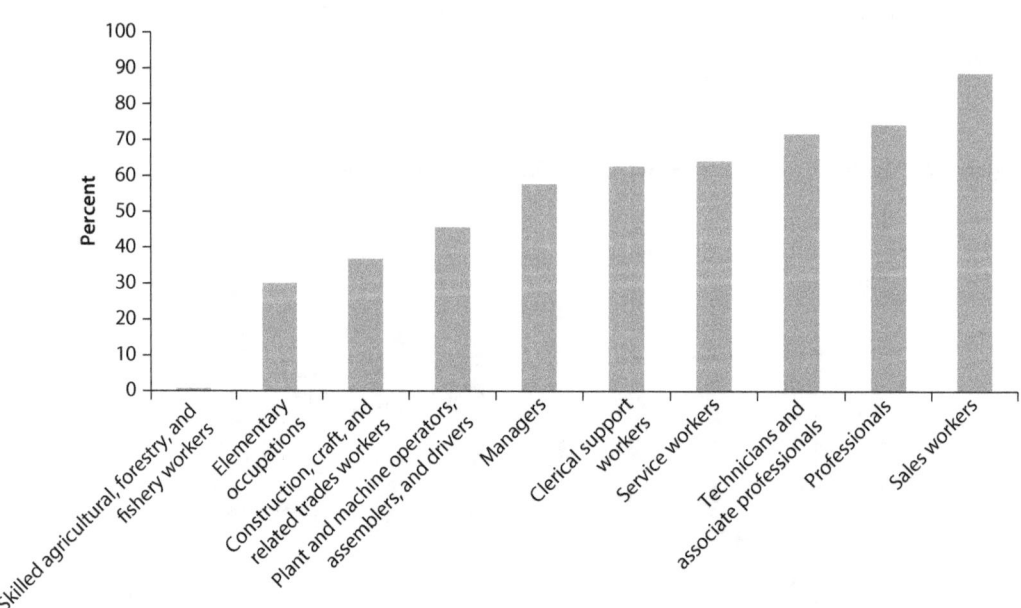

Source: STEP Employer Survey 2012.

Table 2.4 Percent of Firms Encountering Hiring Problems, Type A Occupations

	Managers	Professionals	Technicians and associate professionals
There are no or few applicants	40	38	34
Applicants lacked required skills	58	81	73
Applicants expected wages higher than we can offer	77	56	63
Applicants did not like working conditions	22	32	51

Source: STEP Employer Survey 2012.
Note: The two most common problems are highlighted in gray.

Table 2.5 Percent of Firms Encountering Hiring Problems, Type B Occupations

	Clerical support workers	Service workers	Sales workers	Skilled agricultural, forestry, and fishery workers	Construction/ craft and related trades workers	Plant and machine operators, assemblers, and drivers	Elementary occupations
There are no or few applicants	20	25	35	34	71	43	9
Applicants lacked required skills	60	61	66	32	51	91	77
Applicants expected wages higher than we can offer	65	56	76	38	61	27	74
Applicants did not like working conditions	49	73	66	34	24	23	88

Source: STEP Employer Survey 2012.
Note: The two most common problems are highlighted in gray.

operators/assemblers/drivers. Further, in hiring construction/craft and related trade workers, over 70 percent of the firms encounter the problem of "no or few applicants." Unmatched wage expectation is also a common problem in the hiring of clerical support workers, service workers, skilled agricultural/forestry/fishery workers, and elementary occupations. Working conditions have posed challenges in hiring service workers and elementary occupation workers.

Drivers of Future Demand for Skills

As China's economic reforms deepen and spread to the interior provinces, the enormous opportunities for development in Yunnan will also bring new skills challenges. The central government has projected three major transformations as the guiding principles for China's economic growth in the new era moving from: (1) investment-led to consumption-led growth; (2) a high-energy to a low-carbon based economy; and (3) relying on low-cost manufacturing to relying on science, technology, and innovation. Guided by these principles, Yunnan has been pursuing its own development strategy of building a strong province with a green economy, diverse culture, and a bridgehead for opening China to South Asia and Southeast Asia. Economic growth and structural changes, as well as the Bridgehead Strategy, as specified in Yunnan's 12th Five-Year Economic Development Plan (12th Five-Year Plan), are expected to further drive the demand for skills.

Driver 1: Economic Growth and Structural Changes

Yunnan's real GDP has been growing at an annual rate of over 10 percent in recent years. The 12th Five-Year Plan sets goals for Yunnan of maintaining its annual growth rate and reaching a GDP of more than Y1,163 billion in 2015. Table 2.6 lists some of the other goals set out in the plan pertaining to economic growth and structural changes.

How much of the GDP growth can be translated into employment and jobs? Although the number of people employed has been increasing with real GDP, employment growth rates are much lower than GDP growth rates. Figure 2.26 illustrates the trends in GDP growth and employment in Yunnan over the past decades.

The relationship between real GDP growth and job growth rates also varies by sector, as shown in figure 2.27. The primary sector, while employing the largest number of laborers, has seen the slowest growth in real GDP. Further, total employment has been decreasing in recent years. The secondary sector in Yunnan has seen rapid growth in real GDP, but employment has remained flat with slight increases in recent years. In comparison, while the tertiary sector hasn't grown as quickly as the secondary sector in terms of real GDP, it has the fastest growth in demand for labor.

Over the next five years, the secondary and tertiary sectors are expected to continue to grow, with the tertiary sector expected to generate increasing employment. The structure of the economy is to be further optimized and diversified, leveraging Yunnan's unique resources and advantages. The composition of Yunnan's economy has been gradually moving away from one dominated by agriculture. In 2010, the secondary sector contributed the most to Yunnan's economy

Table 2.6 Selected Goals Specified in Yunnan's 12th Five-Year Plan

Indicator	2010	2015	Annual growth	Total growth
Yunnan GDP (2010Y)	722 billion	>1,163 billion	>10%	n.a.
Industrial composition[a] (%)	15:45:40	12:46:42	n.a.	n.a.
Light:heavy sector (%)	46.2:53.8	48.2:51.8	n.a.	n.a.
Value added by tertiary sector (%)	40	>42	n.a.	>2
Share of employment in tertiary sector (%)	28.8	35.7	n.a.	6.9
Urbanization rate (%)	36	45	2	9
New urban employment (persons)	24 million	22 million	n.a.	n.a.

Source: Yunnan 12th Five-Year Plan (2011–15).
Note: n.a. = not applicable.
a. Consisting of primary, secondary, and tertiary sectors.

Figure 2.26 Real GDP and Number of People Employed in Yunnan, Real and Projected, 1957–2015

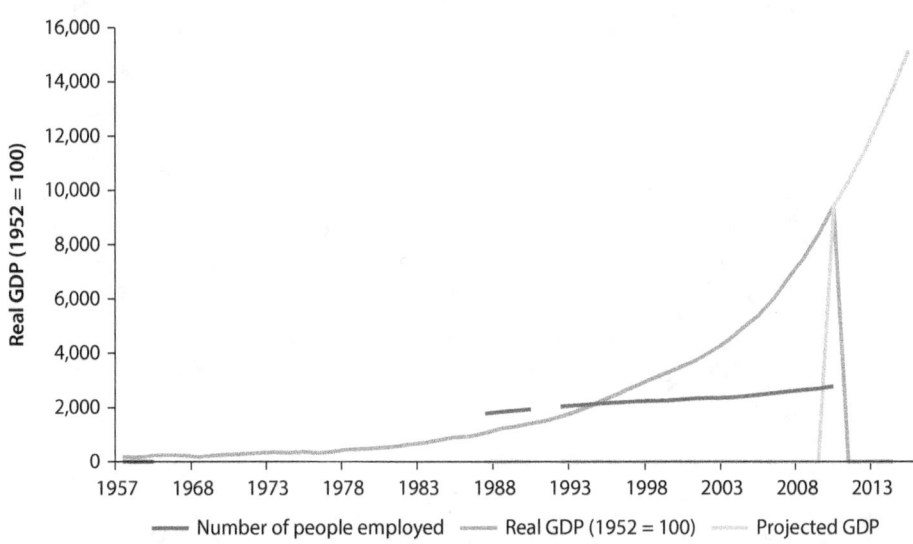

Sources: Yunnan Statistical Yearbook 2011; Yunnan 12th Five-Year Plan (2011–15).

(45 percent), followed by the tertiary sector (40 percent) and the primary sector (15 percent). The shares of the secondary and tertiary sectors in the economy are expected to continue to grow by 2 percent each over the next five years. Within the secondary sector, the government particularly encourages the development of the labor-intensive light sector. Furthermore, the tertiary sector is expected to account for 36 percent of total employment by 2015, a 7 percent increase from 2010.

Driver 2: Bridgehead Strategy

Recognizing its strategic location, the Chinese government has formulated a Bridgehead Strategy (桥头堡) to position Yunnan as: (1) a strategic gateway to the Southwest; (2) an experimental zone for opening up China's southwestern borders; (3) a base for export-oriented, distinct, and competitive industries in the western region; (4) a treasure house of biodiversity and a safety net for the ecosystem in the Southwest; and (5) a national-level model zone for ethnic harmony and border stability.

The national strategy is expected to further accelerate Yunnan's provincial development and strengthen its openness and exchange with neighboring countries and provinces. Yunnan has been upgrading its transportation infrastructure connecting to Southeast Asia and building a pipeline for oil and gas supplies. More cooperation and exchange is expected, both internationally with the Greater Mekong Sub-region and domestically with other economic zones within China.

Yunnan will adopt both the strategy of "coming in," by allowing more foreign investment and attracting financial and human capital from abroad, and

Figure 2.27 Real GDP and Employment by Sector, 1957–2008

a. Primary sector

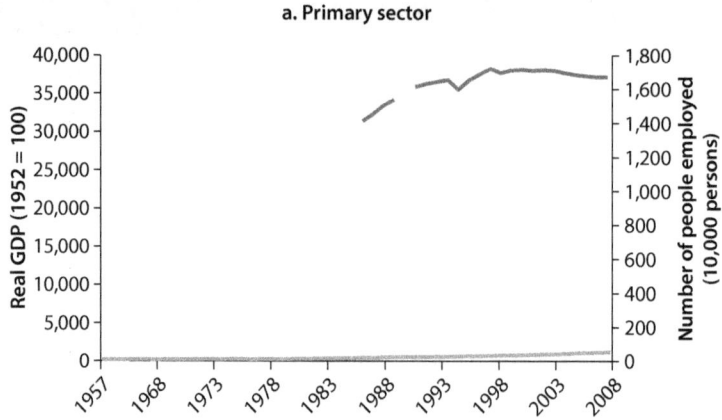

b. Secondary sector

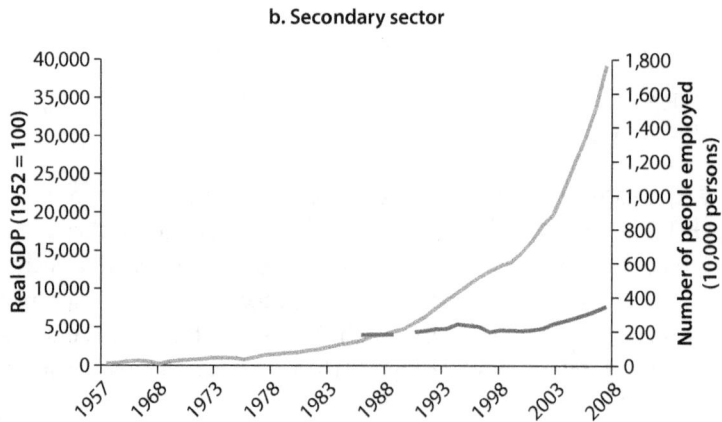

c. Tertiary sector

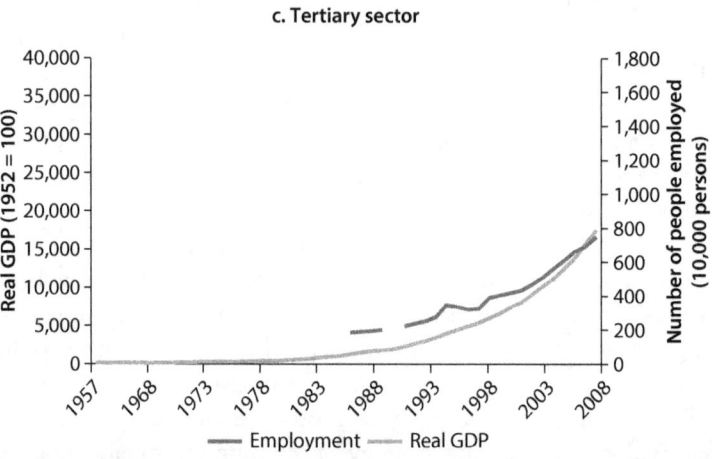

—— Employment —— Real GDP

Source: Yunnan Statistical Yearbook 2011.

the strategy of "going out," by leveraging the resources and demand in the foreign market and increasing the scale and effectiveness of investments abroad. The Bridgehead Strategy will not only create more employment in the secondary sector, but, more importantly, will drive the demand for high-skilled professionals and technicians in transportation, logistics, international trade, and finance.

In order to sustain economic growth and reach its development goals, Yunnan will need to increase the number of skilled laborers, improve the quality of human resources, and optimize the skills composition of its labor force. Specific targets have been laid out in Yunnan's 12th Five-Year Plan, as well as in its Medium- and Long-term Plan for Talent Development. Table 2.7 lists Yunnan's

Table 2.7 Projected Demand for Skills in Yunnan, 2010–20

	2010	2015	2020
Overall goals			
Average years of education received by new labor force (years)	8	12.5	n.a.
Total amount of talent resources (millions of people)	2.51	n.a.	5
Talent share of total human resources (%)	n.a.	n.a.	13
Proportion of GDP spent on human resources (%)	n.a.	n.a.	10
Talent contribution rate (%)	n.a.	n.a.	20
GER[a] at upper secondary level (%)	65	85	n.a.
R&D[b] spending as percent of GDP (%)	0.6	1.5	n.a.
Develop high-level innovative talent			
Proportion of labor force with tertiary education (%)	n.a.	n.a.	15
R&D[b] employees per 10,000 laborers	n.a.	n.a.	15
Selected types of talent			
Party and government officials holding college degree and above (%)	n.a.	n.a.	87
Enterprise management talent	n.a.	575,400	729,500
Professional and technical talent (millions)	n.a.	1.36	1.58[c]
High-skilled workers[d]			
Total number of high-skilled workers	420,000	613,900	811,900
Number certified at Levels 1 and 2	45,000	70,000	100,000
High skilled workers' share of total skilled labor (%)	21	25	26
Rural practical talent (millions of people)	n.a.	1.03	1.57
Ten industries urgently needing talent	Tobacco, energy, nonferrous metals, black metals, petroleum and chemicals, biotechnology, tourism and culture, commercial and trade circulation, equipment manufacturing, optic-electronics		

Sources: Yunnan 12th Five-Year Plan; Yunnan Talent Development Plan (2010b), Yunnan High-Skilled Talent Cultivation Medium- and Long-Term Plan (2010–20).
Note: n.a. = not applicable.
a. GER = gross enrollment ratio.
b. R&D = research and development.
c. Target distribution is senior (10 percent), medium (40 percent), and junior (50 percent).
d. High-skilled workers are roughly defined as technicians who are certified as senior (Level 3), technicians (Level 2), and senior technicians (Level 1).

most important targets, a list that can also be read as the projected demand for skills. Consistent with our previous analysis, Yunnan has aimed to raise its overall level of human resources, with a focus on developing professional and technical skills. The plans also list ten key sectors of strategic importance, as well as urgent needs for skills concentrated in the secondary and tertiary sectors.

Summary

In this chapter, we have reviewed the education and skills composition of the current workforce in Yunnan, which reveals an increasing demand for skills. Labor force and employer surveys shed light on the specific skills in demand and reveal emerging skills gaps and mismatches in Yunnan.

Employment in Yunnan has been historically dominated by the agriculture sector, but the shares of secondary and tertiary employment have been on the rise over the past decade. In recent years, employment has been driven mostly by the tertiary and secondary sectors. At the same time, employment in SOEs and collectives has been declining. Today the non-public sector absorbs nearly half of the total employment in Yunnan.

Although the education levels of the labor force have been increasing, the skills levels of the labor force in Yunnan remain low compared to the national average, as well as to other parts of China. A majority of workers have completed only compulsory education or less. Further, the primary and secondary sectors, employing the largest number of workers, are composed mostly of frontline/operative skilled workers. Skill certification rates are also low among technical, professional, and frontline/operative skilled workers.

Nevertheless, a rising demand for skills in Yunnan is indicated by the rising wage returns to education. Rates of return for an additional year of education in Yunnan have increased from more than 3 percent in 1988 to more than 7 percent in 2002. During the same period, returns to every level of education beyond the junior secondary level increased in Yunnan, with the most dramatic increase occurring at the tertiary level. Gaps in returns between tertiary and secondary education and between Bachelor's degrees and associate degrees have been widening, indicating a particularly strong demand for higher-skilled workers with tertiary education, especially those with Bachelor's degrees.

A number of cognitive, non-cognitive, and technical skills measured by the STEP Household survey are associated with higher wages—even after controlling for level of education. According to our analysis of data from Kunming, higher-wage jobs require more intense reading, writing, and thinking skills. In addition to higher levels of education, computer and foreign language skills are technical skills in demand across occupations and sectors. Among non-cognitive skills measures, openness appears consistently associated with higher wages.

Demand for higher skills is further revealed from employers' perspectives. Firms in Yunnan increasingly seek to hire high-skilled professionals and technicians, and the demand for frontline/operative skilled workers remains high. Apart from job-specific technical skills, firms also consider "leadership skills" and "communication skills" to be among the most important job-related skills. Conscientiousness has been cited by over 70 percent of the firms as the most important non-cognitive skill.

As the demand for skills has grown, skills shortages and mismatches have begun to emerge. Among various labor factors, "finding workers with previous experience" and "[TVET] of workers" appear to be the factors most severely impeding the operation and growth of businesses. Skills shortages and mismatches have caused problems for firms trying to hire new employees and prevented them from filling job vacancies. Particularly, in hiring for managerial, professional, and technical positions, the "lack of required skill" and "mismatch of wage expectation" are the two most common problems. For frontline/operative skilled workers, "lack of required skill" and "lack of applicants" are the two major problems.

The latest policy developments specified in Yunnan's 12th Five-Year Plan are expected to intensify the demand for skills in the future. To sustain economic growth and carry out the Bridgehead Strategy, Yunnan will need to increase the overall quality of human resources and optimize the composition of skills within its labor force. A key to bridging the gaps and addressing the skills challenges faced by firms in Yunnan lies in strengthening its education and training system. How can the quality and goals of the formal education and training system be better aligned with the skills demands of employers? How can Yunnan promote the access to, relevance, and quality of non-formal training to improve the skills of employees? These issues will be addressed in detail in the following chapters.

Notes

1. Except for 1988, where we estimated the number of years according to the highest level of education reported by individuals.
2. Years of experience = age − years of schooling − 6.
3. Due to the limitations of the data, ethnicity is not controlled for in estimating returns for Yunnan (Kunming) 2012.

Bibliography

Behrman, J., N. Birdsall, and M. Szekely. 2003. "Economic Policy and Wage Differentials in Latin America." Center for Global Development Working Paper 29, Washington, DC.

Blom, A., L. Holm-Nielsen, and D. Verner. 2001. "Education, Earnings and Inequality in Brazil, 1982–1998: Implications for Education Policy." *Peabody Journal of Education* 76 (3–4): 180–221.

Chinese Household Income Project Series [database]. ICPSR03012-v2. Inter-university Consortium for Political and Social Research [distributor], Ann Arbor, MI. http://www.icpsr.umich.edu/icpsrweb/DSDR/series/00243.

National Bureau of Statistics of China. 2011. *China Labor Statistical Yearbook*. Beijing: China Statistics Press.

———. 2011. *China Statistical Yearbook*. Beijing: China Statistics Press.

Colclough, C., G. Kingdon, and H. Patrinos. 2010. "The Changing Pattern of Wage Returns to Education and Its Implications." *Development Policy Review* 28 (6): 733–47.

Fiszbein, A., H. A. Patrinos, and P. I. Giovagnoli. 2007. "Estimating the Returns to Education in Argentina Using Quantile Regression Analysis: 1992–2002." *Economica* 53 (1, 2): 53–72.

HRSS (Yunnan Department of Human Resources and Social Security). 2010a. *Quarterly Vacancy Data.*

———. 2010b. *Yunnan Medium- and Long-Term Plan for Talent Development.* http://yn.yunnan.cn/html/2010-12/13/content_1438313.htm.

———. 2011. *Quarterly Vacancy Data.* http://www.ynhrss.gov.cn/list.aspx?KindID=000100030007.

———. n.d. *Yunnan High-Skilled Talent Cultivation Medium- and Long-Term Plan (2010–20).*

Keith, G., and R. Zhao. 1993. *The Distribution of Income in China.* London: Macmillan.

Li, S., C. Luo, Z. Wei, and X. Yue. 2008. "Appendix: The 1995 and 2002 Household Surveys: Sampling Methods and Data Description." In *Inequality and Public Policy in China*, edited by B. Gustafsson, S. Li, and T. Sicular, 337–54. Cambridge, U.K.: Cambridge University Press.

Liu, X., A. Park, and Y. Zhao. 2010. "Explaining Rising Returns to Education in Urban China in the 1990s." Discussion Paper Series No. 4872, Institute for the Study of Labor, Bonn, Germany.

Longitudinal Survey on Rural Urban Migration in China (RUMiC) [database]. Institute for the Study of Labor, Bonn, Germany. http://idsc.iza.org/?page=27&id=58.

Mincer, J. 1974. *Schooling, Experience, and Earnings.* New York: NBER Press.

Riboud, M., Y. Savchenko, and H. Tan. 2007. *The Knowledge Economy and Education and Training in South Asia.* Washington, DC: World Bank.

Riskin, C., Z. Renwei, and L. Shi. 2001. *China's Retreat from Equality: Income Distribution and Economic Transition.* Armonk, NY: M.E. Sharpe.

Sanchez-Puerta, M. L., A. Valerio, G. Pierre, and S. Urzua. 2012. STEP Skills Measurement Surveys Methodology Note Draft. World Bank, Washington, DC.

Skills Toward Employment and Productivity Employer Survey. 2012. World Bank, Washington, DC.

World Bank. 2005. *Investment Climate Assessment.* Washington, DC: World Bank.

———. 2012. *China 2030 Conference Edition.* Annex Table 10, p. 214.

World Development Indicators (database). World Bank, Washington, DC. http://data.worldbank.org/data-catalog/world-development-indicators.

Yunnan Bureau of Statistics. 2008. *Yunnan Non-public Enterprise Survey.* Beijing: China Statistics Press.

———. 2002–11. *Yunnan Statistical Yearbook.* Beijing: China Statistics Press.

Zhang, J., Y. Zhao, A. Park, and X. Song. "Economic Returns to Schooling in Urban China, 1988 to 2001." *Journal of Comparative Economics* 33: 730–52.

CHAPTER 3

Overview of Yunnan's Education and Training System

Yunnan's education and training system is the key to improving the skills of its population and ensuring a sufficient supply of skills to meet future challenges. This chapter offers an overview of the formal and non-formal education and training systems in Yunnan.

According to the provincial Department of Human Resources and Social Security, Yunnan's population totaled 46 million in 2010 and grew at a rate greater than 6 percent. In 2010, 72 percent of Yunnan's population was of working age. The total workforce amounted to 36 million in 2010, of whom 0.67 million were new entrants into the labor force. Demographically, Yunnan has a high birth rate of 13 percent as of 2010, which is more than 1 percent higher than the national average. Youth aged birth to 14 years account for 21 percent of Yunnan's total population.

Although the total supply of labor seems to be sufficient, the large population does not seem to ensure an attendant high stock of skills. Less than 15 percent of the total population has attained education beyond the compulsory level, compared to 23 percent nationwide. The illiteracy rate remains at 6 percent, almost 2 percent higher than the national average. At the same time that skills gaps are starting to emerge, Yunnan is also faced with a labor surplus, especially among the 65 percent of its population still residing in rural areas.

In China, education and training take place in both formal and non-formal settings. In this report, all diploma-oriented education programs are treated as part of the formal education and training system. Also included are adult learning and distance learning programs. Non-formal education and training include various non-diploma-oriented training programs.

Formal Education System

Figure 3.1 illustrates the structure of the formal education system in China. Highlighted in gray is the vocational track at different levels. The system starts with kindergarten and preschool for early childhood development at the

Figure 3.1 Structure of the Formal Education System, Yunnan

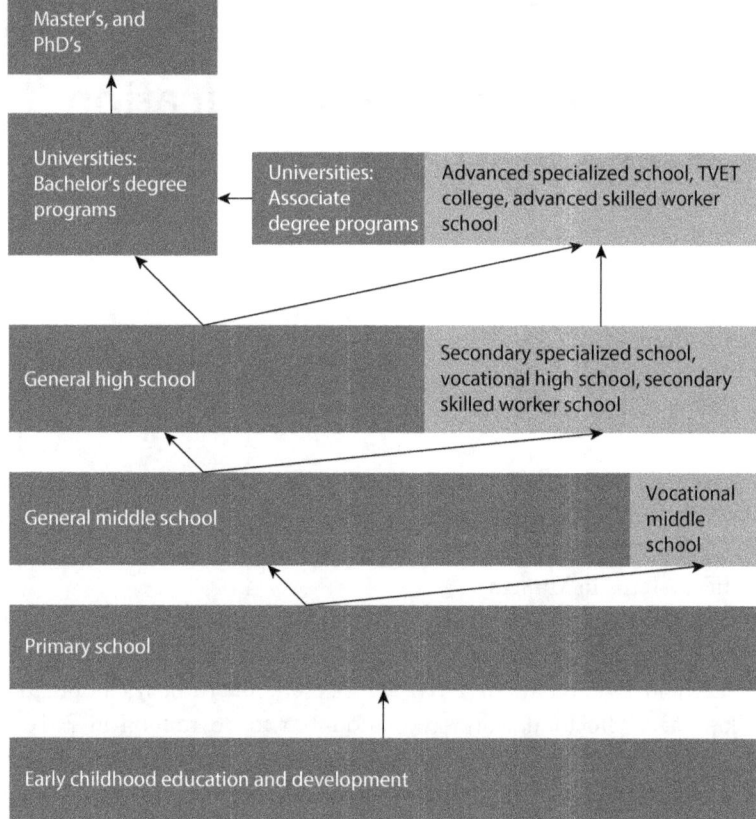

pre-primary level. Compulsory education starts at age six, with a duration of nine years through the end of middle school at the lower secondary level. There are a small number of vocational schools at the lower secondary level.

At the upper secondary level, Technical and Vocational Education and Training (TVET) is provided at vocational high schools, secondary specialized schools, and secondary skilled-worker schools. The main governance bodies are the Ministry of Education, which supervises vocational high schools and secondary specialized schools, and the Ministry of Human Resources and Social Security, which supervises secondary skilled-worker schools. At the tertiary level, TVET is provided mostly in TVET colleges, advanced specialized schools, and advanced skilled-worker schools. Some universities also offer vocational programs. Most of the TVET programs grant associate degrees. Although the majority of secondary TVET graduates enter the job market, some of them advance into tertiary-level programs, mostly associate degree programs or other TVET programs.

The share of Yunnan's students in basic-level education (currently enrolling over 6 million students), although gradually decreasing, is more than four times that of students in upper secondary-level education (table B.1). The shares of students in the secondary and tertiary education systems are expanding, as the number of students admitted is greater than the number of graduates. At the secondary level, the size of the general education and the vocational tracks are about the same, with each enrolling about 0.6 million students. At the tertiary level, Bachelor's degree programs currently enroll more students (0.26 million) than associate degree programs (0.18 million) and are expanding more quickly.

Despite the large number of students enrolled, enrollment rates and advancement rates are low and vary greatly across cities and prefectures within Yunnan (figure 3.2). For example, although the net enrollment rates at the primary level have exceeded 99 percent, only 96 percent of the primary school graduates advance to the lower secondary level. In the city of Baoshan, the advancement rate is only 85 percent. Further, only 73 percent of middle school graduates advance to the upper secondary level, and in 10 out of the 16 cities and prefectures, advancement rates to the senior secondary level are even lower than the provincial average. The highest advancement rate (94 percent in Yuxi) is more than double the lowest rate of 46 percent in Nujiang.

The relevance and quality of the formal education system are also called into question. According to the Skills Toward Employment and Productivity (STEP) Survey, among employers in Kunming (table 3.1), only 56 percent of the firms agree that the current TVET system meets the skill needs of employers adequately. More specifically, as many as 65 percent of the firms agree that the current TVET system does not produce enough workers with up-to-date knowledge of methods, materials, and technology. Over half of the firms also agree that the current TVET system does not produce enough people with a "good attitude and self-discipline" or "practical skills."

Likewise, fewer than half of firms consider the general education system to be adequately meeting the skills needs of employers. Sixty-seven percent of firms think that the general education system fails to produce enough people with up-to-date knowledge of methods, materials, and technology. Over half of the firms think that the current general education system does not produce enough people with either the level or the kinds of skills needed. Aside from job-related skills, 55 percent of firms think that the general education system does not produce people with a "good attitude and self-discipline." Employers' evaluations shed light on the weaknesses of the current formal education and training system. Specifically, the current system fails to keep up with the ever-evolving skills needs of employers, and both the TVET and general systems are unable to produce enough students with important non-cognitive skills, such as good attitude and self-discipline.

Non-Formal Training

According to the 2011 quarterly job vacancy data, the largest group of job applicants in Yunnan is the unemployed (including the newly unemployed, employment-to-unemployed, and others), followed by rural laborers, new

Figure 3.2 Advancement Rates Across Cities and Prefectures

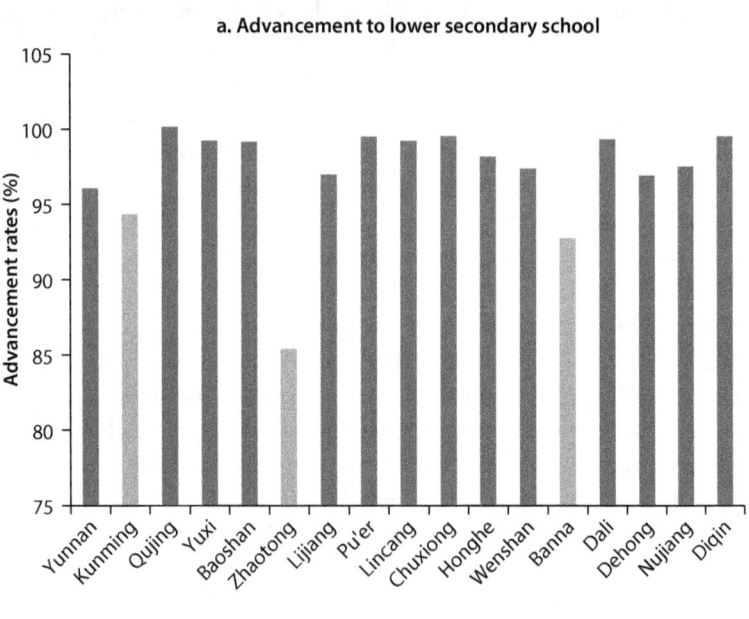

a. Advancement to lower secondary school

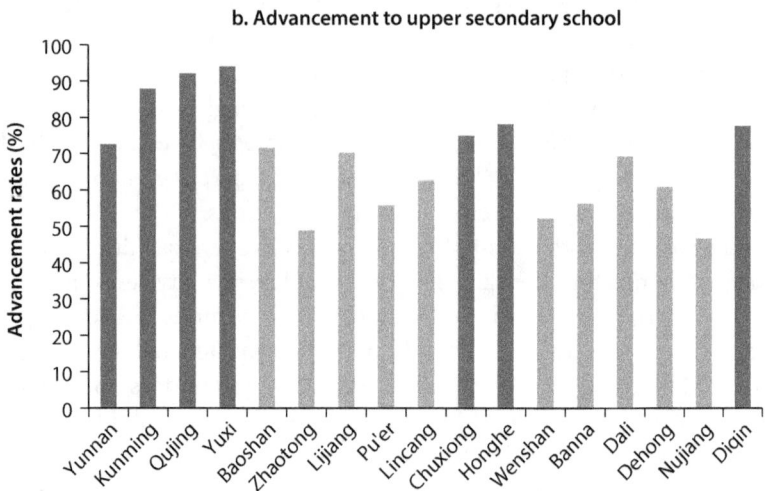

b. Advancement to upper secondary school

Source: Yun, Liu, and Li 2011.
Note: Darker and lighter bars represent advancement rates above and below the provincial average, respectively.

college graduates, and laid-off workers. Efforts to improve the skills and retrain the current labor force rely on various training programs outside of the formal education system.

In 2010, the Yunnan Department of Human Resources and Social Security, the Development and Reform Commission, and the Department of Finance jointly issued an Announcement on Implementing Special Vocational Training Plan (HRSS 2010). The Announcement identifies six major types of training

Table 3.1 Impressions of the TVET and General Education Systems, Yunnan (% of firms)

	TVET	General education system
Meets the skill needs of employers adequately	56	47
Does not produce enough people with the level of skills needed by employers	40	56
Does not produce enough people with the kinds of skills needed by employers	47	50
Does not produce enough people with up-to-date knowledge of methods, materials, and technology	66	67
Does not produce enough people with practical skills	58	49
Does not produce enough people with good attitude and self-discipline	59	55

Source: STEP Employer Survey 2012.

programs to be subsidized by public funds: (1) in-service and transfer training for employees; (2) migrant employee training; (3) rural labor transfer training and labor preparatory training; (4) reemployment training for the unemployed; (5) entrepreneurship training; and (6) urgently needed talent training.

The Announcement states that the government should devote at least 15 percent of its Employment Categorical Fund to subsidizing providers of vocational training. Training providers, including skilled worker schools, public employment training centers, and private institutions wishing to participate in subsidized training programs (such as migrant worker training, reemployment training, and rural labor transfer training) have to go through the initial application and review process, followed by regular inspection. Training providers participating in public vocational training programs also get government support for improving infrastructure and operating conditions.

For work-based training directed at employees, such as in-service, transfer, and migrant employee training, the government mandates that enterprises retain 1.5–2.5 percent of the total payroll for an Employee Education and Training Fund. In addition, at least 60 percent of the employee training fund should be spent on technical workers, especially frontline/operative workers. The government also provides additional subsidies to help employers suffering financial difficulties, and as incentives for enterprises and individuals (box 3.1).

There are three major types of external training providers: skilled-worker schools, employment training centers, and non-public training agencies. According to government statistics, non-public training agencies provided training to the largest number of people in 2009, followed by public employment training centers, and then skilled-worker schools (table B.2). Employment training centers, training mostly laid-off, unemployed workers, and rural workers, are characterized by high proportions of part-time teachers, high student-teacher ratios, and the short duration of their training programs: 77 percent of the trainees at public employment training centers receive training for less than six months.

Participants may or may not be certified upon completing non-formal training. According to 2009 statistics (table B.2), almost all trainees who attend skilled-worker schools are certified upon finishing, and 15 percent are certified

Box 3.1 Government Subsidies for Non-Formal Training in Yunnan

- *In-service and transfer training for employees.* Enterprises suffering financial difficulties that are participating in the unemployment insurance program can draw funds from unemployment insurance to finance training and subsidize up to 50 percent of training fees. Unemployed personnel receive Y700 upon completion of training programs, Y800 upon certification, Y1,300 upon completion of entrepreneurship training, with an additional Y100 for securing new employment.
- *Migrant employee training.* Employers can draw from the Employee Education Fund to provide training for rural migrant workers within six months of their employment. For each migrant worker who gets certified, employers receive a subsidy of Y400, equal to 50 percent of training fees.
- *Rural worker training.* Rural students graduating from middle school or high school who are unable to continue their studies are encouraged to participate in labor preparatory training, and receive Y800 in subsidies upon certification.
- *Reemployment training for the unemployed.* Subsidies of Y688–800 upon certification or reemployment. Without reemployment, payment of 60 percent of the subsidy for training and certification.
- *Entrepreneurship training.* Y300 for participating in training. Y1,000 for starting up a company hiring three to five persons. Y2,000 for starting up a company hiring more than five persons. An additional Y1,000 for first-time college graduate entrepreneurs.
- *Urgently needed talent training.* Companies are encouraged to set up an employment category fund. Government subsidies are granted on the principle of "whoever pays for training gets subsidies."

Source: Announcement on Implementing Special Vocational Training Plan (HRSS 2010).

at Level 3 (senior), Level 2 (technicians), or Level 1 (senior technicians). Non-public agencies, training the highest number of people, also have a certification rate of 90 percent among their trainees. Moreover, the average employment rates among graduates from employment training centers and non-public agencies are around 76 percent.

Studies on non-formal training in China are scarce, and there is no systematic review of how well the formal and non-formal education and training systems perform. We fill this gap by offering an in-depth analysis in the following chapters. Chapter 4 reviews the formal TVET system of Yunnan, critically examining its legal framework, governance, curriculum, and finance. Chapter 5 evaluates the impact of rural labor transfers and skills training. Chapter 6 offers insights into employee training in urban enterprises in Yunnan. Finally, Chapter 7 draws on Shanghai's Program for International Student Assessment data to shed light on the role of schools in developing student literacy, numeracy, and science skills.

Bibliography

HRSS (Yunnan Department of Human Resources and Social Security). 2010. Announcement on Implementing Special Vocational Training Plan. http://www.ynhrss.gov.cn/readinfo.aspx?InfoId=9987.

———. 2011a. *Quarterly Vacancy Data.* http://www.ynhrss.gov.cn/list.aspx?KindID=000100030007.

———. 2011b. 年云南省人力资源和社会保障事业发展统计公报. http://www.ynhrss.gov.cn/readinfo.aspx?InfoId=82abbe9f37444b379de71346ac0b1262.

Skills Toward Employment and Productivity (STEP) Employer Survey. 2012. World Bank, Washington, DC.

Yun, B., H. Liu, and Y. Li. 2011. "云南省职业技术教育发展研究报告."

CHAPTER 4

Strengthening Technical and Vocational Education and Training

A central part of any skills development system is the formal Technical and Vocational Education and Training (TVET) system. In 2010, there were more than 300 secondary and 51 tertiary TVET institutions in Yunnan, enrolling 663,400 and 183,300 tertiary students, respectively (table B.3). Between 10 and 12 percent of the total TVET enrollment is in private institutions. In addition to enrolling full-time students, many of the formal TVET institutions also offer non-formal training programs to adults. This chapter provides an overview of the legal framework, governance and management, school–industry links, quality assurance, curriculum reforms, and financing of the formal TVET system in the national and provincial contexts.

Legal and Policy Framework

Since the founding of the People's Republic of China in 1949, the government has enforced a series of laws and regulations to guide and regulate the provision of TVET. A relatively established legal and policy framework exists at both the national and provincial levels. In 1986, the Education Law was promulgated, specifying that the responsibility for the provision of post-secondary education lies with the provincial and national governments, while the responsibility for basic education and secondary education lies with local governments. Clause 19 of the Education Law states that government will provide conditions that enable all citizens to receive TVET, including adult education.

In 1995, the Labor Law specified that the state take various measures to promote employment, develop vocational education, set labor standards, and gradually improve the life of workers. The People's Congress promulgated the Vocational Education Law in 1996, which established the guiding principles for TVET and broadly defined the TVET system to include all forms of pre- and in-service training for all ages. The law also established the right of all citizens to receive training and included provisions for establishing nongovernmental TVET institutions, collaborating with enterprises, and financing TVET.

In 2002, the State Council announced the Decision to Vigorously Promote the Reform and Development of Vocational Education. The Decision increased support for and leadership in vocational education and expanded the scale of vocational education. In 2005, the State Council published the Decision to Vigorously Develop Vocational Education, which reiterates the strategic importance of developing vocational education for social economic development and calls for deeper employment-oriented reforms and a higher quality of TVET institutions. The latter Decision encourages the mobilization of non-public resources and links between school and industry. It further pledges to diversify sources of funding and strengthens leadership for TVET.

Most recently, in recognition of the strategic importance of education and training in upgrading labor force skills and facilitating the shift of economic growth patterns, the Chinese government renewed its commitment to education and training by launching two important policy documents in June 2010: the Medium- and Long-Term Education Development Plan (2010–20) and the Medium- and Long-Term Talent Development Plan (2010–20). Both plans emphasize the role of industries and enterprises in TVET development and call attention to the need to develop vocational education and training for rural areas and rural workers. In addition, China is now in the process of revising its Vocational Education Law and developing a Lifelong Learning Law. Following national law and policy, local governments develop specific plans and targets in accordance with the national framework.

Governance and Management

The chief administrative authority in China is the State Council. Provision of education and training is largely public, through authorities in the Ministry of Education and the Ministry of Human Resources and Social Security (HRSS) and their local departments. For certain economic sectors such as transportation, health, and agriculture, line ministries share responsibility in delivering sector-specific training. There is no single government ministry or agency that is in charge of TVET affairs in China, though the Ministry of Education has been charged with a leading role in implementing the TVET system reform under the direction of the Medium- and Long-term Education Development Plan, with input from a broad spectrum of stakeholders including the public and private sectors, donors, and training providers (figure 4.1).

Vertically, there are four levels of government structure: central government, provincial governments, prefectures, and counties or cities (figure 4.2). The central government develops a national policy framework, and local governments undertake the main responsibility for developing and implementing TVET programs.

In an effort to improve TVET coordination, the National Inter-Ministry TVET Coordinating Committee was set up at the national level, composed

Figure 4.1 Horizontal Arrangements of TVET, Yunnan

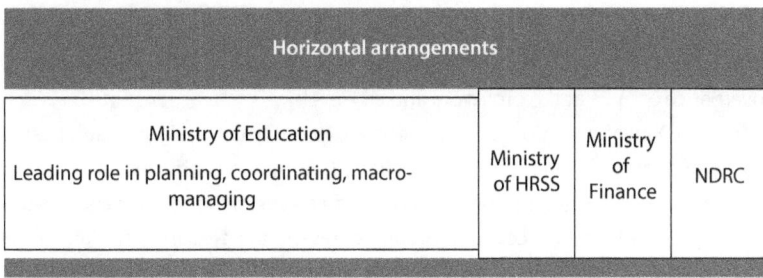

Source: Adapted from Liu 2010.
Note: NDRC = National Development and Reform Commission.

Figure 4.2 Vertical Arrangements of TVET, Yunnan

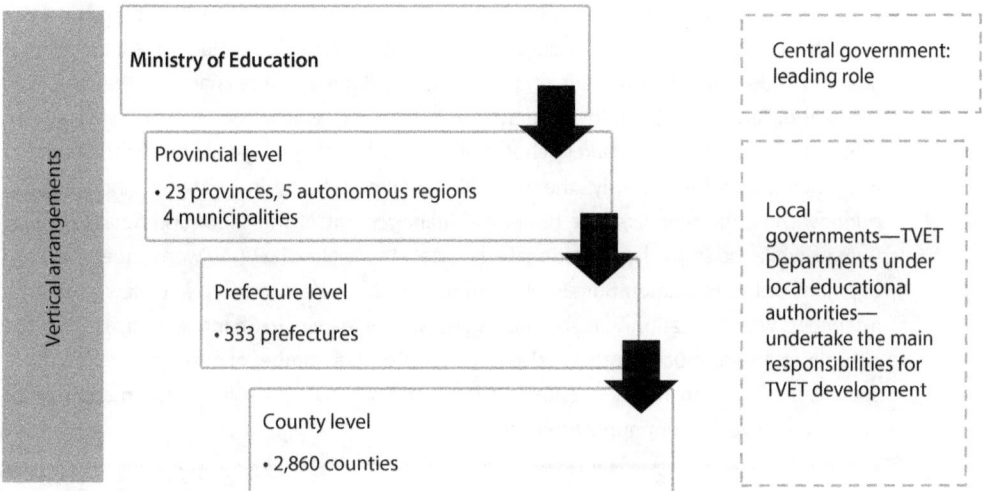

Source: Adapted from Liu 2010.

of members from the Ministry of Education, HRSS, the Ministry of Finance, the National Development and Reform Commission (NDRC), and the Ministry of Agriculture, among others. At the local level, a number of provinces have also established such coordinating committees. Examples can be found in Xinjiang and Shanghai, which provide good models for overcoming fragmented governance of TVET at the provincial level (box 4.1). Xinjiang replicates the national coordination model at the provincial level; Shanghai goes further, however, to consolidate functions such as admissions, curriculum and teaching, teacher management, and student registration under the Education Bureau.

Box 4.1 Overcoming Fragmented Governance of TVET: Xinjiang and Shanghai

Xinjiang and Shanghai have taken two different approaches to addressing the fragmented governance of TVET at the provincial and city levels.

In 2006, Xinjiang set up an overarching Provincial Vocational Education Leading Group in 2006. The deputy secretary of Xinjiang's Party Committee chairs the Leading Group, and the vice president of Xinjiang in charge of education serves as the co-chair and executive director. The 22 members in the Leading Group represent the Departments of Education, HRSS, Organization, Propaganda, Finance, Economy and Trade, and Poverty Relief, the Agricultural Office, the Development and Reform Commission, Labor Union, the Association for the Handicapped, the Women's Federation, and the Youth League.

The Vocational Education Leading Group is jointly operated with the Xinjiang Employment Office. The Leading Group created a platform for coordinating policy development, but it does not consolidate functions from various government authorities.

Shanghai has taken a more comprehensive approach. Starting in the fall semester of 2006, the Shanghai government placed the admission, curriculum and teaching, teacher management, and student registration of skilled-worker schools under the authority of the Shanghai Education Bureau, without changing financing sources or human resources management. Educational authorities on the district level are in direct charge of the establishment, abolishment, inspections, student admissions and registration of local skilled-worker schools. City-level skilled-worker schools are under the direct leadership of the Shanghai Education Bureau. Previously, the 41 skilled-worker schools in Shanghai, including 28 nongovernmental schools, were under the management of the Labor and Social Security Bureau, while the secondary vocational schools and specialized schools were under the management of the Education Bureau. Although there have been no formal reviews, informal interviews with Education Bureau officials and school leaders in Shanghai indicate that the consolidation was much appreciated and has resulted in a number of positive developments, such as more streamlined admissions and registration and equitable teacher management and career development opportunities.

School–Industry Links

Key elements of a demand-driven education and training system include a governance and management structure that can systematically incorporate industry representation at the system level as well as at the school level. In China, governance and management of TVET remain a government affair. Although employers and industry associations are sometimes consulted in the policymaking process, the consultation is often ad hoc, and the role of industry and employers remains advisory. The establishment of coordination bodies for TVET governance has been carried out without formal input from industry. Within Asia, Indonesia's establishment of APINDO, the Employers Association, provides a good example of how to institutionalize the involvement of employers and industries in human resource development on the apex level (box 4.2).

Box 4.2 APINDO, the Employer Association of Indonesia

APINDO (the Employer Association of Indonesia) was recognized in 1975 by decree of the Minister of Manpower, and mandated by KADIN Indonesia (the Indonesian National Chamber of Commerce and Industry), as the sole body representing employers in all the tripartite councils on industrial relations and manpower affairs at the national, provincial, and district levels, and in the international forum.

APINDO is an independent organization. It has approximately 5,000 members in all parts of Indonesia, with branches in each of the 27 provinces and in the many districts or industrial centers. The membership of APINDO includes private enterprises, state-owned enterprises, local companies, joint ventures, and cooperatives. The mission of APINDO is to enhance harmonious industrial relations, represent the Indonesian business community in manpower institutions, and protect, defend, and empower all businesses, especially its member businesses.

At the national level, APINDO is represented in tripartite bodies including the National Council for Tripartite Cooperation, the National Productivity Council, the National Committee for Productivity Award, the National Wages Council, the National Council for Occupational Safety and Health, the National Council for Work Training, and the Central Committee for Settlement of Industrial Disputes. APINDO is also represented in several bodies at the provincial level, such as the Provincial Tripartite Councils, the Provincial Councils on Manpower Affairs, and the Provincial Committees for Settlement of Industrial Disputes.

Service to membership at the national or provincial and district levels includes consultation on industrial relations and manpower development, legal assistance, representation at labor courts, and training programs on manpower affairs.

Strong government policies, as well as a robust economy and labor market, have led TVET institutions across China, including in Yunnan, to collaborate in various ways with business enterprises. Forms of collaboration include contracting with enterprises for graduate employment, teacher training, student internships during their last year of study, equipment donation, and establishing school-run enterprises for training and production.

The capacity of different schools for the planning and management necessary to strengthen links with industry varies greatly. National model secondary TVET schools and tertiary TVET schools tend to have a greater capacity to develop in-depth collaborations with enterprises. Schools constrained by limitations of capacity and resources tend to engage in more rudimentary forms of collaboration with local enterprises. From the employers' point of view, industry has little incentive to provide systematic and sustained inputs to the management of TVET schools. Not all industry settings are conducive to student participation: simulating various production problems for training in a real-time production setting or shutting down production equipment for training purposes may be prohibitively costly. According to the STEP Employer Survey, approximately

57 percent of workplaces in Kunming have regular contacts with educational or training institutions. Among those, most school-enterprise collaborations take the form of staff recruitment and employee training. From 56 to 65 percent of firms also provide work experience for students in either professional or technical occupations or relatively lower skilled and more frontline/operative type B occupations. However, fewer than a quarter of firms are involved in curriculum development for training and educational institutions; even fewer are involved in testing of students. Table 4.1 shows the percentage of enterprises collaborating with schools in various ways for both type A and type B occupations.

Overall, most of these collaborations rely on personal connections and remain ad hoc, idiosyncratic efforts, without system support. No institutionalized mechanism enables schools to formally incorporate industry in their governance, management, and educational affairs. Public TVET institutions do not yet have governance boards that include industry representation. For those schools that have established some kind of board or committee, the role of industry remains mostly advisory. In comparison, private TVET institutions are legally required to have a school board with diverse representation, and they tend to have stronger links with industry than do public institutions. One of the few exceptions is the city of Ningbo in Zhejiang province, which has taken a lead in establishing policy and legal assurances for systematic school–industry collaboration (see box 4.3).

In response to the demand and pressure from industry and interested enterprises, some schools, particularly those in areas with strong and active local private sector involvement, started to experiment with management models within legal constraints. One such model that has emerged in recent years is the vocational education group (职教集团), under which a cluster of similar enterprises and a group of TVET institutions form a joint management group that oversees vocational education. The platform involves resource sharing, student internships in enterprises, industrial experts instructing in schools, and collaboration in development of training materials. The vocational education group provides an integrated approach to linking industry,

Table 4.1 Extent of School-Enterprise Collaboration, Kunming (% of firms)

Type of collaboration	Type A	Type B
Recruitment of staff	85	86
Provides work experience for students (internships and apprenticeships)	56	65
Uses the institution for further training of your firm's existing employees	56	48
Provides feedback to the institution for their curriculum development	19	25
Participation in testing of students	4	4
Other	10	17

Source: STEP Employer Survey 2012.
Note: Type A occupations include managers, professionals, technicians/associate professionals; Type B occupations include clerical support workers, service workers, sales workers, skilled agricultural/forestry/fishery workers, construction/craft and related trades workers, plant and machine operators/assemblers, and elementary occupations.

Box 4.3 Ningbo's Regulation for Promoting TVET School–Industry Collaboration

Ningbo's Regulation for Promoting TVET School–Industry Collaboration was promulgated in 2008 and enacted on March 1, 2009. Selected provisions from the regulation include:

- Government should encourage, support, and promote school–industry collaboration and establish a system guided by government and coordinated by industry associations.
- TVET institutions should take initiative and collaborate with business and industry in the field of student internships, curriculum development, admissions and employment, instructor training, employee training, and continuing education.
- TVET instructors should receive at least two months of industry training every two years.
- Business and industry should accept students and instructors for paid internships and industry training.
- TVET institutions should provide vocational ethics and safety education, provide accidental injury insurance for student interns, and assign guidance instructors to supervise student internships.

In 2012, Ningbo further enacted implementation methods for the regulation. The implementation methods protect the rights and welfare of student interns and propose to establish (1) categorical grants directed at school–industry collaboration, (2) a public online service platform to facilitate collaboration and communication, and (3) a joint conference system involving various stakeholders including government officials, schools, and industries.

---

research and development, and education and training (box 4.4). The model promises to provide an intermediate and practical mechanism for institutionalizing industry involvement in the running of TVET schools, even before Yunnan develops a comprehensive legal and policy framework to sustain the collaboration.

Quality Assurance

Reflecting the education and human resources dual-track provision of TVET, there are also two parallel arrangements for quality assurance for education and training providers in Yunnan. The Ministry of Education first promulgated standards for the establishment of secondary and tertiary TVET institutions in 2000. The standards were revised and the revisions formally adopted in 2010. In 2012, HRSS updated its previous skilled-worker school standards and issued the latest standards for the establishment of skilled-worker schools, advanced skilled-workers schools, and technicians' academies. In addition, Yunnan started implementing an updated version of its Non-public Education Institute Management Measures in May 2012, including additional establishment standards for private secondary TVET schools (in accordance with the national standards for secondary TVET) and private vocational training providers offering non-diploma-oriented training.

Box 4.4 Vocational Education Groups in Yunnan

As of 2010, Yunnan had 20 provincial-level vocational education groups, covering light industry, tourism, mining, transportation, agriculture, economic management, art and crafts, construction, forestry, and energy. Additionally, there are 10 prefecture- and city-level vocational education groups in Kunming, Yuxi, Dali, Honghe, and Zhaotong.

For example, the Yunnan Forestry Vocational Education Group, initiated by the Southwestern Forestry University, integrates 26 entities in forestry, including TVET colleges, skilled-worker schools, research institutions, and businesses. Drawing on resources from each institution, the Group provides students with industry-commissioned training and effectively integrates vocational education with industry training. The Group also facilitates research and development in forestry and, importantly, supports the use of research and development in products and services. The Group also explores new ways to finance vocational education.

Table 4.2 lists areas of requirement according to existing standards. The standards are input-based, requiring a minimum level of school infrastructure, training facilities and equipment, number of majors, and qualifications of institutional heads and teachers. They also require schools to have a stable source of financing and to set up specific curriculum and teaching plans. At the tertiary level, HRSS requires schools to have teaching research groups and an academic leader for each major. For skilled-worker schools at both the secondary and tertiary levels, HRSS also requires each school to have a system for industry–school collaboration: Skilled-worker schools are required to set up a school–industry collaboration committee, and each major in advanced skilled-worker schools or technician academies has to partner with a minimum number of enterprises.

Minimum standards are also specified for the number and qualifications of teachers (table 4.3). Qualifications are often measured by teachers' professional ranking or skills certification. Faculty at TVET schools is composed of teachers teaching general courses and teachers and trainers teaching technical courses and workshops. Rather than setting the same minimum qualifications and experience level for all teachers, the standards are set up to ensure the faculty is composed of a minimum percentage of teachers with skills certifications or professional rankings at a certain level. For example, technical teachers and trainers should constitute at least 70 percent of the faculty at skilled-worker schools, and all of them are required to obtain skills certification at level 5. For secondary TVET, at least 20 percent of the full-time teachers are required to have previous experience in the industry. Part-time teachers, though often rich in industry experience, cannot exceed a third of all faculty members in skilled-worker schools.

These standards serve as the basis for the initial licensing of institutions and for the annual inspection conducted by the local government authorities. Schools

Table 4.2 Standards for the Setup of Secondary and Tertiary TVET Institutions, Yunnan

	Secondary TVET	Tertiary TVET	Skilled-worker school	Advanced skilled-worker school	Technician academy	Private vocational training provider
Campus area	√	√	√	√	√	√
Training facilities and equipment	√	√	√	√	√	√
Minimum enrollment	√	√	√	√	√	√
School leader and management	√	√	√	√	√	√
Teacher number and qualification	√	√	√	√	√	√
Stable source of financing	√	√	√	√	√	√
Curriculum and teaching learning plan	√	√	√	√	n.a.	√
Teaching research group; major leaders	n.a.	n.a.	n.a.	√	√	n.a.
Minimum majors	n.a.	√	√	√	√	n.a.
Industry-school link	n.a.	n.a.	School–industry collaboration committee	At least three enterprises per major	At least five enterprises per major	n.a.

Sources: HRSS 2012a, 2012b, 2012c; Ministry of Education 2000, 2010b; and Yunnan Department of Education 2012.
Note: n.a. = not applicable.

not meeting the standards are issued a warning and put on probation. Schools that do not improve during the probation period may be prohibited from admitting any students. Local governments are encouraged to help schools reach the standards through macro-level planning, targeted public investment, and integrating and reallocating resources.

In reality, however, these accreditation standards serve more as targets for existing schools than as minimum standards. The current operating conditions of many TVET schools across China, especially at the secondary level, are below the specified accreditation standards. For example, none of the provinces meet at least five of the six major indicators listed in table 4.4. Shanghai, Guangdong, and Zhejiang, all in eastern China, perform relatively better, reaching four of the standards. A number of provinces in western China, including Yunnan, do not reach any of the six standards.

In comparison, some tertiary TVET institutions operate at levels higher than the national standards. Tertiary TVET institutions in all provinces have reached minimum enrollment and minimum value of equipment and facilities. Seven provinces meet all seven indicators listed in table 4.5. Yunnan meets only three

Table 4.3 Selected Teacher Qualifications and Standards for Secondary and Tertiary TVET Institutions

	Secondary TVET	Tertiary TVET	Skilled-worker school	Advanced skilled-worker school	Technician academy	Private vocational training provider
Number of full-time teachers	>60	>70 with Bachelor's degree	n.a.	n.a.	n.a.	Provincial (20); city (15); county (10)
Maximum share of part-time teachers (%)	n.a.	n.a.	33	33	33	75
Teacher:student ratio	1:20	n.a.	1:20	1:20	1:18	n.a.
Minimum share of teachers with practical experience (%)	20	n.a.	20	20	25	n.a.
Minimum share of technical teachers and trainers (%)	n.a.	n.a.	70	70	70	n.a.
Qualifications	Senior professional ranking (20 percent); double qualifications[a] (30 percent); at least two teachers per major with medium professional ranking	Associate senior professional ranking (20 percent); at least two teachers per major with double qualifications[a]	Technical teachers certified at Level 5 or above (100 percent), at Level 4 (30 percent); trainers certified at Level 3 (100 percent)	Technical teachers certified at Level 5 (100 percent), at Level 4 (40 percent); trainers certified at Level 3 (100 percent), at Level 1 or 2 (45 percent); 50 percent technical teachers and trainers are all-around[b]	Technical teachers certified at Level 5 (100 percent), at Level 4 (60 percent); trainers certified at Level 3 (100 percent), certified at Level 1 or 2 (50 percent); 60 percent of technical teachers and trainers are all-around[b]	Medium professional ranking (at least 15 percent)

Sources: HRSS 2012a, 2012b, 2012c; Ministry of Education 2000, 2010b; and Yunnan Department of Education 2012.

Note: n.a. = not applicable.

a. Teachers with both teacher qualifications and technical skills certification.
b. All-around teachers can teach both theoretical and technical classes.

Table 4.4 Provinces Meeting the Establishment Standards for Secondary TVET by Region, 2009

	Enrollment	Student:teacher ratio	Full-time teachers with both degrees and skills certification (%)	Floor area per student (m²)	Value of equipment/ facility per student (Y)	Number of computers per 100 students
National standards	>1,200 students	20:1	30	20	2,500	15
East	All	Tianjin, Beijing, Liaoning	0	0	All except Hunan, Fujian, Hebei	All except Jiangsu, Fujian, Shandong, Hebei, Hainan
Middle	All except Heilongjiang, Jilin, Shanxi, Hunan	Jilin	0	0	0	Hunan
West	All except Inner Mongolia, Gansu, Yunnan, Xinjiang	0	Ningxia, Xinjiang	0	Tibet	Xinjiang
Number of provinces not meeting the standards	8	27	29	31	26	23

Source: Zhang and Ma 2011.

indicators: enrollment, percentage of teachers with post-graduate degrees, and value of equipment and facilities.

Quality assurance is also exercised in the Chinese TVET system by skills certification. Students obtain an education diploma upon graduation, but, increasingly, they also sit for skills certification tests administered by HRSS, usually at the end of their study, to increase their employability. In Yunnan's skilled-worker schools alone, 77 percent of graduates in 2010 were certified at Level 4 (medium-skilled workers), and 18 percent were certified at Level 3 (senior-skilled workers).

In 1999, under the leadership of HRSS, China started to implement its own occupational classification. There are eight main categories of occupations and 1,838 occupations. Although over the years the government has made revisions to the definitions and standards for some occupations, most were developed during China's planned economy period. Moreover, the Chinese classification of occupations differs significantly from the International Standard Classification of Occupations (ISCO), last revised in 2008. There is no direct correspondence between China's and the international classifications, making international comparisons a challenge (table 4.6).

Table 4.5 Provinces Meeting the Establishment Standards for Tertiary TVET by Region, 2009

	Enrollment	Student-teacher ratio	Full-time teachers with post-graduate degrees (%)	Floor area per student (m²)	Value of equipment/ facilities per student (Y)
National standards	>2,000 students	18:1	15	14	4,000
East	All	All except Shanghai, Shandong, Hebei, Tianjin, Jiangsu, Liaoning, Beijing	All	All except Hainan	All
Middle	All	All except Henan, Shanxi, Jilin, Heilongjiang, Jiangxi	All	All except Anhui, Jilin, Shanxi	All
West	All	All except Guangxi, Yunnan, Chongqing, Xinjiang, Qinghai, Xizang	All except Qinghai	All except Guizhou, Gansu, Yunnan, Qinghai, Sichuan, Ningxia	All
Number of provinces not meeting standards	0	18	1	10	0

Source: Zhang and Ma 2011.

Table 4.6 Comparison of ISCO-08 and China's Occupational Classifications by Major Groups

ISCO-08	China
• Managers • Professionals • Technicians and associate professionals • Clerical support workers • Service and sales workers • Skilled agricultural, forestry, and fishery workers • Craft and related trades workers • Plant and machine operators and assemblers • Elementary occupations • Armed forces occupations	• Unit head (of government organization, party organization, enterprise, or public institution) • Professional and technical workers • Clerical and related workers • Business and service personnel • Agricultural, forestry, fishery, and water conservancy workers • Production and transport equipment operators and related workers • Military • Other unclassified

Similarly, China's existing competency standards for occupations have not kept up with the evolving demands of industry and do not reflect the competencies required. Not all existing competency standards have been broken down into discrete modules, which would allow flexibility in training. Both occupations and the corresponding competencies required have been changing

> **Box 4.5 Turkey: Involving Industry and Training Providers in the Development of the National Qualification Framework (NQF)**
>
> Although qualification frameworks are government-led initiatives in many countries, social partners can be actively involved in the process.
>
> The NQF in Turkey dates back to a Technical and Vocational Education and Training (TVET) reform process begun in the 1990s and supported by the World Bank, through which occupational standards were developed to link both formal and non-formal training to the labor market. In 2006, the Vocational Qualifications Authority was established under the Ministry of Labor and Social Security.
>
> One of the strengths of the emerging Turkish NQF is the voluntary participation and involvement of stakeholders. Social partners (state, employers, employees, and education and training providers) are represented on the general board of Vocational Qualification Authority, enabling them to express their needs and priorities and to set strategies for the system accordingly. Stakeholders have a say at every stage of the process, and the system is shaped through consensus. This involvement enhances the sense of ownership and has a positive effect on the outcomes in the system.
>
> Specifically, industries are represented by various institutions and organizations in the General Assembly of the Vocational Qualification Authority. By signing the protocols of cooperation with the Vocational Qualifications Authority, members of these institutions and organizations are authorized to take part in NQF-related activities (such as occupational standards development).
>
> *Source:* Allais 2010.

rapidly, and the classification and competency standards need to be updated accordingly with further input from industry. Box 4.5 describes how Turkey involved stakeholders in the development of its National Qualification Framework (NQF).

Because skills certification is a key mechanism linking labor market demand with education and training, developing a skills certification system with updated and industry-led competency standards and occupational classifications reflecting industry demand and recognized by employers is vital for the development of a demand-driven skills development system. The lack of regular reviews and involvement of industry in the development and update of competency standards may have contributed to the seeming lack of credibility of the current certification system. Evidence shows that existing skills certificates do not carry much weight among employers. According to the non-public enterprise survey in Yunnan, only 24 percent of the professional and technical personnel and 12 percent of frontline/operative skilled workers have obtained professional or vocational certification. The most recent quarterly job vacancy data also show that only about 20 percent of job openings in Yunnan require a skills certification.

The experience of Hong Kong shows how a comprehensive qualification framework not only involves industry in developing competency standards, but also includes mechanisms for assuring quality of training programs, facilitating articulation between academic and vocational studies and recognizing prior learning (box 4.6).

Box 4.6 Hong Kong SAR, China's Qualification Framework

Hong Kong SAR, China endorsed the establishment of a seven-level cross-sector qualification framework and its associated quality assurance mechanism in February 2004. Qualifications recognized under this framework are outcome-based and apply to both academic and vocational sectors.

Industries play a pivotal role in developing competency standards in the vocational sector. The Specification of Competency Standards (SCS) comprises both the competency standards at various levels and the assessment guidelines. SCSs are formulated by Industry Training Advisory Committees (ITACs), consisting of representatives from employers, employees, and relevant professional bodies. So far, ITACs have been formed for 18 industries. To ensure continued relevance of an SCS, the ITACs concerned must review and update the SCS regularly to keep abreast of the latest manpower requirements. The SCSs developed by industries also support the Applied Learning Courses under the new academic structure for senior secondary education. Upon completion of industry-wide consultation on the draft SCSs, training providers develop appropriate training programs. The programs and related qualifications will be recognized under the qualification framework if they are quality-assured by the Hong Kong SAR, China Council for Accreditation of Academic and Vocational Qualifications.

The competency standards are presented as "units of competency." In this way, trainees will be free to acquire any units of competency specified in the SCS according to their own needs and to accumulate credits for obtaining various qualifications. These may be qualifications at different levels within the same functional area, qualifications at the same level across a number of functional areas, or whole qualifications (such as certificates and diplomas). A credit accumulation and transfer system enables learners to systematically accumulate the credits of learning and training gained from various courses with a view to converting the accumulated credits into a recognized qualification. By referring to the SCSs, employers may also provide tailor-made in-service training to individual employees or use the SCSs as yardsticks for identifying personnel with suitable skills and knowledge for recruitment or promotional purposes.

Qualifications are not confined to academic and training attainment. A recognition of prior learning (RPL) mechanism developed by individual industries enables employees of various backgrounds to receive formal recognition of the knowledge, skills, and experience already acquired. The RPL mechanism operates based on the SCSs formulated by the respective industries to ensure its credibility. The RPL mechanism has been implemented in seven industries and will be extended to more sectors by phases.

Source: Hong Kong SAR Qualification Framework 2004.

Curriculum Reform

In 2002 the State Council published the Decision to Promote the Reform and Development of Vocational Education (大力推进职业教育改革与发展的决定) and set the overall direction for TVET reform in china. An important clause stated:

> Vocational schools and training institutions should adapt to the structural adjustment in economy, the technological progress and the changes in the labor market. This includes adjusting the major programs, developing majors facing the newly developed industries and modern service industries, increasing the relevance and unique features of the programs. The training of technical workers, especially senior technicians, should be strengthened. To promote curriculum reform, developing curriculum that reflects new knowledge, technology and techniques and that is unique to vocational education. To strengthen the link between school and enterprises, between school and industries, building systems for tight connection between vocational school and the labor market. (§ 3, cl. 8)

TVET institutions across China have become keenly aware of the importance of delivering relevant training programs. Schools across the country are engaged to varying degrees in the process of updating training programs. To examine the implementation and impact of the TVET curriculum reform, we commissioned a survey sampling 40 TVET institutions at both the secondary and tertiary levels from Liaoning, Guangdong, Shandong, Yunnan, Shanghai, and Chongqing. Box 4.7 lists the major findings of the survey. Overall, the survey shows that TVET curriculum reform has been commonly recognized and implemented across China and focused on school–industry collaboration and practice-theory combination. The majority of schools surveyed have conducted skills-demand analyses, set up a sector-specific advisory committee and a school–industry collaboration committee, developed and implemented new curriculum standards, conducted evaluations of teachers, and solicited feedback on the reforms.

However, our study also reveals several challenges encountered in the process of reform. First and foremost, the overall lack of up-to-date, industry-led, competency-based occupational standards seems to have hampered the overall quality of training programs at the school level. For 23 percent of the majors surveyed, schools had to develop their own standards. Only 40 percent of the majors surveyed are able to use HRSS-developed competency standards as the basis for revising their training programs. For a third of the majors, schools used standards developed by industry. Updating the existing standards and developing standardized competencies are crucial for reducing the costs and improving efficiencies of curriculum development on the school level.

Second, schools have reported a lack of participation and involvement by industry. Existing efforts are often the result of personal connections between school leaders and industry representatives. Without sufficient industry participation, schools do not have enough expertise to develop new curriculums. Although a majority of schools have started conducting demand analyses, only 42 percent are able to use the information from the analysis to change the

Box 4.7 Main Results and Outputs of the Implementation of TVET Curriculum Reform in China

Demand Analysis
- Two-thirds of the majors surveyed have conducted skills-demand analyses; however, only 42 percent of schools use this information to adjust and optimize curriculums and programs
- Sources of information include enterprises (36 percent), industry associations (23 percent), Internet (20 percent), and HRSS authorities (10 percent)

Industry Participation
- Sector-specific advisory committees have been established by 85 percent of schools and 73 percent of majors
- School–industry collaboration committees have been established by 76 percent of schools and 65 percent of majors
- Among those involved in developing competency-based training standards（人才培养方案）, industry experts account for only 25 percent; others include teachers (25 percent), principals (21 percent), TVET experts (14 percent), and skills certification experts (11 percent)

Curriculum Development and Implementation
- Forty percent of majors comply with national vocational qualification standards, 33 percent use industry standards, and 23 percent have developed their own competency standards
- Before implementing a new curriculum, 41 percent of schools need approval by a sector-specific advisory committee, 24 percent need approval by academic deans, 21 percent need approval by the school principal, 9 percent need approval by a higher authority such as the Department of Education, and about 4 percent need approval by an industry authority
- Sixty-nine percent of majors have strictly followed their new curriculums, 28 percent have implemented most parts

School Resources
- Only 37 percent of majors have a student-teacher ratio lower than 20 to 1
- Only 90 percent of schools and majors have established teacher files and teacher training plans
- Facilities and equipment meet the instructional requirements of only 32 percent of majors

Evaluation and Quality Assurance
- Seventy-six percent of majors have developed teacher evaluation systems, 79 percent have developed regular graduate tracer studies and employer surveys
- Only 35 percent of schools have a third-party education quality evaluation report
- Seventy-four percent of majors conduct feedback surveys among teachers, students, and administrators during the process of curriculum implementation
- Ninety-five percent of graduates must take vocational qualification tests to get certified

Source: Background Study by Shanghai Academy of Education Science.

curriculum and programs. Industry involvement in the development of standards and curriculum can be further strengthened. Industry experts account for only one quarter of those involved in the development of new training programs. Only 41 percent of schools require the new training programs to be approved by a sector-specific advisory committee before implementation.

Last but not least, schools are ill suited to be the sole designers and implementers of curriculum reform. For example, schools lack the resources and information, which could be provided by the government and other authorities on the macro-level, to conduct a scientific and comprehensive analysis of a market. Moreover, the lack of school resources has impeded the successful implementation of curriculum reform in TVET: The capacities of teachers are limited, the student-teacher ratio is high, and facilities and equipment are inadequate for instruction. For the most part, only 28 percent of the newly developed training programs can be implemented.

Employment and Pathways

To further examine the relevance and quality of Yunnan's TVET system, we look into the employment rates among graduates of different levels of education (figure 4.3). On the secondary level, the overall employment rate among secondary TVET graduates has been around 95 percent in recent years. According to the statistics provided by the Graduate Employment Service Center, in 2008 73 percent of the graduates were employed by enterprises of varied ownership, 12 percent became individual business owners, and 15 percent went on to the next level of education. The majority of the graduates found employment in the tertiary sector. In addition, approximately 35 percent of the graduates found employment outside Yunnan, including a small number working abroad. The same statistics show that culture/art/athletics, information technology, medicine/health, manufacturing, and commerce/trading/tourism had the highest employment rates.

At the tertiary level in 2011, the initial employment rate among graduates was 84 percent, and the year-end employment rate was almost 96 percent. The 2011 year-end employment rates were 96 percent for Bachelor's degree holders and associate degree holders. According to the statistics in 2010, however, although overall employment rates were similar, as many as 44 percent of the graduates with associate degrees had flexible, that is, part-time or temporary, employment (table 4.7).

To improve the attractiveness of TVET, there are multiple pathways within TVET and between TVET and general education. In recent years, policies expanding admissions and diversifying admissions criteria increasingly encourage secondary TVET students to advance their studies. For example, an increasing number of Bachelor's degree programs in universities have opened admission to secondary TVET graduates. Some colleges and universities set admissions quotas specifically for secondary TVET graduates from counterpart schools or programs. Some secondary TVET schools have even established collaboration agreements with institutions overseas. Guangdong recently gave autonomy to over ten tertiary TVET institutions for the purposes of organizing entrance exams and admitting secondary TVET graduates. Unlike general track programs, admissions to tertiary TVET programs often take into account students' specialized skills and skills certification in addition to their academic scores on the entrance examination.

Figure 4.3 Pathways Taken by Secondary TVET Graduates in Yunnan, 2008
Percent

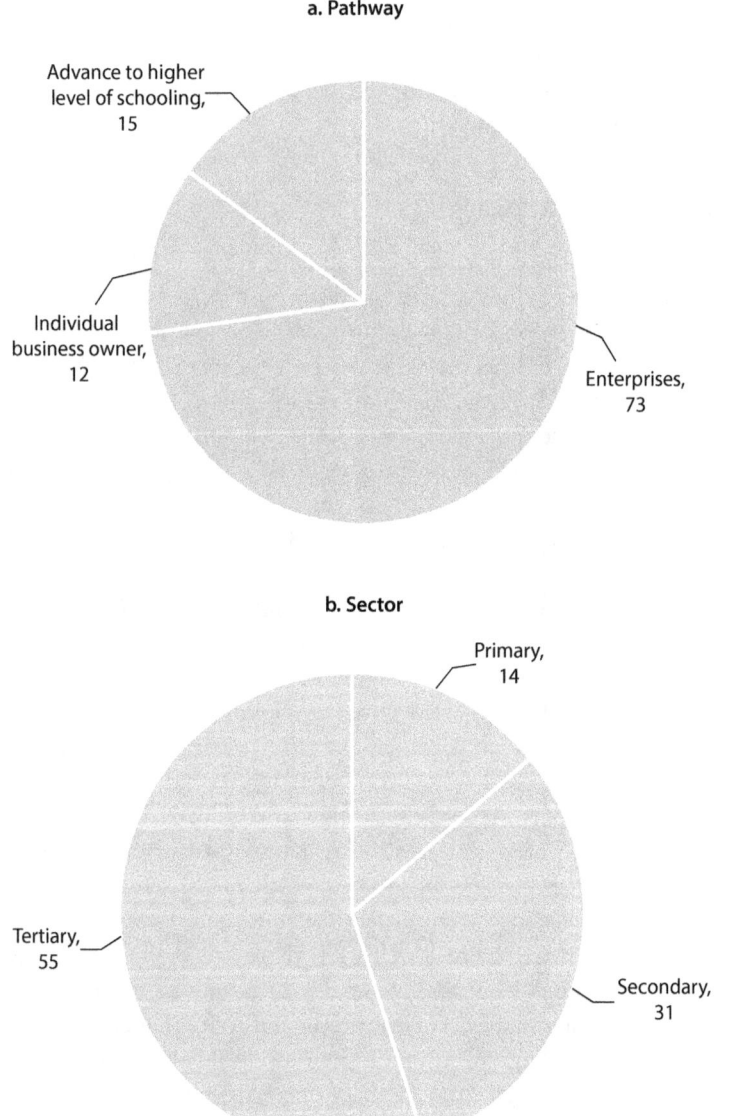

a. Pathway

- Advance to higher level of schooling, 15
- Individual business owner, 12
- Enterprises, 73

b. Sector

- Primary, 14
- Tertiary, 55
- Secondary, 31

figure continues next page

Figure 4.3 Pathways Taken by Secondary TVET Graduates in Yunnan, 2008 *(continued)*
Percent

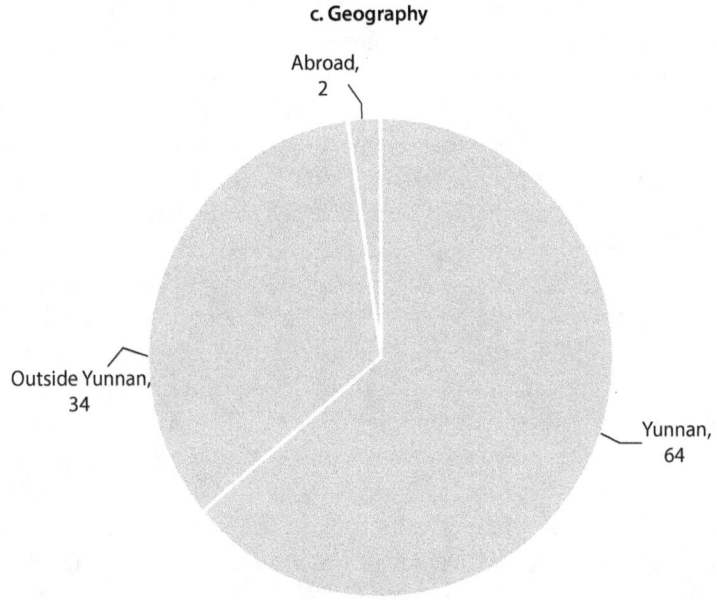

c. Geography

Abroad, 2
Outside Yunnan, 34
Yunnan, 64

Source: Yun, Liu, and Li 2011.

Table 4.7 Year-End Employment Rates in Yunnan, 2010

	Post-graduate		Bachelor's		Associate		Total	
	Number	Percent	Number	Percent	Number	Percent	Number	Percent
Graduates	6,212	100	47,757	100	48,113	100	102,082	100
Employed	5,854	94	45,408	95	45,803	95	97,065	95
Government and political parties	429	7	2,369	5	1,007	2	3,805	4
State and collective institutions	2,661	43	6,524	14	4,254	9	13,439	13
Non-public institutions	143	2	644	1	657	1	1,444	1
State-owned enterprises	978	16	7,184	15	5,989	12	14,151	14
Non-public enterprises	761	12	9,737	20	7,471	16	17,969	18
Flexible employment	413	7	10,370	22	21,081	44	31,864	31
Continued education	311	5	3,207	7	2,152	4	5,670	6
Unemployed	358	6	2,349	5	2,310	5	5,017	5

Source: Yun, Liu, and Li 2011.

There are also opportunities for students to move from the vocational to the general education track (专升本). There are three types of entrance examinations for vocational students seeking to transfer to general academic programs. First, students completing their associate degrees or tertiary TVET programs can transfer for two more years of study to a Bachelor's degree program through entrance examinations. Another type of degree program is called "self-study" for certain degree holders. A second entrance examination is organized every year specifically for "self-study" students holding tertiary TVET or associate degrees. Upon completing the program, they are granted a certified "self-study" Bachelor's degree. In addition, an adult college entrance examination, held every fall, provides the chance for any associate degree holder to enter an adult Bachelor's degree program.

Creating pathways alone, however, is not sufficient to enhance the status and attractiveness of TVET programs in Yunnan. In 2010, the actual rate of advancement to further education was only about 15 percent among secondary TVET graduates and 5 percent among tertiary TVET graduates (figure 4.3 and table 4.7). These rates are relatively low compared to more developed economies, such as Shanghai, where in 2012 as many as 33 percent of secondary TVET graduates advanced to tertiary institutions. In the Republic of Korea, more than two-thirds of secondary TVET graduates continued to tertiary education in 2010.

Financing Formal TVET

Financing of education in China comes from five main sources: government fiscal allocations to public schools, income from undertakings (including tuition and student fees), investment by private school sponsors, external donations, and other income (table B.4). Government fiscal allocations constituted about 85 percent of total financing for TVET in Yunnan in 2009.

Resource Allocation

Public TVET schools in China and Yunnan rely heavily on fiscal allocations from the central government's categorical funds and equity projects and local governments. The government employs a combination of supply- and demand-side allocation mechanisms. At the secondary TVET level, schools receive block grants from the relevant authority, based on the number of enrolled students, at an average of Y2,700 recurrent expenditure minimum per student in secondary TVET. The actual amount of allocation varies by area. Provincial-level schools tend to receive the highest amounts, followed by city-level and county- and district-level schools. At the tertiary level, there are 34 provincial-level tertiary institutions in Yunnan. In 2011, the allocation was Y10,000 per student for students in Bachelor's degree programs and Y5,000 for students in associate degree or TVET programs. In 2012, the allocation is expected to reach Y12,000 per student in Bachelor's degree programs and Y6,000 per student in associate degree or TVET programs. Schools use this block funding, combined with student fee income and revenues from other income generating activities, to carry out all educational functions, including the payment of teaching staff.

In recent years, the central government, through the Ministry of Education, the Ministry of Finance, and the NDRC, has introduced schemes to boost the funding for TVET. The most prominent program is the National Model TVET School Project at both the secondary and tertiary levels. Usually these are nationally competitive multiyear grants. Proposals are evaluated by a panel of national experts; thus only schools with quality proposals are awarded grants and the accompanying status. Typically the Model TVET School grant requires a 1:1 counterpart contribution from the provincial government. A competition-based approach provides incentives and motivation for improving quality and innovation in TVET, but tends to benefit schools with more resources, which are more likely to produce high-quality proposals and meet the criteria for grants, at the expense of weaker schools. Similarly, Yunnan's provincial government allocates on average Y20 million in categorical grants each year to vocational education, mostly for buying new equipment, building new facilities, employing experienced teachers, and training teachers for secondary TVET institutions. TVET institutions in rural and ethnic minority areas are further supported by funds for poverty alleviation, science and technology promotion, ethnic minorities, and migrant settlement. Initially these grants were also allocated on a competitive basis, which presented the same equity issues as those that arise under the Model TVET School Project.

Other than block grants based on enrollment and special funds earmarked for development, however, there is not yet a regular performance-based funding arrangement for TVET schools.

Government Spending on Education

In 2010, China's total education financing from all sources was Y1,956 billion, of which Y1,467 billion were fiscal allocations for education (including budgetary allocations, education surcharges at all levels of government, and enterprise- and school-generated funds), which accounted for almost 4 percent of gross domestic product. Budgetary allocations, together with education surcharges at all levels of government, totaled Y1,416 billion, accounting for nearly 16 percent of total government spending.

Yunnan's total spending on education amounted to Y44 billion in 2009. Fiscal allocation accounted for a larger proportion of the total allocation to education in Yunnan (over 84 percent) compared to the national average (74 percent). Yunnan's budgetary allocation, mostly from the provincial and local governments, accounted for 82 percent of the total funding on education. If we include both the budgetary allocation and the education surcharges, public spending on education in 2010 was Y44 billion in Yunnan, accounting for 19 percent of the total government spending, the highest share in the southwestern region and among the top five provinces in the nation (figure 4.4). The total amount of public spending on education ranked second in the southwestern region, after Sichuan province. Even compared to developed countries, Yunnan's public spending on education is high as a percentage of its total government expenditure and gross domestic product (figure 4.5).

Figure 4.4 Public Spending on Education as a Share of Total Government Spending, 2010

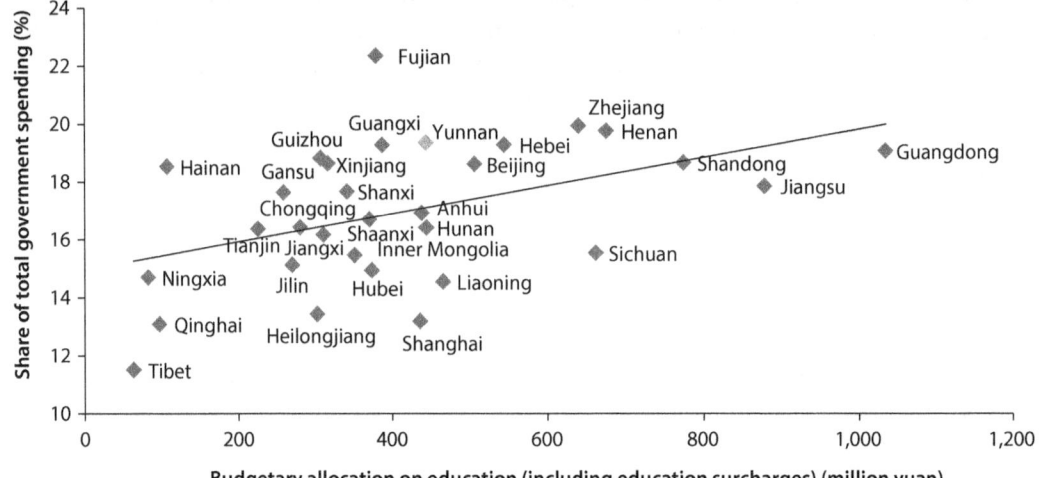

Source: Ministry of Education 2010a.
Note: The lighter-colored symbol indicates Yunnan.

Although the high share of government spending demonstrates Yunnan's commitment to education, the amount of public spending per student appears inadequate. Yunnan's budgetary recurrent expenditure per student is lower than the national average at every level of education (table B.5). The gaps are particularly pronounced at the compulsory level: for 2010, the per student recurrent expenditure is approximately 18 percent lower than the national average. At the tertiary level, including Bachelor's and associate degree programs, the recurrent expenditure reached Y8,526 per student (figure 4.6). At the secondary level, per student recurrent expenditure is Y4,728 for secondary TVET, slightly higher than that for general secondary schools.

Recurrent expenditure can be further divided into personnel expenditure (including wages, allowances, bonuses, social security benefits, and financial aid) and public expenditure (operating expenses, administrative and office expenses, purchasing of equipment and facilities, and maintenance expenses). At the tertiary level, over half of the recurrent expenditure is public, whereas at the lower levels of schooling the majority of the expenditure is devoted to personnel expenses (figure 4.6). In particular, at the compulsory level and in general high schools, approximately three-quarters of the total recurrent expenditure is devoted to personnel. For secondary TVET, over 61 percent of recurrent expenditure was spent on personnel.

As education finance is largely decentralized in China, the level of public spending on education varies greatly by city and prefecture within Yunnan. The variance is most pronounced for secondary TVET schools and ranges from Y10,788 recurrent expenditure per student in Pu'er to Y2,600 per student in Chuxiong (figure 4.7). More than half of the cities and prefectures spend less than the provincial average of Y4,265.

Figure 4.5 International Comparison of Yunnan's Public Expenditure on Education, 2009

a. Total government expenditure

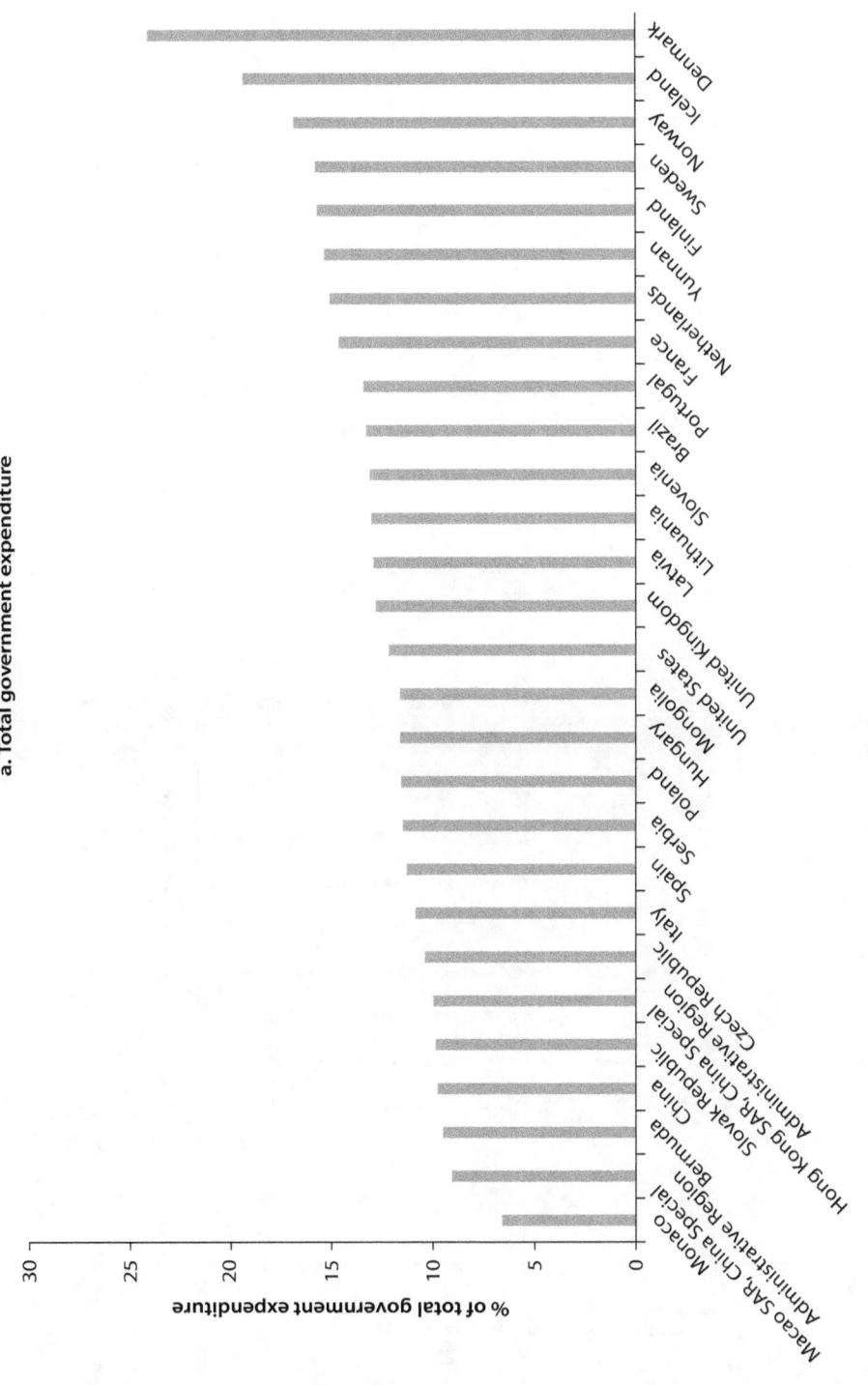

figure continues next page

Figure 4.5 International Comparison of Yunnan's Public Expenditure on Education, 2009 *(continued)*

b. Gross domestic product

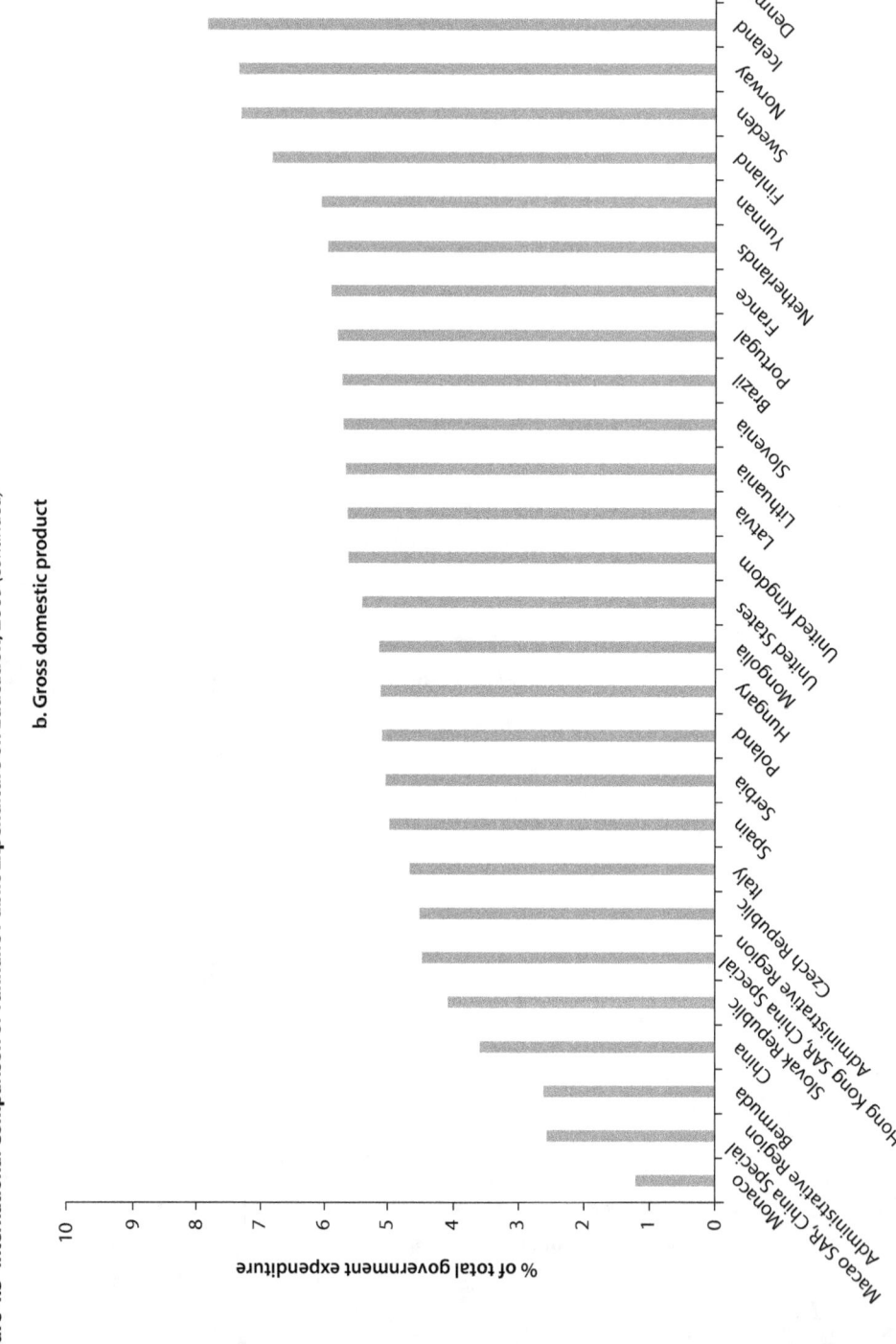

Sources: OECD.Stat; Ministry of Education 2009.

Strengthening Technical and Vocational Education and Training

Figure 4.6 Budgetary Recurrent Expenditure per Student by Level of Education in Yunnan, 2010

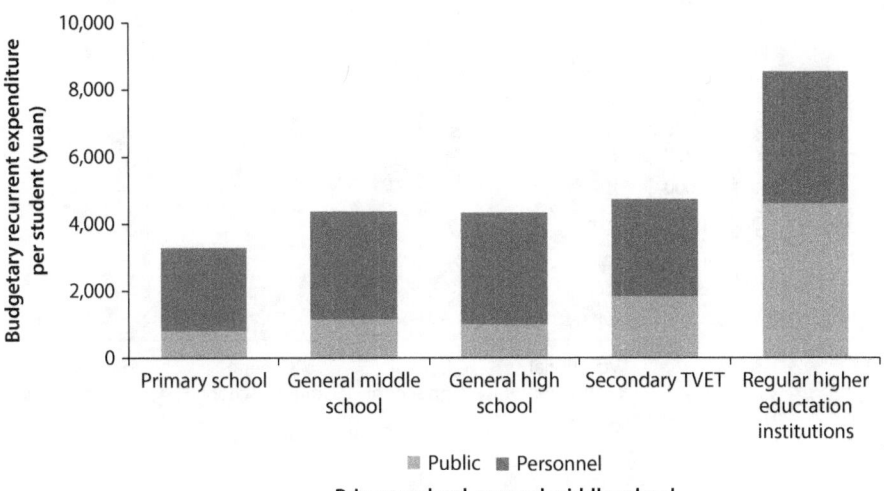

Sources: China Education Finance Statistical Yearbook 2010; table B.5.

Figure 4.7 Budgetary Recurrent Expenditure per Student on Secondary TVET, 2009

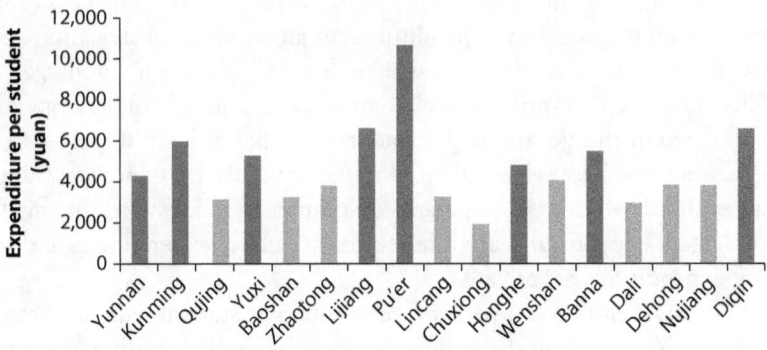

Source: Yun, Liu, and Li 2011.
Note: Darker bars indicate expenditures above, and lighter bars indicate expenditures below, the provincial average.

Inequalities in spending across cities and prefectures are correlated with the urban-rural gap. Per student expenditure in rural schools is lower than average at all levels of schooling with the exception of primary schools in Yunnan (figure 4.8). The gap is most pronounced in vocational high schools; per student expenditure at rural vocational high schools is 41 percent lower than the provincial average. Further, public expenditure and personnel expenditure in rural vocational high schools are as much as 64 percent and 28 percent, respectively, lower than the total averages.

Figure 4.8 Budgetary Recurrent Expenditure per Student in Yunnan, 2009

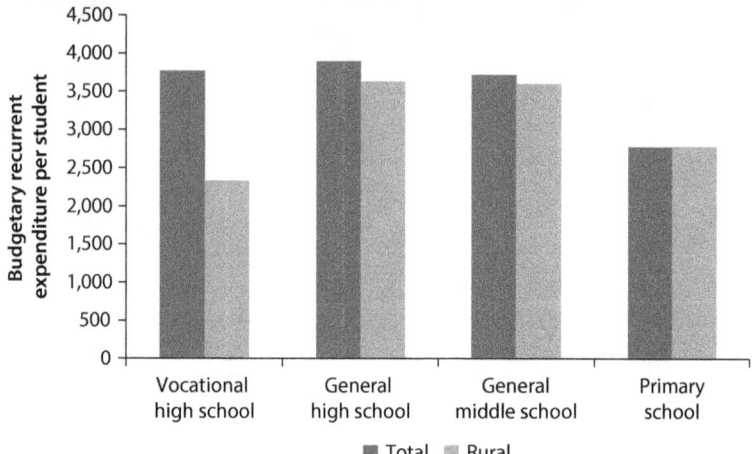

Source: China Education Finance Statistical Yearbook 2010.

Private Spending and Provision of Education

Since the early 1980s, the financing of education in China has been shifting rapidly toward a decentralized system with a diversified revenue base (Tsang 1996). In addition to budgetary expenditures coming from fiscal allocation and categorical funds, nonbudgetary sources include local education surcharges and levies, allocations by enterprises, social contributions, and school fees. Specifically, it is stipulated in the Vocational Education Law that at least 30 percent of the local education surcharges have to be allocated to vocational education (20 percent for areas that have not yet popularized compulsory education). In this subsection, budgetary expenditures are referred to as "public" expenditures and nonbudgetary expenditures as "private."

Private spending as a percentage of total per student expenditure is generally lower in Yunnan than the national average (table B.7). Within Yunnan, the share of private funding is the highest for tertiary associate degree programs (45 percent), followed by tertiary Bachelor's degree programs and pre-primary school (figure 4.9). For secondary TVET, nonbudgetary expenditure accounts for about 39 percent of the total expenditure per student, lower than the national average of 43 percent.

Table 4.8 further illustrates the proportion of students enrolled in private schools at different levels in Yunnan. Most private education in Yunnan takes place at the pre-primary and tertiary levels. For TVET, although the proportion of non-public spending is relatively low, 26 percent of students are enrolled at the 10 non-public tertiary institutions, and 12 percent are enrolled at the 54 secondary TVET institutions, levels similar to the national average. In comparison, Yunnan has much lower levels of private provision at the primary and

Figure 4.9 Total Budgetary and Nonbudgetary Expenditure by Level of Schooling in Yunnan, 2009

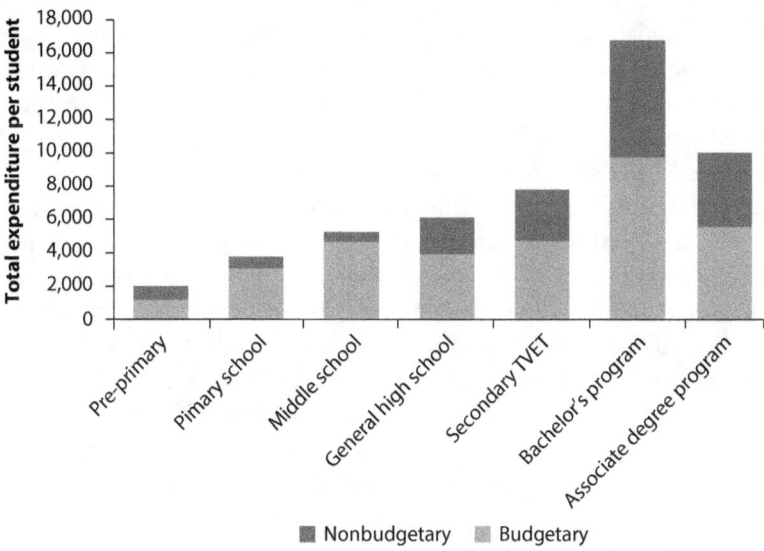

Source: China Education Finance Statistical Yearbook 2010.

Table 4.8 Private Provision of Education in Yunnan, 2010

Level	School type	Number of schools	Enrollment	Total enrollment, Yunnan (%)	Total enrollment, China (%)
Tertiary	Regular HEIs	17	107,101	24	n.a.
	Independent academies	7	59,905	23	n.a.
	TVET/associate degrees	10	47,196	26	n.a.
Upper secondary	TVET	54	85,795	12	14
	General	50	36,347	6	10
Lower secondary	General	79	48,524	2	8
Primary	General	114	100,531	2	5
Pre-primary	n.a.	2,906	415,481	42	47

Sources: Yun, Liu, and Li 2011; National averages are authors' calculations based on Ministry of Education 2010a statistics.
Note: HEI = Higher Education Institution; n.a. = not applicable.

lower secondary levels (only about 2 percent) and for general upper secondary education (only about 6 percent).

Private spending on education also includes funds provided by students' families. To investigate household expenditures on TVET, we draw on a survey conducted in 2010 among 900 students from 10 schools in Kunming, Qujing, Dali, and Tengchong. Students at secondary TVET are subsidized Y1,500 per year nationwide for living expenses. Most recently, rural students, students from poor families, and students studying in agricultural programs have been exempted from secondary TVET tuition fees by the State Council. On average, personal education expenditures are Y5,739 per student per year, accounting for about 27 percent of per capita family income. Tertiary TVET students spend the most on education (Y7,353), accounting for 40 percent of their per capita family income. At the secondary level, skilled-worker school students spend the most, accounting for 25 percent of their per capita family income (see figure 4.10).

The survey also asks students about their perception of the financial burden posed by education. On average, only 7 percent of the students surveyed expressed "no difficulties," and nearly 53 percent reported "with some difficulties but bearable." As many as 37 percent of the students think the cost of TVET education is "unbearable" and were forced to borrow money, and 51 percent of tertiary TVET students agree. At the secondary level, although the majority of students consider the financial burden to be bearable, 17–29 percent of the students think the cost is "unbearable" and also rely on borrowed money.

Efficiency of Public Spending on TVET

Because we do not have data on TVET graduates' labor market outcomes across Yunnan, we use enrollment rates and advancement rates, as well as indicators of education resources, such as student-teacher ratios, floor areas per student, and construction areas of school buildings (total size of school building divided by number of students) to examine the efficiency of Yunnan's financing of formal TVET.

Figure 4.10 Household Income and Educational Expenditure in Yunnan, 2010

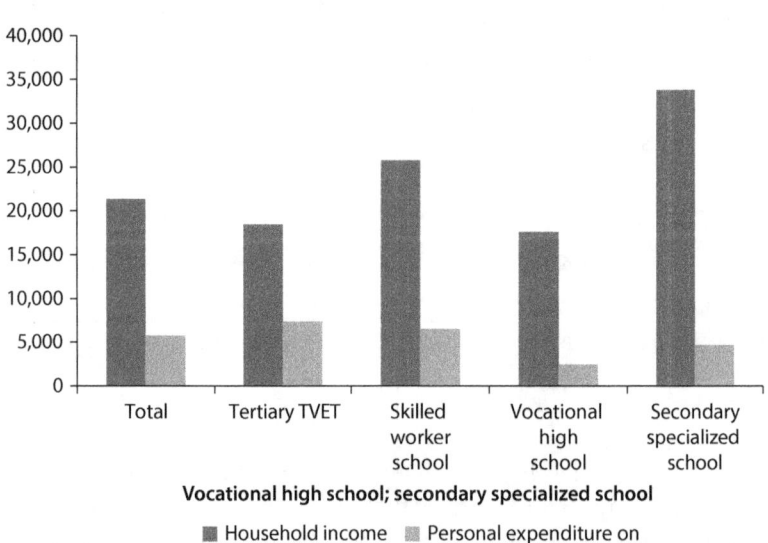

Source: Yun, Liu, and Li 2011.

Figure 4.11 Perceptions of Financial Burden Posed by Education Expenditures in Yunnan, 2010

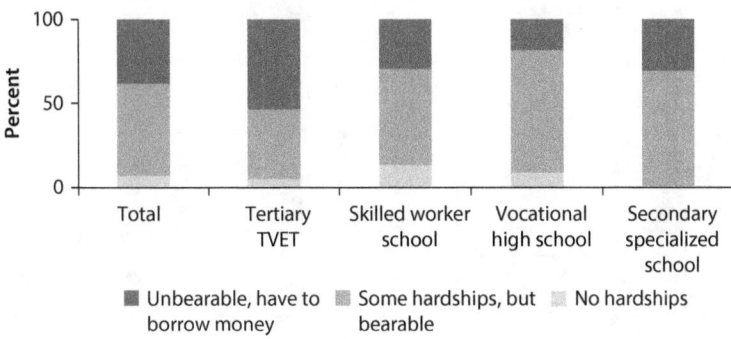

Source: Yun, Liu, and Li 2011.

Table 4.9 Comparison of Enrollment Rates and Advancement Rates in Yunnan and China, 2010

	Yunnan	China
Enrollment rates of school-age children	100	100
Advancement rates to lower secondary school	96	99
Advancement rates to upper secondary school	73	88

Sources: Yunnan Statistical Yearbook (Yunnan Province Statistical Bureau 2011); Yun, Liu, and Li 2011.

Although standardized testing scores are not available for benchmarking the performance of Yunnan's education system against other provinces, enrollment rates and advancement rates beyond the primary level lag behind the national average (table 4.9). Only 73 percent of the middle school graduates continued on to the upper secondary level, 15 percent lower than the national average. Even at the compulsory level, only 96 percent of primary school graduates continue on to the lower secondary level. Gross enrollment rates in Yunnan at the senior secondary level are only 65 percent in 2010, as compared to the gross enrollment rate at the senior secondary level in Shanghai of nearly 97 in 2009. Among cities and prefectures in Yunnan, Qujing has achieved a gross enrollment ratio of 91 percent at the upper secondary level, in sharp contrast to the 34 percent in Zhaotong, the lowest rate in the province (figure 4.12).

Poor operating conditions suggest that the average investment in TVET is insufficient, especially at the secondary level. Although TVET schools face difficulties meeting the national standards across China, the issue is particularly compelling for Yunnan. For example, table 4.10 compares the actual operating conditions of schools in Yunnan against the national standards and the national average on major indicators. In secondary TVET institutions, the student-teacher

Figure 4.12 Gross Enrollment Ratio in Yunnan at Upper Secondary Level by City and Prefecture, 2010

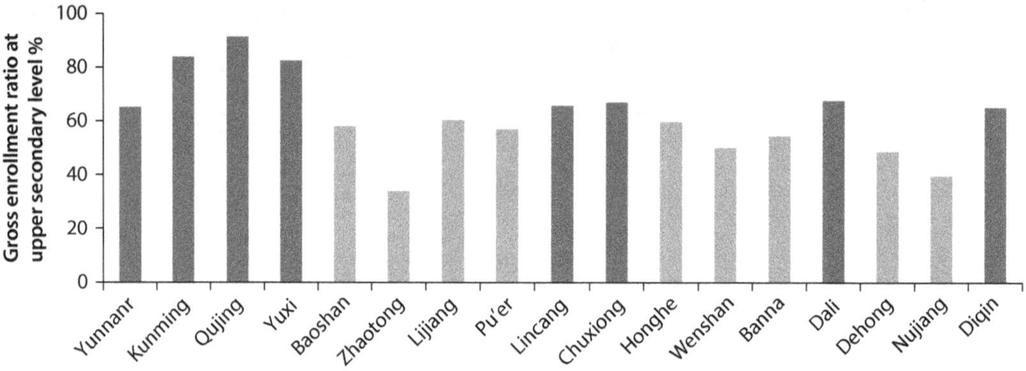

Source: Yun, Liu, and Li 2011.
Note: Darker bars indicate rates above, and lighter bars indicate rates below, the provincial average.

Table 4.10 Selected Standards for Secondary TVET Institutions in Yunnan, 2010

	Enrollment (persons)	Student-teacher ratio	Full-time teachers with both degrees and skills certification (%)	Floor area per student (m²)	Value of equipment/facilities per student (Y)	Number of computers per 100 students
National standards	>1,200	20:1	30	20	2,500	15
National average	1,672	27:1	21	12	2,331	13
Yunnan	1,414	29:1	17	9	1,337	11

Sources: China Education Finance Statistical Yearbook 2010; Ministry of Education 2010b.
Note: Secondary TVET institutions in this table include secondary specialized schools and vocational high schools, but do not include skilled-worker schools.

ratio in Yunnan (29:1) far exceeds the national standard of 20:1, while the 17 percent of full-time teachers with both degree and skills certifications is well below the national minimum of 30 percent and the national average of 21 percent. In terms of the infrastructure and facilities, Yunnan is also lagging behind: floor area per student is only 9 square meters, well below the national standard of 20 square meters and the national average of 12 square meters. The value of equipment and facilities per student and the number of computers are also far from adequate to meet the national standard and match the national average.

On the tertiary level (table 4.11), Yunnan's TVET institutions meet the national standards and exceed the national average on major indicators. For example, Yunnan has achieved an average student-teacher ratio of 18:1. The percentage of full-time teachers with post-graduate degrees has reached nearly 33 percent, more than double the national minimum standard of 15 percent. The value of equipment and facilities and floor area per student, although slightly lower than the national average, meet the national standard.

In vocational high schools, Yunnan's recurrent expenditure per student and average student-teacher ratio are close to the national average. With similar levels

Table 4.11 Selected Standards for Tertiary TVET Institutions in Yunnan, 2010

	Enrollment (persons)	Student-teacher ratio	Full-time teachers with post-graduate degrees (%)	Floor area per student (m^2)	Value of equipment/ facilities per student (Y)
National standards	>2,000	18:1	15	14	4,000
National average	7,754	17:1	32	15	6,115
Yunnan	5,236	18:1	33	14	4,615

Sources: China Education Finance Statistical Yearbook 2010; Ministry of Education 2000, 2004.
Note: Secondary TVET institutions in this table include secondary specialized schools and vocational high school, but do not include skilled-worker schools.

of per student expenditure, Yunnan has a lower student-teacher ratio than Guizhou, Sichuan, and Shaanxi in southwestern China. However, compared to Qinghai, also with a similar level of per student expenditure, Yunnan has a much higher student-teacher ratio. For secondary specialized schools, Yunnan spends slightly more than the national average and yet has a higher student-teacher ratio. Compared to Gansu and Shaanxi, Yunnan appears to have a higher level of expenditure per student but also a higher student-teacher ratio (see figure 4.13).

Efficiency gaps can be further illustrated by inequalities in educational resources available to secondary TVET institutions within Yunnan. The national standards specify a minimum of 33 square meters of floor area per student, 20 square meters of construction area of school building per student and a maximum student-teacher ratio of 20:1. However, as indicated by figure 4.14, basic operating conditions vary greatly across the province, and only a few cities and prefectures meet the national standards. For example, floor area per student ranges from 127 square meters in Nujiang to only 15 square meters in Lincang. Only five cities and prefectures have a student-teacher ratio of lower than 20:1, while Qujing and Lincang have student-teacher ratios of 50:1.

Summary

This chapter provides a comprehensive review of the formal TVET system in Yunnan, with a specific focus on governance and management, industry involvement, curriculum reforms, quality assurance, and finance.

Although management of the formal TVET system in China has traditionally been fragmented, involving multiple ministries and departments, in recent years interdepartmental TVET coordination committees have been established at the national level and in a few provinces. Governance and management of TVET in China are still the responsibility of government, with limited industry involvement. Although employers and industry associations are sometimes consulted in the policymaking process, their role remains advisory and their involvement is often ad hoc.

With the wide implementation of curriculum reforms, schools have become more aware of the need to align training programs and curricula with labor market demand. Efforts to establish formal school–industry links through

Figure 4.13 Student-Teacher Ratio Compared to Recurrent Expenditure per Student in Yunnan, 2010

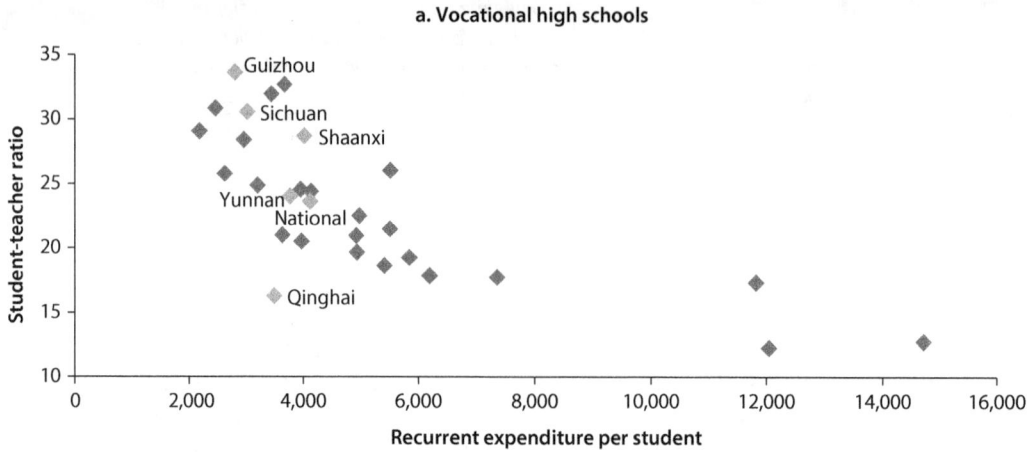

a. Vocational high schools

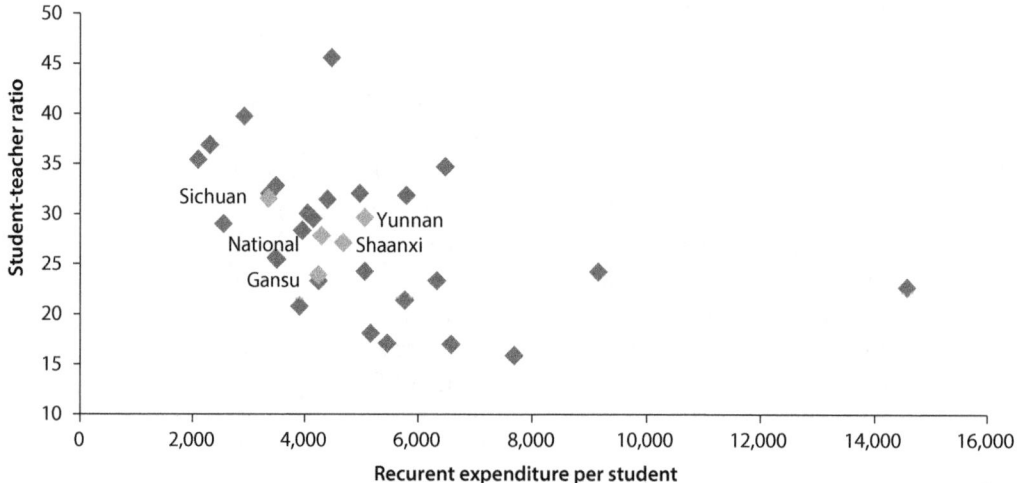

b. Specialized secondary schools

Sources: Expenditure data from Ministry of Education 2010a; student-teacher ratio from Yunnan Statistical Yearbook (Yunnan Province Statistical Bureau 2011).
Note: Lighter colors indicate regions and nation.

collaborative advisory and sector-specific advisory committees have started to emerge, with support from the National Model TVET School project and development partners such as the World Bank. However, the links are often limited to recruiting graduates or providing internships and training. Very few enterprises are involved in curriculum development or assessment of students. Furthermore, the limited capacity of teachers, inadequate facilities and equipment, and lack of school resources have impeded the implementation of the TVET curriculum reform.

Quality assurance is carried out through enforcement of standards for training providers and a nationwide skills certification system. Responding to the

Strengthening Technical and Vocational Education and Training　　97

Figure 4.14　Operating Conditions of Secondary TVET Institutions in Yunnan, 2010

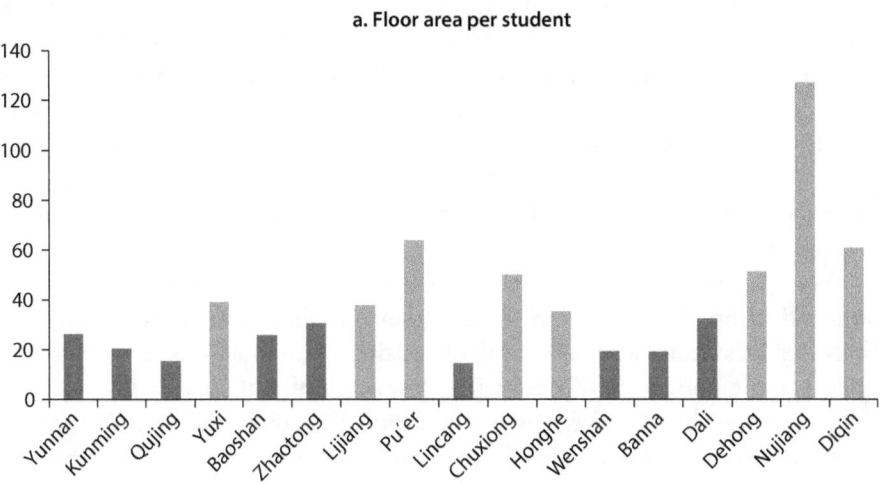

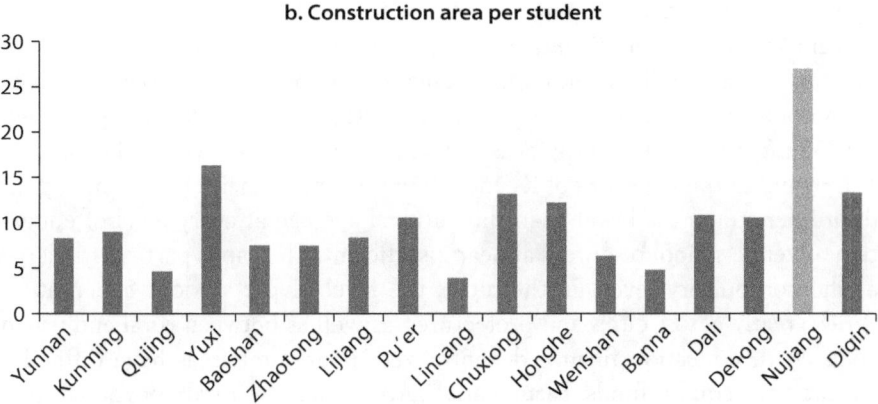

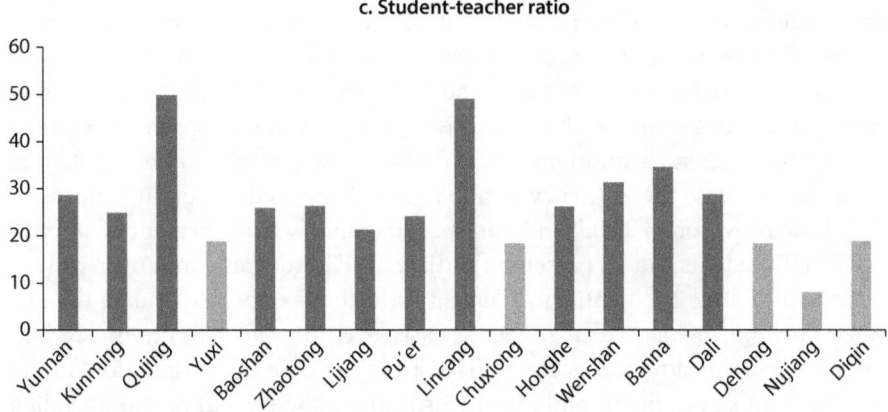

Source: Yun, Liu, and Li 2011.
Note: Light-colored bars indicate city and prefecture averages not meeting national standards.

most recent national policies, the Ministry of Education and HRSS have updated the standards for establishing TVET institutions on both the secondary and tertiary levels. Although the standards are comprehensive and specific to the types of institutions, many existing TVET institutions, especially those at the secondary level, face difficulties in attaining them. The issue is particularly pressing for resource-constrained provinces such as Yunnan. The standards continue to serve as benchmarks for local governments as they strive to improve the overall conditions of TVET institutions through better resource allocation and planning.

Quality assurance is also exercised at the student level through a certification system developed by the HRSS. An increasing number of students are pursuing skills certificates in addition to their academic diplomas upon graduation. However, the current certificates suffer from lack of authority and are not yet fully recognized by employers. Only a minority of existing workers in Yunnan has obtained certification, and only 20 percent of the new job openings over the past year required a skills certification for new hires. The existing occupational classification and competency standards for each occupation have not been fully updated to reflect the changing demands of the market.

Yunnan's education *finance* relies mostly on public sources of funding. Yunnan's total public spending on education amounted to 6 percent of its gross domestic product and 19 percent of total government spending—a high level compared to other provinces in China and even to developed countries. Yet, owing to the large size of its education system, Yunnan's recurrent expenditure per student is lower than the national average at every level of education. Overall, school resources appear insufficient. The gap is particularly large at the compulsory level. Furthermore, the level of per student expenditure varies greatly across cities and prefectures, as well as between rural and urban areas. With education finance decentralized, poor rural areas have difficulty allocating adequate funds. Particularly hard hit are the rural vocational high schools.

The poor performance of the education system in Yunnan is suggested by enrollment and advancement rates that are lower than the national average. Within Yunnan, there exist huge disparities in school resources and educational quality across cities and prefectures, and between rural and urban areas. In particular, disparities among TVET institutions appear even more pronounced than those among general institutions. These disparities suggest that there is potential to further increase the efficiency of public spending on education in Yunnan.

Private provision of TVET in Yunnan is emerging with 12 percent of secondary TVET students and 25 percent of tertiary TVET students enrolling in private institutions. There is potential for Yunnan to further explore expanding the private provision, in particular at the tertiary level, beyond its current level to mobilize additional resources and to have a healthy dose of "competition" in the system. Across both public and private institutions, the level of private spending on TVET in Yunnan remains lower than the national average. Indeed, private support could be more strongly mobilized.

The allocation of public funds in TVET is primarily driven by student enrollment and a per student expenditure formula. In addition, the government provides special funding opportunities, which have been mainly competition based. Although competition-based funding provides incentives and motivation for improving quality and innovation in TVET, equity-based resource allocations for disadvantaged schools can enable these schools to make critical improvements in educational quality. Demand-side financing is limited to waiving fees for poor rural students and the RMB 1,500 across-the-board subsidy for living expenses. There is no other demand-side financing such as training vouchers.

Bibliography

Allais, S. 2010. *The Implementation and Impact of National Qualifications Frameworks: Report of a Study in 16 Countries*. Geneva: ILO.

National Bureau of Statistics of China. 2010. *China Education Finance Statistical Yearbook*. Beijing: China Statistics Press.

Hong Kong SAR Qualification Framework. 2004. http://www.hkqf.gov.hk/.

HRSS (Yunnan Department of Human Resources and Social Security). 2010. *Quarterly Vacancy Data*.

———. 2011. *Quarterly Vacancy Data*.

———2012a. *Advanced Skilled Worker School Establishment Standard (Provisional)*. http://www.gov.cn/gongbao/content/2012/content_2163427.htm.

———. 2012b. *Skilled Worker School Establishment Standard (Provisional)*. http://www.gov.cn/gongbao/content/2012/content_2163427.htm.

———. 2012c. *Technicians Academy Establishment Standard (Provisional)*. http://www.gov.cn/gongbao/content/2012/content_2163427.htm.

Liu, P. 2010. "TVET System and Its Innovation Strategy in China." Presentation at the South-South Study Visit on Skills and TVET, "TVET System & Its Innovation Strategy in China—For a More Flexible, Responsive and Attractive System," Guangdong, China, November 1.

Ministry of Education. 2000. *No. 14: Tertiary TVET Establishment Standard (Provisional)*. http://www.moe.edu.cn/publicfiles/business/htmlfiles/moe/moe_621/200409/3208.html.

———. 2004. *No. 2: Regular Higher Institutions Basic Operating Condition Indicators (Provisional)*. http://www.moe.edu.cn/publicfiles/business/htmlfiles/moe/moe_2/201006/88606.html.

———. 2009. 教育部国家统计局财政部关于2009年全国教育经费执行情况统计公告 [Announcement on 2009 National Education Finance Implementation]. http://www.moe.edu.cn/publicfiles/business/htmlfiles/moe/s3040/201012/112378.html.

———. 2010a. 教育部国家统计局财政部关于2010年全国教育经费执行情况统计公告, http://www.moe.edu.cn/publicfiles/business/htmlfiles/moe/s3040/201112/128871.html.

———. 2010b. *No. 12: Secondary TVET School Establishment Standard*. http://www.gov.cn/gongbao/content/2010/content_1745852.htm.

OECD.Stat extracts (database). Organisation for Economic Co-operation and Development, Paris, France. http://stats.oecd.org/.

State Council. 2002. 大力推进职业教育改革与发展的决定 [Decision to Promote the Reform and Development of Vocational Education]. http://www.gov.cn/gongbao/content/2002/content_61755.htm.

STEP (Skills Toward Employment and Productivity) Employer Survey. 2012. World Bank, Washington, DC.

Tsang, M. C. 1996. "Financial Reform of Basic Education in China." *Economics of Education Review* 15 (4): 423–44.

Yun, B., H. Liu, and Y. Li. 2011. "云南省职业技术教育发展研究报告."

Yunnan Bureau of Statistics. 2011. *Yunnan Statistical Yearbook.* Beijing: China Statistics Press.

Yunnan Department of Education. 2012. *Yunnan Non-public Education Institute Management Measures.* http://www.mbjyw.com/html/201208/20120829306.shtml.

Zhang, C., and S. Ma. 2011. "我国职业学校办学条件评价和预警机制研究." 中国高教研究杂志 8.

CHAPTER 5

Non-Formal Training

The previous chapter provided an in-depth review of the formal Technical and Vocational Education and Training (TVET) sector. In this chapter, we turn to the non-formal training sector. Recognizing the importance of creating second chances and building a lifelong learning framework for their citizens, many countries are taking steps to improve their non-formal education and training systems through increasing both access and quality. China must also aggressively face these challenges.

As China's economic reforms and urbanization accelerate, a large population of rural laborers, previously engaged in agricultural activities, has become idle. The training of surplus rural labor is of paramount importance in facilitating the transfer of rural workers to the secondary and tertiary sectors and preparing them for migration across regions.

This chapter presents an overview of the context of rural labor training, the evolution of the policy framework, and the major training projects implemented in rural Yunnan. The analysis is further enriched by a quantitative evaluation of the impact of rural training on household income using data drawn from a survey of 3,000 rural households in Honghe Prefecture, Yunnan.

Rural Work Force and Surplus Labor Transfer

Training the largely unskilled rural working population is a key strategy of the Chinese government's poverty alleviation efforts. China has set target urbanization rates of 44 percent in 2015 and 50 percent in 2020, up from the current rate of 31 percent. In order to reach those targets, a significant number of rural unskilled laborers must be transferred to the secondary or tertiary sector. Those who remain in the agricultural sector need training in both higher-value-added agricultural activities and technology to improve their productivity.

Yunnan's structural adjustment in agriculture started in the 1990s, with policies such as "shrinking grain production and expanding trading" and the later promotion of "characteristic," "highly efficient," "large-scale," and "export-oriented" agriculture. These policies are aimed at improving agriculture efficiency and increasing rural income. Yet, because the rural population is large and farmland is limited, rural poverty remains an issue. Governments at both the central and local levels are aware that the solution lies in reducing the number of farmers, transferring rural surplus labor to the secondary and tertiary sectors, turning producers of agricultural produce into consumers, and reducing agricultural production while increasing the demand for it. These strategies are expected not only to increase the income of the rural population, but also to promote the development of "socialist new rural areas" and a "well-off society," and to bridge the urban-rural gaps.

Yunnan has a more than sufficient stock of rural labor engaged in agricultural activities. Since 1978, the size of the rural workforce has almost doubled, although its share of the total labor force has gone down by 5 percentage points (figure 5.1). As of the end of 2010, the rural labor force totaled 22 million, constituting approximately 78 percent of Yunnan's total labor force. Two-thirds of the rural labor force is between the ages of 16 and 40. Among the rural workers, 78 percent were engaged in agricultural activities, while 9 percent and 13 percent were engaged in the secondary and tertiary sectors, respectively.

The provincial Department of Human Resources and Social Security (HRSS) estimated in 2011 that surplus labor was 7.6 million, one-third of Yunnan's total rural labor force (HRSS 2011). By the end of 2011, more than 5 million of the surplus rural laborers found employment in the secondary or tertiary sector, while 2.5 million remain to be transferred. In 2011 alone, 1.7 million rural surplus laborers were transferred, with 1.3 million finding employment within

Figure 5.1 Number of Workers in Rural Areas and Share of Total Employment in Yunnan, 1978–2010

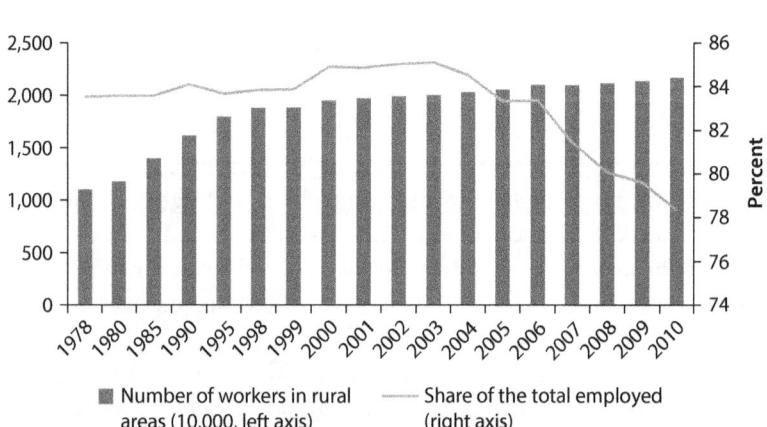

Source: Yunnan Statistical Yearbook 2011.

Yunnan and 0.4 million outside Yunnan (HRSS 2012). The rate of transfer of rural labor in Yunnan is lower than the national average.

Yunnan's rural working age population averages only seven years of education. Nearly 9 percent of the rural working age population is illiterate; most have attained only primary school (32 percent) or lower secondary education (39 percent). Only about 20 percent have had upper secondary education or beyond. Furthermore, as many as 86 percent of the rural workers have not received any training (National Bureau of Statistics of China 2008). The number of rural professional and technical personnel amounted to less than 0.2 percent of the total human resources in rural Yunnan.

The rural laborers who manage to transfer also lack skills and training. Transferred laborers average a little more than eight years of education, slightly higher than the average for Yunnan's rural population, but still less than the level of compulsory education. The majority of transferred workers have attained only lower secondary education. Only 2 percent of the current transferred labor force received training before their transfers.

Rural-to-Urban Migration and Employment: Policy Evolution

Since 1949, China's national policy on rural-to-urban migration and employment has undergone three major phases:

Phase 1: Planned period (1949–77)

During this period in the broader context of China's planned economy, labor mobility was restricted between rural and urban areas, as well as across provinces. The residential registration (*hukou*) policy strictly prohibited unplanned migration.

Phase 2: Restricted migration (1978–99)

With China's economic reforms, the "family contract responsibility system" was introduced in rural areas. Formerly collectively owned lands were contracted to households, releasing some farmers from agricultural activities. During the same period, rural laborers were permitted, but only on a restricted basis, to migrate to and get employment in urban areas. Gradually, the government started regulating the recruitment process for rural migrants, including issuing urban employment permits and temporary urban residential permits.

Phase 3: Guided and facilitated migration (2000 to present)

As the migration rate accelerated, the government has adapted its role from restricting migration toward guiding it. For example, the national government initiated the Sunshine Project, the Rural Labor Skills Training and Employment Project, and the Rain and Dew Project to prepare migrants for the migration process and their ultimate employment in the cities. Yunnan has also issued a series of provincial policies to implement training projects among rural workers (box 5.1).

Box 5.1 Yunnan's Policies on Rural Worker Training, 2004–08

2004
The policy entitled Suggestions on Accelerating Rural Labor Force Transfer by Yunnan Provincial People's Government proposed the Project of Training a Million Rural Workers.

2005
The Announcement on Distributing the 2005–10 Training Plans for Rural Workers of Yunnan by the General Office of Yunnan Provincial People's Government set an annual target of providing training to 500,000 transferring workers. The ratio of guidance training to skills training was set at 4:1.

2006
The Announcement on Distributing the Implementation of Enhancing Employment and Re-employment by Yunnan Provincial People's Government pledged to provide policy assurance for subsidizing Yunnan's rural workers seeking employment in urban areas.

2008
The Announcement on Distributing the Implementation of the Employment Promotion Law by Yunnan Provincial People's Government specified that "unemployed ex-servicemen and rural workers in urban areas who participate in training will have their training fees subsidized."

Demand for and Supply of Rural Worker Training

Rural laborers need training in order to transfer to secondary and tertiary industries or across regions. They need not only to acquire technical skills specific to the sector they are transferring to, but they also need guidance training that prepares them for migration to urban areas. Guidance training usually consists of an orientation covering topics such as basic rights at the work place, laws and regulations, and advice on urban living and employment. Rural laborers who remain in agricultural activities need training that would equip them with practical skills to improve productivity.

Various training providers serve the rural population, including the TVET schools, employment training centers, and employers, all of which also serve urban workers. In addition, the agricultural broadcasting schools and agricultural training centers under the Department of Agriculture and the Poverty Alleviation Office deliver training, especially agricultural skills training, to rural workers in local villages. Figure 5.2 illustrates the training demand and supply among rural workers.

During the 11th Five-Year Plan period (2006–10), 6.5 million rural workers received training, of whom nearly 5 million received guidance training and over 1.5 million received skills training. A total of nearly 870,000 took part in the skills certification, over 750,000 of whom have successfully obtained skills qualifications.

Figure 5.2 Demand for and Supply of Rural Labor Training

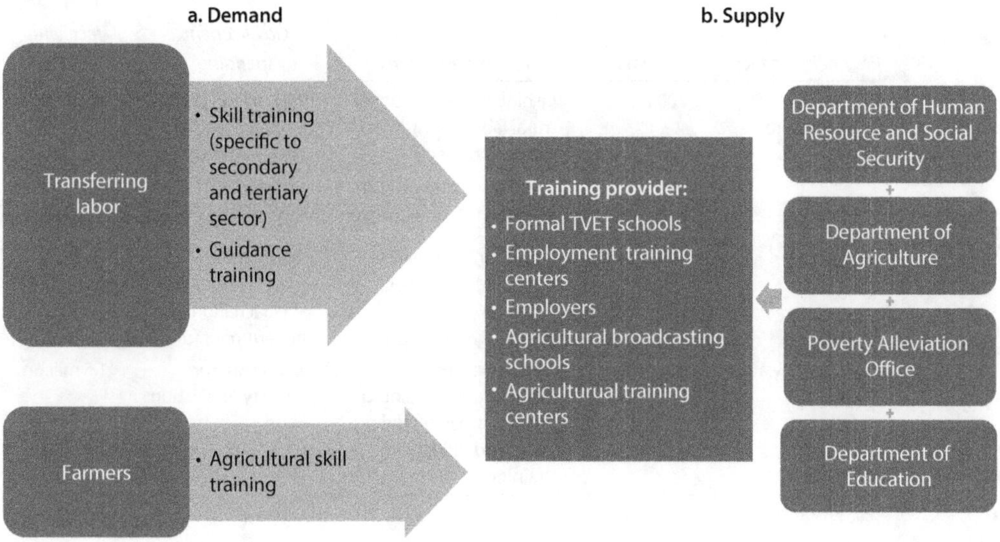

a. Demand

- Transferring labor
  - Skill training (specific to secondary and tertiary sector)
  - Guidance training
- Farmers
  - Agricultural skill training

Training provider:
- Formal TVET schools
- Employment training centers
- Employers
- Agricultural broadcasting schools
- Agriculturual training centers

b. Supply

- Department of Human Resource and Social Security
- Department of Agriculture
- Poverty Alleviation Office
- Department of Education

Note: TVET = Technical and Vocational Education and Training.

Managing and Financing Rural Worker Training Programs

Table 5.1 lists the major rural training programs carried out in Yunnan in recent years, organized by Department of Agriculture, HRSS, and the Poverty Alleviation Office. In addition, Yunnan's Department of Education has been involved in training school-aged youth in rural Yunnan on topics such as agriculture as part of the formal education curriculum. There are also training programs initiated by the Trade Union, the All China Women's Federation, the CCP Youth League Committee, and the Department of Science and Technology.

The costs of training are shared between public finance (at the central, provincial, and local levels) and participants. Governments at all levels have set up categorical funds for rural training, which are disbursed to rural trainees in the form of cash, vouchers, or reduced training fees. In addition, the All China Women's Federation and the Youth League raise donations through foundations devoted to conducting rural training for target groups.

Several measures are in place to assure the quality of training. For example, Yunnan's provincial rural transfer labor training program requires that a panel of experts review the qualifications, facilities, experience working with rural areas, and proximity to rural areas of participating training providers. Potential training providers are not eligible to enter the bidding process if the employment rate of their trainees is under 80 percent. Furthermore, to ensure the employability of trainees, public training funds are allocated so as to give priority to targeted programs contracted by employers.

Table 5.1 Major Training Programs for Rural Workers in Yunnan

Provincial agency	Years	Training programs	Government spending	Number receiving training
Department of Agriculture	2004–09	Sunshine Project (national rural labor transfer training project) Provincial-level rural labor transfer training project	Y194.3 million (Y104.3 million from the national fund; Y90 million from the provincial projects)	1 million
HRSS	Since 2006	Rural Labor Skills and Employment Project	Through 2009, Y314 million from special national government fund	804,000
Poverty Alleviation Office	2004–09	Rain and Dew Project (labor transfer training in poor areas, including skills and guidance training)	Y452 million from Poverty Alleviation Fund	1.5 million

Source: Li 2012.

The existing governance and finance of non-formal training suffer from three major challenges. First, fragmented governance and financing reduce the efficiency and effectiveness of the system. For example, the management of rural labor transfer training alone involves the Departments of Finance at all governmental levels, along with HRSS, Education, Science and Technology, and Construction. In poor areas the Poverty Alleviation Offices participate as well. Yunnan has set up a provincial-level rural labor transfer leadership office (operating in the Agriculture Department), but it is unknown whether or to what extent the coordinating efforts have been effective.

Second, although competitive bidding is used for some training programs and training providers are given autonomy in admitting students, conducting training, and establishing connections with employers, there are no accountability measures to assure the quality of training. Allocation of training funds is based mostly on the number of trainees and the unit cost of training, instead of on training outcomes such as certification and employment rates. In some cases, trainees and training providers are reimbursed on the condition that the trainees pursue skills certification. Given the low credibility among employers of skills certification in general, certification rates do not necessarily translate into higher employment rates or guarantee a high quality of training. In addition, the requirements for auditing and monitoring are only roughly implemented, giving training providers room to misuse public resources for their own interests.

Finally, overall training funds appear insufficient. The total government spending on rural worker training in Yunnan was Y60 million in 2009 and Y65 million in 2010. The maximum subsidy of Y600 per person is far below the cost of training a primary lathe worker or a welder, which exceeds Y2,000, or the cost of training a chef, which exceeds Y1,300. As a result, rural training has been limited mostly to short-term, non-skill-oriented guidance training.

Content and Delivery of Rural Labor Training

Rural labor training programs in Yunnan are managed by three different government agencies: HRSS, the Department of Agriculture, and the Poverty Alleviation Office. The programs offered by each agency vary in duration, focus, and form of delivery. Table 5.2 shows the range of program characteristics for each agency.

The training programs usually comprise a combination of orientation, covering basic legal and policy knowledge, and skill-specific courses. Trainings conducted by the Department of Agriculture tend to focus on agriculture-related technical skills, whereas Poverty Alleviation Office and HRSS programs offer a variety of courses geared toward urban employment, mostly in the construction and service sectors. An important characteristic of rural training is the form of delivery: Although many sessions are conducted in county vocational schools and other accredited training agencies, training sessions are also conducted in local villages and sometimes in homes.

The content of training provided through HRSS is based on a standard framework that leads to skills certification. Trainees who receive training through HRSS are required to pay for the final certification tests. A higher proportion of those who receive training through HRSS obtain skills certificates compared to those in other training programs. Those who fail the tests still obtain module

Table 5.2 Content and Provision of Rural Worker Training Programs in Yunnan

Government agency	Types	Areas	Duration	Entry requirements	Training provided by	Final certification
Yunnan Department of Agriculture: Sunshine Project	Guidance training	Law and policy concerning urban employment	7–16 days	Middle school graduate, healthy	County vocational high schools, rural broadcasting school	No
	Skills training	More than 20 agriculture-related fields				
Yunnan HRSS	Guidance training	Law and policy concerning urban employment	At least one month; cooking approximately 45 days	No	Accredited training providers, at home or local villages	Qualified trainees obtain skills certificates; those not qualified receive module attendance recognition
	Skills training	Computer, horticulture, animal husbandry, stitching and sewing				
Yunnan Poverty Alleviation Office: Rain and Dew	Guidance training	Law and policy concerning urban employment	Three days	Middle school graduate, healthy	County vocational high school, at home or local villages	Usually no, but students can take skills tests administered by HRSS
	Skills training	Hospitality, computer skills, sewing	One month			

Source: Li 2012.

attendance recognition, which entitles them to work toward final certification in the specific technical area. In comparison, programs organized by the Poverty Alleviation Office often do not lead to certification. The Department of Agriculture generally provides short-term agriculture courses, which also do not lead to any certification.

Impact of Rural Training: Evidence from Honghe Prefecture

Despite the increased investment made by the government at various levels, there has been very little analysis of the impact of rural training. Honghe Prefecture is one of the target areas participating in the national and provincial rural labor training projects. Given the low socio-economic level and diverse demographic and geographic features, Honghe is an ideal site for studying the effects of rural labor training in Yunnan. Fortunately, we are able to access data from a longitudinal household survey conducted from 2006 to 2010 in rural Honghe Prefecture in Yunnan. The unique data allow us to conduct a quantitative analysis to investigate the impact of rural training on household incomes.

The Honghe Hani and Yi Autonomous Prefecture ("Honghe") is located in southeast Yunnan, bordering Kunming, Yuxi, Qujing, and Vietnam. Honghe has an area of 32,931 square kilometers, 85 percent of which is mountainous area. As of the end of 2006, Honghe's registered population totaled over 4 million, 57 percent of whom belong to ethnic minorities. The largest ethnic minority groups in Honghe are Yi and Hani, accounting for 24 percent and 17 percent, respectively, of the total population. In 2006, Honghe had six national-level poverty counties and one provincial-level poverty county. Population below the poverty line numbers 734,000, nearly 18 percent of its total registered population.

A description of the Honghe Rural Household Survey and the sample restrictions used in this study can be found in box 5.2. In our final analytic sample, 1,260 members from 571 households participated in training in 2006. The vast majority attended training organized by government, while a small number sought training programs on their own or attended training organized by enterprises. Table C.1 further tracks our treatment and control groups in the years following 2006.

Households members participated in training in 2006 differ significantly in both village-level and household-level characteristics from those whose members did not (table C.2). On the village level, as many as 84 percent of households whose members did not participate in training are from villages with a high concentration of ethnic minorities. Moreover, over 80 percent of them are located more than 20 kilometers away from county towns or in mountainous areas. Among households receiving training, however, about half are from non-ethnic-minority villages, and only 43 percent live in mountainous areas. These findings imply that geographic barriers might have prevented rural laborers from receiving training. During the survey, when asked why they did not participate in training, "training is not available locally" is

Box 5.2 The Honghe Rural Household Survey and Analytic Sample

This study draws on data from the Honghe Rural Household Survey conducted by the Honghe Statistics Bureau and the Statistical and Mathematical College at the Yunnan University of Finance and Economics. The sample of 3,000 households was selected randomly using two-stage cluster sampling from 295 villages in 13 counties. The surveyed households record their income from different sources and expenditures on a daily basis. In addition, the survey collects information on household members' education, training, migration, and work background. We include in our analytic sample 2,143 households who participated in the survey each year from 2006 through 2010. We analyze the trends for labor transfer across industries, migration, and training participation over the five years.

In order to estimate the effects of training on income, we further restrict our sample to include (1) households with at least one member attending training in 2006 (the treatment group) and (2) households with no members attending training from 2006 through 2008 (the control group). We measure the net income per person in the household in 2007 and 2008. Incomes are adjusted using 2006 as the base year, according to the price indices provided by the Honghe Statistics Bureau. Table B5.2.1 lists the three major training projects implemented in rural Honghe since 2005.

Table B5.2.1 Training in Rural Honghe

Organizer	Starting date	Types	Spending per student(Y)	Duration	Number of participants
Honghe Poverty Alleviation Office: Rain and Dew	2005	Guidance training	2005–07: 100 2008 to date: 200	2005–07: seven days 2008 to date: three days	40,000
		Skills training	2005–07: 500 2008 to date: 800	One month	
Honghe Bureau of HRSS	2006	Guidance training and skills training leading to certification	2006–08: 500 2009 to date: 500 (400 training fee and 100 certification fee)	At least one month; cook's training approximately 45 days	60,000
Honghe Bureau of Agriculture: Sunshine Project	2006	Guidance training; agricultural skills training	400	7–16 days	60,000

Source: Li 2012.

the second most-cited reason. In addition, households whose members participated in training tend to come from villages with high participation rates.

On the household level, households that did not participate in training seem to be characterized by much lower literacy rates: In 7 percent of those households, all members are illiterate, much higher than the 1 percent among households whose members participated in training. Similarly, in only 13 percent of the households without training, are there members with education levels beyond high school, compared to 26 percent of the households with training. Some of the training programs require participants to have attained at least junior secondary level education, which prevents many less-educated and uneducated rural laborers from receiving training. Furthermore, households whose members participated in training had higher total net income and agricultural income than those households without training. Finally, 17 percent of the households who participated in training had cadres, as compared to only 9 percent of the nonparticipating households.

Using propensity score matching estimators, we match households whose members participated in training with similarly situated households without training.[1] We then used the matched sample to estimate the effects of training. The results are presented in table 5.3. Overall, we find a positive and significant effect of training on the net income of family members. Average treatment effect on the treated (ATT) tells us the extent to which the households whose members attended training benefit from it. Households whose members participated in training in 2006 showed an average increase in their 2007 net income per person of Y1,471, an increase that is 26 percent higher than if they did not attend training. The effects are slightly smaller on 2008 income, but still positive and significant. In contrast, as shown by the average treatment effect on the controls (ATC), households in the control group would have increased their income by Y1,041 (24 percent) in 2008 had they participated in training in 2006. On average, having member(s) receiving training in 2006 increased the real net income per person in the household by Y996 (22 percent) in 2007 and Y962 (20 percent) in 2008, as indicated by the average treatment effect (ATE). We have tested the robustness of the results employing other methods and models. These results are available upon request.

Summary and Policy Implications

As Yunnan's economic development and urbanization advance, a significant number of rural unskilled laborers need to be transferred to the secondary or tertiary sector. Those who remain in the agricultural sector need training to

Table 5.3 Estimated Effects of Training on Net Income per Person, 2007 and 2008

	2007		2008	
	Income	*log(income)*	*Income*	*log(income)*
Average treatment effect on the treated (ATT)	1471.2***	0.259***	761.08*	0.10912
	(416.21)	(0.06)	(387.41)	(0.07)
Average treatment effect (ATE)	996.3**	0.22395**	962.08*	0.20404*
	(379.79)	(0.08)	(412.90)	(0.08)
Average treatment effect on the controls (ATC)	810.25	0.21021	1040.8*	0.24123*
	(429.53)	(0.11)	(515.32)	(0.11)

Source: Honghe Household Income Survey.
Note: Abadie-Imbens (AI) standard errors in parenthesis. *** $p < 0.001$, ** $p < 0.01$, * $p < 0.05$.

upgrade their skills to improve productivity. Both the central and provincial governments have introduced training schemes targeted at rural surplus laborers.

Using data collected in Honghe, we were able to evaluate the impact of training by estimating the effects of household members who received training in 2006 on the net income per person in the household in 2007 and 2008. The propensity score matching estimators illustrate a positive and significant effect of training: Households whose members participated in training in 2006 earned 26 percent more income per person in 2007, and 11 percent more income per person in 2008 than households that did not participate. On average, households whose members attended training showed an increase in their net income per person in 2007 and 2008 of over 20 percent. Our results provide evidence of the economic returns of training and further highlight the value of rural labor training. It is particularly worth noting that, although training is given to individual household members, the training effect goes beyond the individual and extends to the net income of the entire family.

Despite the positive economic effects, our analysis and interviews in the field have revealed several areas of potential improvement in the effectiveness and efficiency of rural worker training programs. The participation rates in rural training are low, as reflected by official statistics and our survey data. Rural laborers face geographic barriers that prevent them from attending training projects. Many rural laborers do not have the minimum education level (usually completion of middle school) required as a starting point by certain training programs. Some are unaware of the value of training, and some are concerned that the training might take too much of their time away from paid agricultural activities. Households in ethnic minority villages are also less likely to participate. Training materials should be tailored to the specific needs of the rural training participants, bridging the gaps between their level of previous education and knowledge, and the training curriculum. Extra effort should also be made in outreach and marketing in the field.

There are also issues concerning the quality of training, especially its effectiveness in helping participants migrate and obtain employment. Because training programs are relatively short, they can provide only limited skills development. Many participants need retraining after they start work. Likewise, the current guidance training programs, accounting for the majority of the training programs, provide only basic work- and living-related orientation for rural workers before migration. Only a quarter of all the training programs actually equip participants with practical skills.

The quality issue reflects in large part insufficient funding, which has prevented training providers and instructors from delivering quality training. Because funding for rural workers' training programs comes from multiple resources and is managed by a range of government departments, training efforts are not coordinated. Experience from other countries has shown how a national training fund can consolidate multiple funding sources and allocate resources across a range of training projects (box 5.3).

Further, accountability measures need to be in place to assure the quality of training and improve efficiency. In addition to the prescreening of training

Box 5.3 Consolidating Funds for Non-Formal Training

The Asian Development Bank–funded Employment-oriented Skills Development Project in Papua New Guinea established a Skills Development Trust Fund to provide a sustainable source of financial support for informal-sector training. By requiring individual provinces to contribute to the fund's capital in order to qualify for its resources, the Fund increased the financial commitment to skills training at the provincial level. Moreover, the Fund adopted cost sharing for both providers and participants, resulting in broad-based ownership. The Fund also became a catalyst for mobilizing additional resources for informal sector training. Furthermore, the fund's capital (about K50 million) was invested and managed by an experienced professional. The accrued interest from the invested capital was, in turn, used to cofinance short-term employment-oriented skills training.

In some countries, the National Training Fund is allocated according to predetermined quotas for funding "windows." For example, in 2002, Chile's National Training Fund financed twelve different programs of widely varying sizes, such as apprenticeship subsidies for youth, trade training for low-income youth, short courses for those without qualifications, youth job retention, individual training scholarships, and training for those in the military and security services. When funding windows are predetermined, it is important to set a reasonable number of windows within available administrative capacity.

The World Bank-funded Labor Force Training Support Project in Côte d'Ivoire took a different approach. A sponsor (such as a mayor, nongovernmental organization, or company) sends a training proposal to the national Vocational Training Development Fund. Training advisers for the Fund then work with the sponsor along with representatives of the beneficiary group to develop the idea into a training program design. The proposed training program is then sent to three to six prequalified training providers for competitive bidding. Such allocations are open-ended and responsive to applications, allowing stakeholders to generate their own proposals. However, technical assistance is needed to convert a training request into a complete training program design, including objectives and specifications that address beneficiaries' needs.

Source: Johanson 2009.

---

providers, requirements for regular auditing of the funds and monitoring of training need to be implemented. Moreover, outcome-based funding mechanisms could be adopted, linking public fund allocation to employment and certification rates. This would further require a skills certification system with improved relevance and credibility.

Note

1. A detailed account of the method is presented in appendix C.

Bibliography

HRSS (Yunnan Department of Human Resources and Social Security). 2011. 云南省农村劳动力转移就业对策研究（征求意见稿）[Yunnan Rural Transfer Labor Employment Policy Study (Working Paper)].

———. 2012. *2011年云南省人力资源和社会保障事业发展统计公报* [2011 Yunnan Human Resources and Social Securities Development Statistical Announcement]. http://www.ynhrss.gov.cn/readinfo.aspx?InfoId=df0ff02e5aa74c4aaed19e6e8c03c978

Johanson, R. 2009. "A Review of National Training Funds." SP Discussion Paper No. 0922, World Bank, Washington, DC.

Li, X. 2012. Background study (unpublished) commissioned for this report. World Bank, Washington, DC.

National Bureau of Statistics of China. 2008. http://www.stats.gov.cn/tjfx/dfxx/t20080220_402463674.htm.

Yunnan Bureau of Statistics. 2011. *Yunnan Statistical Yearbook*. Beijing: China Statistics Press.

CHAPTER 6

Work-Based Training in Urban Yunnan

In addition to the formal Technical and Vocational Education and Training (TVET) system that primarily trains young students before they enter the labor force, and the non-formal training that targets rural worker and the unemployed, enterprises play an important role in training and upgrading the skills of the labor force. Globally available evidence shows that investment in work-based training is correlated with firm productivity. In this chapter, we provide a snapshot of work-based training in Yunnan's urban areas and examine the challenges encountered by small and medium-sized enterprises (SMEs) in providing training. We also propose potential approaches to improving the quality and relevance of work-based training.

Data and research are scarce on work-based training in China. Our analysis draws on official statistics as well as survey data collected during 2004 and 2005. To supplement the data, qualitative interviews and observations were conducted at the end of 2011 at six enterprises in Yunnan. The Skills Toward Employment and Productivity (STEP) Employer survey conducted in 2012 also provides insights based on data from 300 non-public enterprises in Kunming.

Demand for and Supply of Work-Based Training in Urban Yunnan

Yunnan has a total of 6 million employed workers in the urban areas. For them, training is often delivered through staff orientation, on-the-job training, training to upgrade skills, and licensing training. Training can be outsourced to external training providers or delivered in-house by a trainer or fellow worker. Training takes place in or outside the workplace, during or outside working hours. Figure 6.1 demonstrates the demand for and supply of work-based training in urban Yunnan.

Our analysis focuses on the work-based training financed, organized, or provided by enterprises that targets currently employed workers. It does not include

Figure 6.1 Demand for and Supply of Work-Based Training in Urban Yunnan

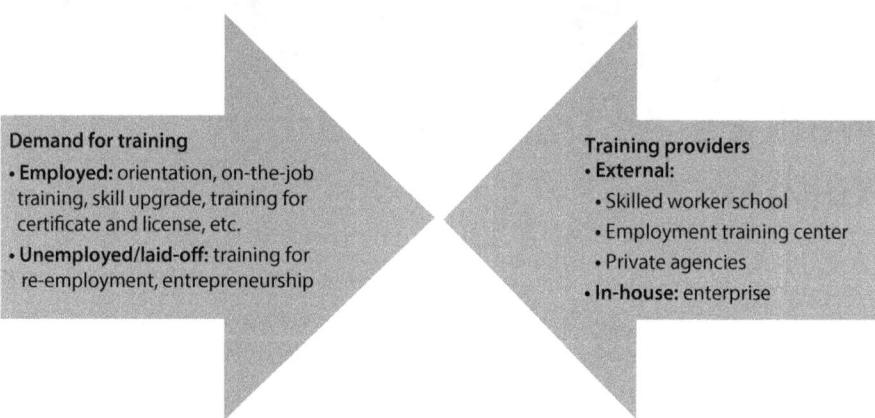

public training programs, such as reemployment training and entrepreneurship training, provided or subsidized by the government that targets unemployed and laid-off workers. We also do not address diploma-oriented adult education programs.

Policy Framework

The government's role in work-based training has shifted from one of planning and commanding to one of providing guidance. A regulatory system for work-based training has been gradually taking shape. In 1994, the Labor Law of China was issued, which, for the first time, guaranteed to laborers, as a matter of law, the right to professional skills training and established the obligation of employers to provide it. In June 1995, the then–Department of Labor issued Regulations on Compulsory Pre-service Training for Technical Workers, which made training compulsory for all technical workers. In 1996, the Law of Vocational Education and the Regulations for Enterprise Employee Training successively specified the types of trainees and the sources and uses of training funds, as well as training methods. Beginning in 2001, managers of enterprises were accredited for their professional qualifications. Training for employees at both the managerial and operational levels has been guaranteed ever since.

In 2008, Suggestions on Bringing into Full Play of the Function of Industries and Enterprises in Vocational Education specifically required that the enterprises retain 1.5–2.5 percent of their wage bill and compensation fund as designated employee training funds. In 2010, after soliciting public opinion, the State Council issued Opinions on Enhancing Vocational Training and Boosting Employment, specifying that no less than 60 percent of the total employee training funds be spent on frontline/operative workers. In December 2010, the

Central Government and the State Council announced the Outline of the National Medium and Long-Term Development Plan for High-Skilled Workers 2010–20, which presents some groundbreaking policies, including the proposal that high-skilled workers in private enterprises, institutions, and organizations should receive the same training subsidies and bonuses for starting a new business as those in the public sector.

To enforce the central government's regulations and policies, the Yunnan provincial government has implemented policies adapted to its local needs. For example, the Yunnan government announced the adoption of the Implementing Special Vocational Training Plan in 2010, detailing the allocation of subsidies to support in-service and transfer training for employees, migrant employee training, and urgently needed talent training (see box 3.1).

Participation in Work-Based Training

There is little data on the participation in and efficiency of training organized, financed, or provided by employers. According to the 2005 World Bank Investment Climate Assessment, 91 percent of the 300 firms surveyed in Yunnan provided formal training in 2004, higher than the average in China. Among the three cities in Yunnan, Yuxi has the highest proportion of firms providing training (96 percent), followed by Kunming (92 percent), and Qujing (85 percent).

Although over 90 percent of the firms surveyed in Yunnan provided training, only a small proportion of employees received training. As shown in figure 6.2, the distribution is skewed toward the high and low extremes, with the majority of firms providing training to fewer than 10 percent of their employees. This is particularly true in Yuxi and Qujing. In comparison, in cities like Guangzhou most firms train the majority of their workers.

The 2012 STEP Employer Survey conducted among enterprises in Kunming also revealed that about 91 percent of firms have provided some form of training on the premises of the workplace for both their type A and type B employees. As shown in figure 6.3, most workers have received on-the-job training, either through an apprenticeship or by learning as they worked. Many are trained by a firm's managers, technical personnel, or peers, or by the firm's dedicated trainers. Only a small proportion of employees have received training on a firm's premises with external trainers. Similarly, on average, employees receive 15 days of on-the-job training per year, and an additional 11–12 days of training by firms' managers, technical personnel, or peers. Training by an external trainer on the firm's premises accounts for only two days per year.

Although the provision of in-house training is relatively consistent across levels of occupations, as shown in figure 6.4, on average, only 41 percent of type A workers and 38 percent of type B workers have received training through private training providers, the most common form of external training. Public TVET schools and equipment suppliers are also common providers of outside training.

Figure 6.2 Percentage of Employees Receiving Training, China and Various Cities, Histogram and k-Density Plot

a. China

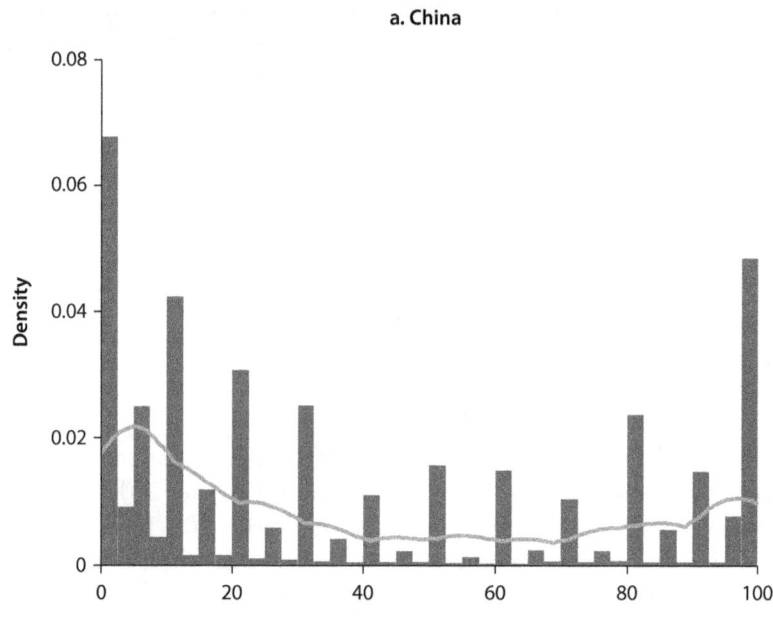

b. Yunnan

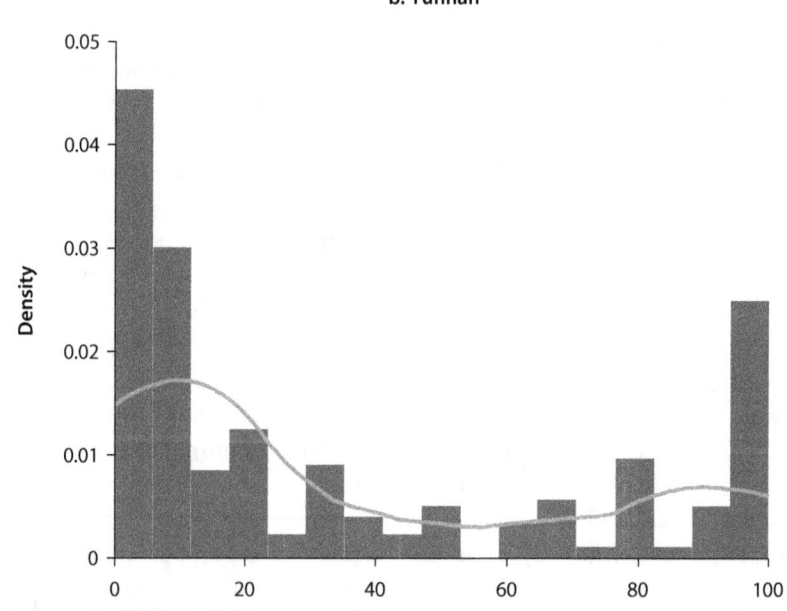

figure continues next page

Figure 6.2 Percentage of Employees Receiving Training, China and Various Cities, Histogram and k-Density Plot *(continued)*

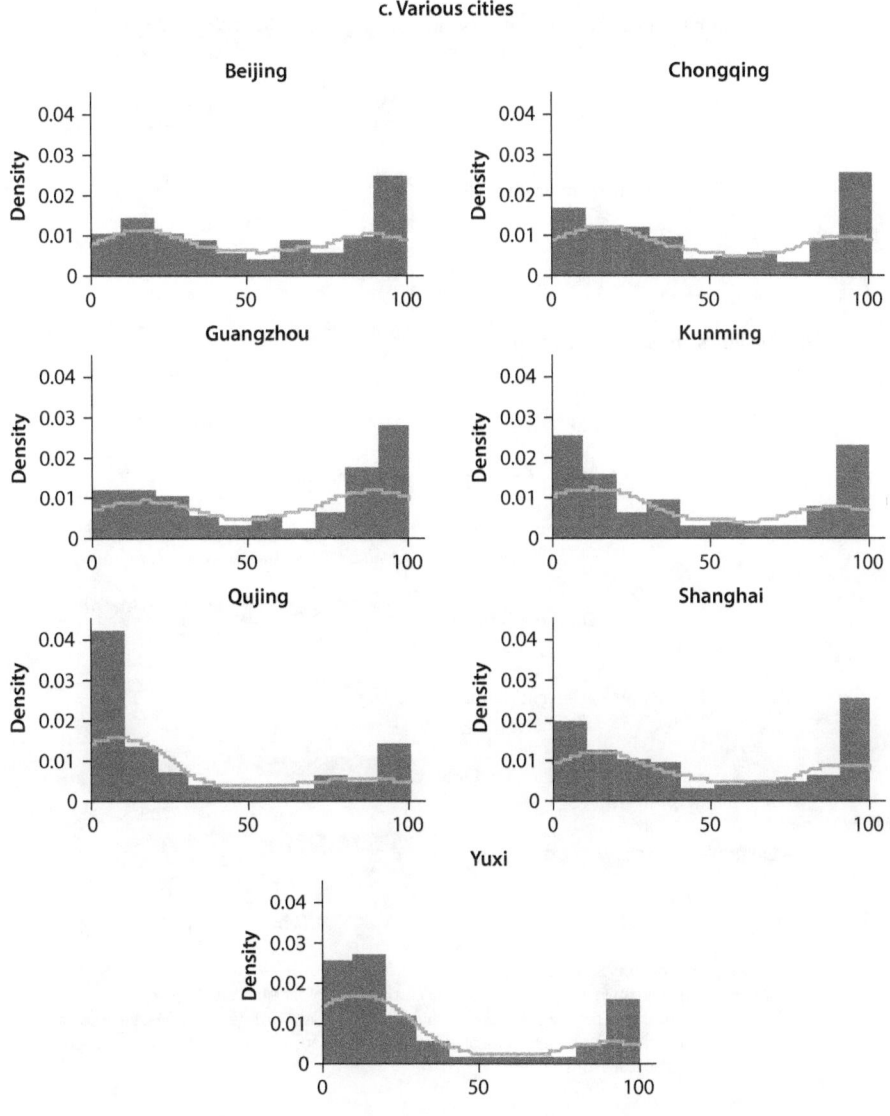

c. Various cities

Source: World Bank 2005.

Overall, employers have provided formal training outside the workplace to a higher proportion of type A workers than type B workers.

Financial Input in Work-Based Training

Law and regulations have specified the amount of training funds that should be derived from enterprise revenues. For example, the Labor Law states that all employers should retain and allocate training funds, "according to the reality of the enterprise." For employees in technical positions, "pre-work training should

Figure 6.3 Provision and Duration of Training on the Premises of the Workplace, Kunming

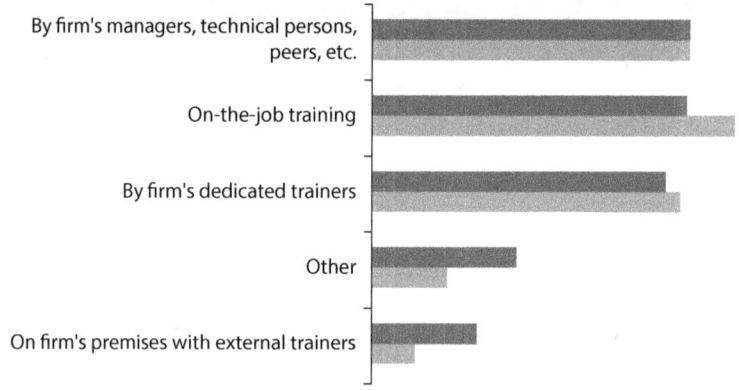

a. Percent of workers by training provider

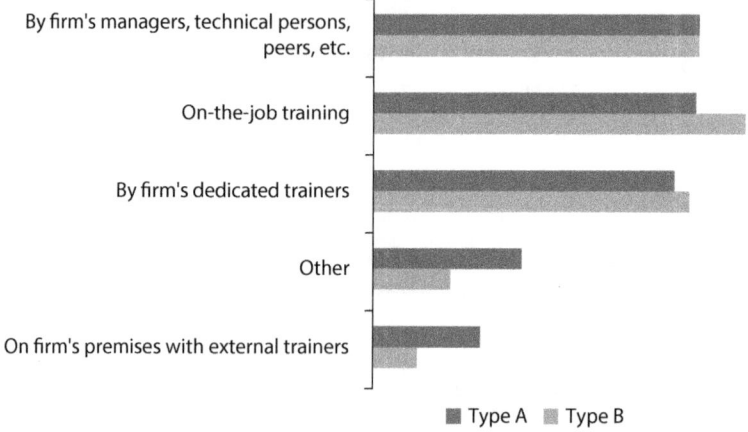

b. Days of training per year by training provider

■ Type A   ■ Type B

Source: STEP Employer Survey 2012.
Note: Type A occupations include managers, professionals, technicians and associate professionals; type B occupations include clerical support workers, service workers, sales workers, skilled agricultural/forestry/fishery workers, construction/craft and related trades workers, plant and machine operators and assemblers, and elementary occupations.

be provided." A related tax regulation requires enterprises to allocate 1.5–2.5 percent of their total payroll for employee training. If training costs are below the allocated amount, the enterprise should pay the costs in full. If training costs are above the allocated amount, the enterprise may pay the excess or negotiate with employees to pay the extra costs themselves.

Yet the law and regulations have in the past left room for employers to avoid compliance. For example, an employer might retain the 1.5–2.5 percent of payroll required (or even exceed the higher limit), but use the funds solely for training at the managerial level. The most recent regulation issued by the State

Figure 6.4 Percent of Workers Receiving Employer-Organized Formal Training Outside the Workplace

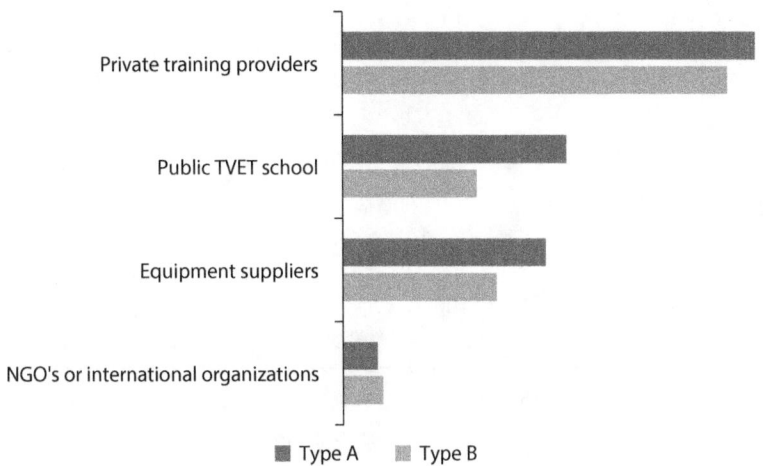

Source: STEP Employer Survey 2012.
Note: Type A occupations include managers, professionals, technicians and associate professionals; type B occupations include clerical support workers, service workers, sales workers, skilled agricultural/forestry/fishery workers, construction/craft and related trades workers, plant and machine operators and assemblers, and elementary occupations. NGO = nongovernmenal organization; TVET = Technical and Vocational Employment and Training.

Council prohibits this by setting a minimum requirement that 60 percent of the employee training funds be spent on frontline/operative workers.

Despite the government's continuing efforts to ensure the enforcement of the laws and regulations, actual investment in training varies greatly among employers. A previous survey (Guo and Lamb 2010) of 18 enterprises in Yunnan in 2004 reveals that 22 percent of employers spent less than 1 percent of their payroll on training. Only 33 percent of the employers surveyed spent more than 2 percent of their payroll on employee training and education. Thirty-seven percent of the employers indicated that their employees had to bear on average 35 percent of the total training cost.

The most recent STEP employer survey also provides information on how much enterprises pay outside training providers. As illustrated in figure 6.3, most training takes place on the premises of the enterprise as on-the-job training or training by personnel from within the firm. Figure 6.5 shows the distribution of the average total amount paid to outside training providers as a percentage of the total wage bill and compensation fund. Almost half of the firms paid nothing to outside training providers. On average, employers in Kunming spent about 0.8 percent of their total wage bill and compensation fund on external training providers. Seventeen percent of the firms spent up to 0.5 percent of their total wage bill and compensation fund on external training providers. Only about 5 percent of the firms spent more than 2 percent of their total payroll on external training providers.

Only about 47 percent of the firms made any payments to outside training providers for training type A workers, and even fewer, 38 percent, paid for any

Figure 6.5 Percent of Wage Bill and Compensation Fund Spent by Firms on Outside Training Providers

Source: STEP Employer Survey 2012.

Figure 6.6 Average Amount Spent per Employee on External Training Providers

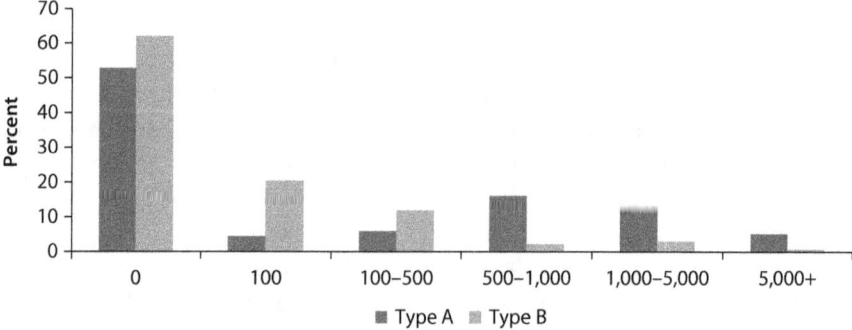

Source: STEP Employer Survey 2012.
Note: Type A occupations include managers, professionals, technicians and associate professionals; type B occupations include clerical support workers, service workers, sales workers, skilled agricultural/forestry/fishery workers, construction/craft and related trades workers, plant and machine operators and assemblers, and elementary occupations.

outside training of type B workers (figure 6.6). On average, firms spent Y866 for each type A worker and Y265 for each type B worker. Moreover, although 16 percent and 13 percent of the firms spent, respectively, Y500 to Y1,000 and Y1,000 to Y5,000 per type A worker on external training, 20 percent of the firms spent no more than Y100 per type B worker on external training. These numbers show that investment in formal training for all types of workers, and particularly for type B workers, is insufficient.

At the end of 2011, we interviewed personnel at a privately owned coal mine. All the technical workers were reaccredited and their vocational qualifications revalidated every two or three years. The coal mine employs more than 600 workers at three different mine sites, and about half of them are technical workers. The mine owner spent about Y3,000 per employee for a 15-day training program administered by training institutions established by the provincial Department of Coal Industry. In contrast, at an automobile maintenance business with 600 employees, the owner said that the company spent only about Y20,000 annually (about Y33 per employee) for an external trainer to come once a week to train the employees after working hours. Although many large enterprises are able to meet the requirements for employee training, others, especially SMEs, do not have sufficient revenue to meet the requirement of 1.5–2.5 percent of payroll for employee training funds. Moreover, employees told us of the many restrictions on accessing training funds and getting reimbursement for training fees. One employee, when asked who paid for his training for certification, said, "My parents and I had to pay for my training for certification. It is difficult to get the employer to pay for them. The employer only gives us a free one-hour training session before or after work hours."

Training Implementation in SMEs

Eighty percent of the enterprises in Yunnan are SMEs. For these enterprises, implementation of work-based training is hampered by insufficient resources. At the end of 2011, we interviewed six SMEs about their work-based training and made several important findings.

First, training in many cases is little more than a formality. For example, an automobile maintenance business and a tourism service business invite an external trainer or an employee to deliver 1–2 hours of training per week outside working hours. This approach is far less costly than providing training organized by accredited training institutions, but it lacks formal structures and methods for delivery, as well as formal evaluation and monitoring processes.

Second, SMEs rarely take a systematic approach to training that includes training management, needs assessment, planning, design, and evaluation. Few have full-time managers specifically in charge of training; most managers have other obligations, and training management is only a small proportion of their duties. Most of the SMEs do not conduct any training needs assessment. As a result, the contents of training seldom align with the development goals of the enterprises. There are no work-based training materials tailored to the needs of specific local industries or to the educational and social backgrounds of the participants.

In some firms we interviewed, neither the employer nor the employees seemed enthusiastic about training: The employer is unwilling to sacrifice work hours for training, and the employees resent being asked to sacrifice their time outside working hours. When asked about training participation, one of the employees of the automobile maintenance business said, "If I have to participate in the training, I have to. If I had a choice, I would not have participated, because I have lots of family commitments outside work and training always takes place after my work hours."

Finally, the high costs of training make it difficult for SMEs to deliver adequate and high-quality training or to access the resources made available by the government. If subsidies are limited, and employers are unable to fully fund training costs, employees are forced to pay for all or part of their training and accreditation or find training opportunities on their own. Although both the central and provincial governments have made great efforts to provide support and guidance, these efforts have not been effective for many SMEs. For example, the government provides enterprises with free online resources about training planning, needs assessment, and course design. However, many SMEs find it difficult to access and utilize these resources. As put by one manager, "We are all overloaded with daily tasks; there is no time and energy to look into that matter."

Summary and Policy Implications

The Vocational Education Law of 1996 stipulated that enterprises devote 1.5–2.5 percent of their total wage bill and compensation fund for employee training. However, compliance with the law and the details of its implementation were left to the determination of the enterprises themselves. As a result, how and the extent to which work-based training is provided varies greatly among enterprises.

Survey results indicate that more than 90 percent of the firms in both Yunnan and China have provided training. However, on closer observation, we found that the majority of enterprises in Yunnan have provided training to fewer than 10 percent of their employees. Most training is conducted in-house by firm managers, technical personnel, or peers, or through on-the-job learning or apprenticeships. Very few firms have paid external trainers to conduct training: Only 41 percent of type A workers and 38 percent of type B workers have received training through private training providers, the most common form of external training. Such patterns of training-resource allocation are not unique to Yunnan. As Professor Thomas A. Kochan (2012) of the Massachusetts Institute of Technology's Sloan School of Management best put it:

> It's a gross misallocation of resources to spend millions on executive education for middle managers or senior executives while systematically underinvesting in people who develop the products, manufacture them, and service them. These middle skills are eroding because firms have given up on training. They expect to be able to buy all these skills on the market, and don't want to invest in training because they're afraid if they do their competitors will hire these newly minted high-skills employees away. Employers need to reinvest by engaging each other in their industry, in their location, sharing the cost and the benefits.

Firms of all sizes face low incentives to train their workers, and the relevance and value of training are constantly called into question. Firms that do not believe in the value of skills certifications will be unwilling to spend the funds needed to enable their employees to obtain them. Diverse financing mechanisms and more effective incentive schemes for work-based training could be used to address these issues. The Republic of Korea's Employment Insurance System (box 6.1) and Singapore's Skills Development Fund (box 6.2) offer two excellent examples.

Box 6.1 The Korean Employment Insurance System (EIS)

Since 1962, Korea's vocational training schemes evolved in response to the demands of the economy and the changing supply of skills (figure B6.1.1). In 1995, an EIS was introduced to address the demand from the knowledge-based economy for continuing training to upgrade the knowledge and skills of incumbent workers, as well as the need for an active labor market policy. EIS consists of three components: (1) an employment security program, which supports the training costs of employees who plan to change their careers; (2) an unemployment benefits program, which provides living expenses for the unemployed; and (3) a vocational competence development program, which provides financial assistance to employers for vocational training of their employees, and to individual employees and the unemployed for their vocational training.

The Employment Insurance Fund is collected differently for each program. For the unemployment benefit program, the employer and the employee each pay an insurance fee of 0.45 percent of an employee's annual total wage. For the employment security and the vocational competence development program, employers pay insurance fees of 0.25–0.85 percent of their employees' payroll, depending on the number of employees.

With EIS, vocational training in Korea has experienced a significant paradigm shift (figure B6.1.2) specifically: (1) the focus of vocational training changed from initial training to continuing training (life-long training); (2) the training market became open to all public and private vocational training institutes, forcing them to compete with each other to attract trainees, which is expected to improve the quality of training and overall efficiency of the system; (3) the operational mode of the training system changed from a government-controlled and supply-driven approach to a demand-driven and incentive-based approach and (4) the training area was expanded from the manufacturing sector to all sectors, including the service sector. The vocational competence development program is a levy-rebate program under which all enterprises pay training levies as part of their insurance fees, but are left free to decide whether to train and what types of training to provide (If they carry out training, the expenses are reimbursed from the Employment Insurance Fund. To provide greater incentives for SMEs, the level of reimbursement for large firms is about 80 percent of the paid training levies, while SMEs receive rebates of up to 270 percent of paid training levies.) The EIS played a crucial role in providing vocational training for the unemployed, whose number increased rapidly during the foreign currency crisis (1997–99), and the EIS has successfully responded to an ever-increasing demand for continuing training of employees.

Figure B6.1.1 Evolution of Vocational Training Funding Schemes in Korea

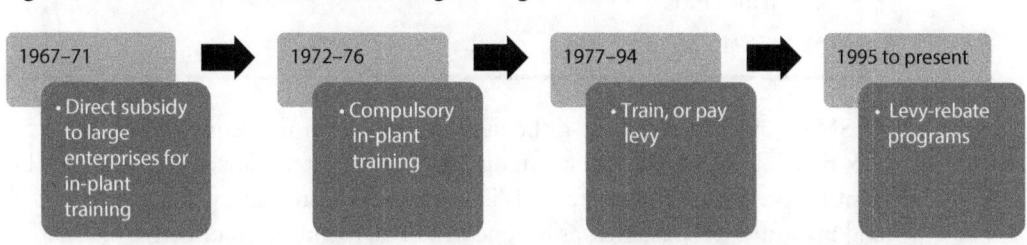

box continues next page

Box 6.1 The Korean Employment Insurance System (EIS) *(continued)*

Figure B6.1.2 Transformation of Korea's Vocational Training System

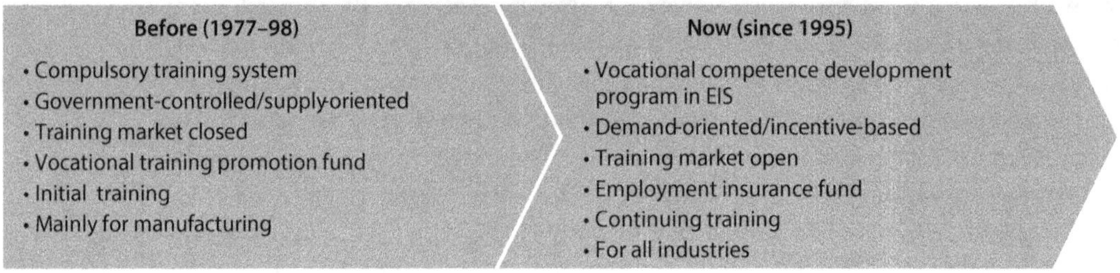

Before (1977–98)	Now (since 1995)
• Compulsory training system • Government-controlled/supply-oriented • Training market closed • Vocational training promotion fund • Initial training • Mainly for manufacturing	• Vocational competence development program in EIS • Demand-oriented/incentive-based • Training market open • Employment insurance fund • Continuing training • For all industries

Sources: Paik 2012; Lee 2006.

Box 6.2 Singapore's Skills Development Fund (SDF)

Singapore established its SDF in 1979 to encourage employers to upgrade the skills of their employees. Employers in Singapore are required to contribute a Skills Development Levy for all employees of up to 0.25 percent of the first $4,500 of gross monthly remuneration, or a minimum of $2, whichever is higher. The payment is added to the SDF, which offers grants supporting up to 80 percent of companies' direct training costs. The SDF provides not only a financial incentive for employers to provide training, but also operates on a cost-sharing principle: to be eligible for the Fund, companies must pay the unfunded portion of the training fees.

The Fund is managed by the Workforce Development Authority, composed mainly of industry representatives (company chairmen and vice-chairmen), along with representatives of government and the labor force. The Fund supports a diverse range of programs, but the selection criteria and review processes incorporate Singapore's development strategies, targeting specific types of training, population, and sectors. For example, the Fund encourages training in strategic sectors, promotes special training programs for upgrading skills, assists SMEs with training in information technology, and targets specific populations such as older workers and low-skilled workers.

The Fund also provides special incentives to encourage smaller firms to offer training. For example, the SDF grants encourage smaller enterprises to hire external consultants to conduct training needs analysis before developing a training plan—giving them access to the specialized resources needed to assess training needs and design appropriate training programs. The Fund also provides preapproved public courses for companies by subscription. This program attracts small companies that have neither the expertise nor the critical mass to create such programs on their own.

Source: Hirosato 1997.

SMEs find it particularly difficult to comply with the requirement that 1.5–2.5 percent of payroll be spent on training. Limited capacity appears to be another constraint. Organizing SMEs into consortiums and providing technical and institutional assistance, as is done in Korea, might be an effective alternative approach to solving these problems (box 6.3).

Box 6.3 Providing Institutional and Technical Assistance to SMEs: Korea's SME Training Consortium

Although Korea's EIS proved to be effective overall, SMEs appear to have benefitted less from its provisions. Specifically, although both large enterprises and SMEs pay training levies, many fewer SMEs actually recover the levies by providing training. SMEs are faced with higher training costs per worker, higher labor mobility, and more limited financial resources and capacity in designing and organizing training.

In response to this situation, the Korean government launched the SME training consortium projects in 2001. Each local chamber of commerce and industry helps a group of some 50 SMEs organize into a training consortium and finances two training managers for each consortium. Each training consortium forms an operating committee composed of representatives from member SMEs, the local chamber of commerce, the Ministry of Labor field office, and training experts. The committee meets periodically for the planning and management of the training needs of the member SMEs.

The two training managers play key roles in the training consortium. They establish an information network among member SMEs, conduct a training-needs survey of each member SME, plan and program training activities, contract outside training institutions or collaborate with them to develop training programs, monitor training activities, and conduct an evaluation upon completion of major training courses on behalf of the member SMEs.

With the institutional and technical assistance provided by the local chamber of commerce through the training consortium, more SMEs have been able to claim rebates of their training levies. The pilot SME training consortium project has achieved significant results and has been replicated both nationally and internationally.

Source: Lee 2006.

Bibliography

Guo, Z., and S. Lamb. 2010. *International Comparisons of China's Technical and Vocational Education and Training System*. Dordrecht, The Netherlands: Springer.

Hirosato, Y. 1997. *Skills Development Fund: A Preliminary Assessment of a Financing Alternative for Enterprise-based Training in the Context of APEC*. Nagoya, Japan: APEC Study Center, Graduate School of International Development, Nagoya University.

Kochan, T. A. 2012. "Interview: Can America Compete? The Workforce." *Harvard Magazine*, September–October: 35–8.

Lee, K. W. 2006. "Effectiveness of Government's Occupational Skills Development Strategies for Small- and Medium-scale Enterprises: A Case Study of Korea." *International Journal of Educational Development* 26(3): 278–94.

Paik, Sung-Joon. 2012. "Korea Employment Insurance Scheme." Unpublished paper, Korea Development Institute School of Public Policy and Management, Seoul.

Skills Toward Employment and Productivity (STEP) Employer Survey. 2012. World Bank, Washington, DC.

World Bank. 2005. *Investment Climate Assessment*. Washington, DC: World Bank.

CHAPTER 7

Developing Cognitive Skills in Schools: Lessons from PISA Shanghai 2009

In the previous chapters, we reviewed the formal Technical and Vocational Education and Training (TVET) system, non-formal training for rural workers, and work-based training provided by employers, and examined their role in developing technical and vocational skills. In this chapter, we turn our attention to the role of general education in developing student cognitive skills.

The Programme for International Student Assessment (PISA) measures the cognitive skills of 15-year-olds in math, reading, and science. PISA scores closely predict students' academic paths and ultimate success in the labor market. Shanghai is the first Chinese province to fully participate in PISA. In the most recent PISA given in 2009, Shanghai placed as the top performer in math, reading, and science among 65 countries and economies.

We draw lessons from the Shanghai experience to infer how general education might contribute to the development of cognitive skills among 15-year-olds. We analyze the 2009 Shanghai PISA data to determine what school-level characteristics correspond to higher math, reading, and science skills. The analysis is followed by a comparison of the education systems in Yunnan and Shanghai, with a discussion on how best to apply Shanghai's experience in the context of Yunnan.

PISA and Skills

PISA tests the knowledge and skills of 15-year-old students using extensive and rigorous surveys. Every three years, PISA compares the scores of 15-year-old students around the world on measures of reading literacy, mathematics, and science, as defined in box 7.1 below. PISA assesses not only how well students have mastered a particular curriculum but, more importantly, whether they can apply the knowledge and skills they have acquired to solving real-world issues.

Box 7.1 Definitions of the PISA Domains

Reading literacy: An individual's capacity to understand, use, reflect on, and engage with written texts, in order to achieve one's goals, to develop one's knowledge and potential, and to participate in society.

Mathematical literacy: An individual's capacity to identify and understand the role that mathematics plays in the world, to make well-founded judgments, and to use and engage with mathematics in ways that meet the needs of that individual's life as a constructive, concerned, and reflective citizen.

Scientific literacy: An individual's scientific knowledge and use of that knowledge to identify questions, to acquire new knowledge, to explain scientific phenomena, and to draw evidence-based conclusions about science-related issues; understanding of the characteristic features of science as a form of human knowledge and enquiry, awareness of how science and technology shape our material, intellectual, and cultural environments; and willingness to engage in science-related issues, and with the ideas of science, as a reflective citizen.

Source: OECD 2009.

Not only does PISA provide a tool for benchmarking different education systems across the world, but PISA scores have also been shown to link directly to students' future academic progress and indirectly to the school-to-work transition. For example, longitudinal studies in Canada (OECD 2010a) have shown that high PISA scores were strongly correlated with the completion of secondary school, participation in post-secondary education, and choice of field of study at university, even after taking students' other background characteristics into account. Figure 7.1 shows the increasing likelihood of university participation associated with higher PISA reading efficiencies according to their PISA reading proficiency levels.

Another study (Bertschy, Cattaneo, and Wolter 2009) using a sample of vocational students in Switzerland confirmed that higher PISA scores are associated with more intellectually demanding vocational training, and students who pursued vocational training with higher intellectual demands had a higher probability of finding an adequate job.

PISA Shanghai 2009

Shanghai participated in PISA for the first time in 2009 and impressed the world with top performances in all three subjects: mathematics, science, and reading (table 7.1). Students in Shanghai scored significantly higher than students from the OECD countries, even though Shanghai's gross domestic product (GDP) per capita is lower than that of the OECD countries. In addition, 33 percent of Shanghai's students come from disadvantaged families, a percentage higher than more than a majority of the OECD countries (figure 7.2).

Figure 7.1 University Participation at Age 21 by PISA Reading Proficiency at Age 15 in Canada, 2009

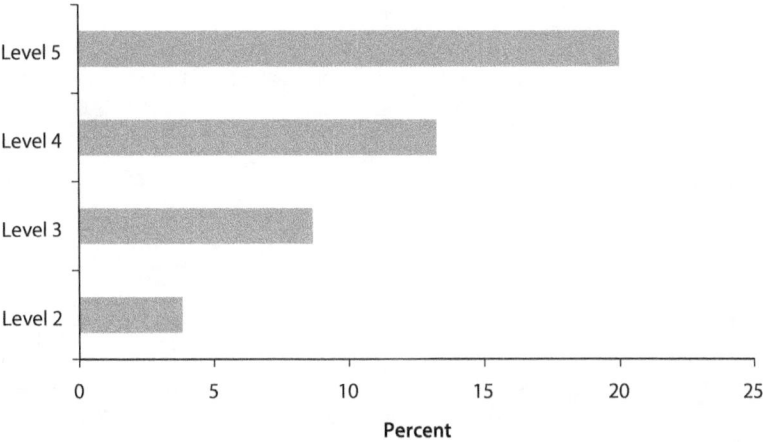

Source: OECD 2010a.
Note: After accounting for school engagement, mother tongue, place of residence, parental education and family income. The reference group for the PISA reading proficiency levels is Level 1, and for the marks in reading it is the group that obtained less than 60 percent.

Table 7.1 Mean PISA Scores, Shanghai and OECD, 2009

	Mean PISA score		
	Math	Science	Reading
Shanghai	600 (2.8)	575 (2.3)	556 (2.4)
OECD average	497 (0.5)	501 (0.5)	494 (0.5)
Shanghai ranking	1	1	1

Source: OECD 2010b.
Note: Standard errors in parentheses.

Not only is Shanghai the highest performing education system among all 65 participating countries and economies, but it has also been shown to be one of the most egalitarian. Nearly 19 percent of the students are resilient achievers,[1] and as few as 0.3 percent are disadvantaged low achievers[2] (figure 7.3). There is a weak relationship between socio-economic background and student performance.[3]

Shanghai's top performance has drawn interest from researchers, policy makers and educators around the world. What are the strengths of Shanghai's education system that have contributed to the high performance on PISA? Because Shanghai and Yunnan are both situated within the Chinese educational system, lessons from the Shanghai PISA will be particularly relevant to Yunnan's efforts to improve its own secondary education system.

Figure 7.2 PISA Reading Performance of Shanghai and OECD Countries, 2009

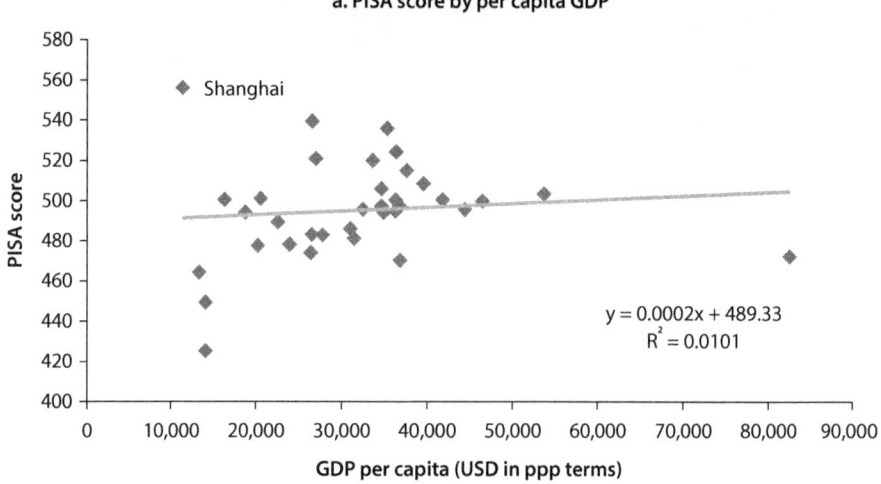

a. PISA score by per capita GDP

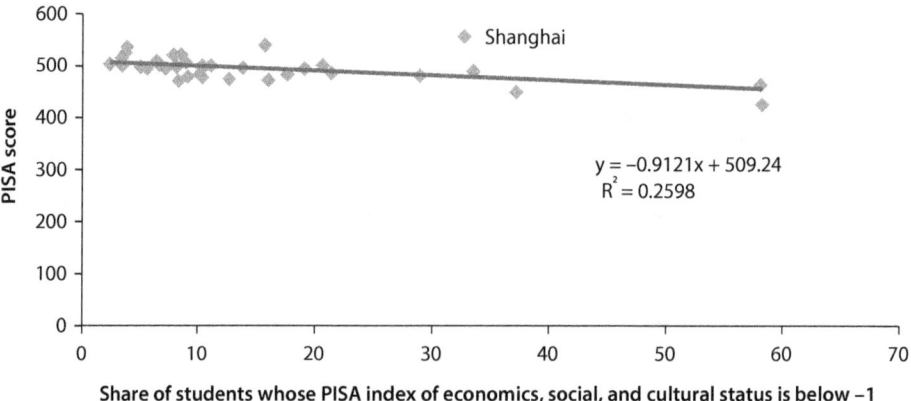

b. PISA reading performance by share of socio-economically disadvantaged students

Share of students whose PISA index of economics, social, and cultural status is below −1

Source: OECD 2009, 2011.
Note: Calculated in purchasing power parity terms.

We analyze the Shanghai PISA data to explore the question: "What school-level characteristics correlate with higher levels of student skills as measured by PISA?" Box 7.2 offers an overview of the Shanghai PISA sample. We study separately lower secondary school (middle school) students, upper secondary general school (high school) students, and upper secondary vocational school (vocational school) students.

PISA scores vary by school type within Shanghai, largely due to the use of high school entrance examinations for admission to the different upper secondary schools (table 7.2).[4] Students in model and experimental high schools, which

Figure 7.3 Proportion of Resilient Achievers and Disadvantaged Low Achievers

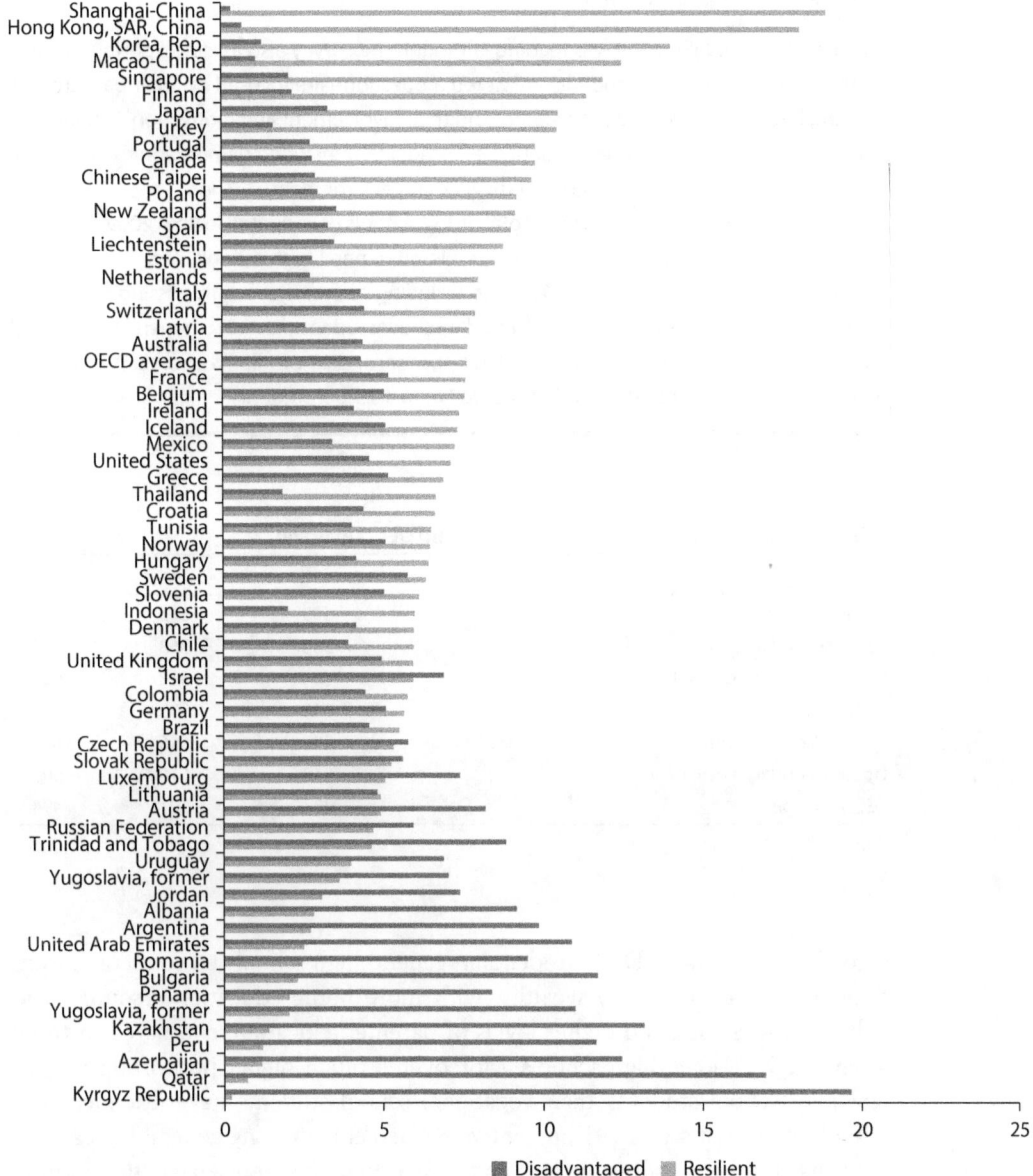

Source: OECD 2010c.

take the highest scoring students on the high school entrance exam, perform the best in PISA. Vocational school students, often lower performing students on the entrance exam, score lower than the middle school students on PISA; their scores are around the OECD average.

Student characteristics and the family backgrounds of students are significantly associated with their selection into different schools on the upper

Box 7.2 PISA Shanghai 2009

The main focus of PISA 2009 was reading, although the survey also assessed performance in mathematics and science. Students answered a questionnaire focused on their background, learning habits, attitudes toward reading, and their involvement and motivation. School principals completed a questionnaire about their school that included demographic characteristics and an assessment of the quality of the learning environment at school.

In Shanghai, 5,115 students from a total of 152 schools participated in PISA 2009, including 52 middle schools, 27 mixed secondary schools, 40 general high schools, and 33 upper secondary vocational schools (table D.1). After excluding observations with missing values, our final analytic samples include (1) 2,041 middle school students, (2) 1,376 general high school students (excluding students who attended upper secondary programs in vocational schools or mixed secondary schools), and (3) 1,063 vocational school students.

Table 7.2 PISA Scores of Schools in Shanghai and OECD Average

	Math	Science	Reading
Shanghai total	600	575	556
Lower secondary	588	568	544
Upper secondary, general	664	618	603
Ordinary	641	598	583
Model, experimental	699	646	631
Upper secondary, vocational	518	515	500
OECD average	497	501	494

Source: OECD 2010b.

secondary level (table D.3). Students in general high schools tend to come from families that are relatively wealthy, with more home education resources and cultural possessions, and higher levels of parental education, compared to those attending vocational high schools. Moreover, a much higher proportion of general high school students than vocational school students have attended preschool for at least a year (91 percent vs. 82 percent). Among general high school students, those attending model and experimental schools have significantly higher levels of family wealth, home education resources, cultural possessions, and parental education (table D.4).

Comparing School Characteristics

As many as 19 percent of middle schools in Shanghai are private, a larger percentage than that for upper secondary schools (table D.5). Moreover, middle schools show the strongest accountability: 87 percent report achievement data to parents, and the achievement data of 84 percent are tracked over time. Compared to general high schools, middle schools tend to have more autonomy over resource allocation and curriculum. On average, however, fewer middle school teachers have tertiary qualifications (86 percent), less than the 97 percent and 92 percent in general high schools and vocational schools, respectively. At the same time, more middle schools are faced with teacher shortages, especially in science and math.

At the upper secondary level, compared to general high schools, vocational schools are characterized by much higher student-teacher ratios, worse teacher-student relations, more disruptive student behavior, and less accountability, but higher levels of autonomy over resource allocation and curriculum. All vocational schools surveyed are public, and 40 percent of them do not consider academic performance as a criterion for admission. To further distinguish between the more competitive, and presumably better quality, general high schools and the less competitive ones, we compare the model and experimental schools with ordinary high schools (table D.6). Although the two types of schools are similar on most measures, the major difference lies in the resources the schools enjoy: model and experimental schools have a higher quality of educational resources and offer more extracurricular activities. Students in model and experimental schools also report better student-teacher relations. More principals of model and experimental schools are evaluated using the school's performance data. In addition, model and experimental schools report a higher level of teacher participation in school governance.

School Characteristics and Student Performance

How do different school characteristics relate to student performance? We run OLS regressions on the three different samples. A Chow's t-test suggests that the relationship between school characteristics and performance varies across the three types of schools, justifying our analytic approach. Findings are presented below for each sample.

Middle Schools

After controlling for background characteristics and grade levels, a number of middle school characteristics are significantly correlated with student performance on PISA (table 7.3). First, private middle school students performed 29 points better than public middle school students. The better performance seems more indicative of the quality of schools than of the students' prior performance; whether or not the school adopts academic performance as an admission criterion is not significant after controlling for other factors. Within-school tracking seems to be related to performance: Middle schools that group students by ability perform worse than those that do not, and the differences are statistically significant for mathematics and science. Third, teacher quality plays a role. Better student-teacher relations are significantly related to better performance. A higher percentage of teachers with tertiary qualifications is related to higher performance in mathematics, while schools that reported a teacher shortage in

Table 7.3 Characteristics and Performance of Middle Schools

	Math	Reading	Science
School characteristics			
Organizational			
Student-teacher ratio	1.69	2.86*	1.48
	(1.60)	(1.10)	(1.21)
Public	−28.94*	−15.81	−17.23
	(13.29)	(9.91)	(10.83)
Competition from other schools	15.76	9.02	17.04
	(15.16)	(11.97)	(12.68)
Policy			
Academic admissions criteria	4.05	3.96	−0.22
	(8.13)	(5.95)	(6.58)
Tracking	−18.82**	−9.75	−13.47*
	(6.52)	(5.21)	(5.73)
Teachers			
Student-teacher relations	12.85***	10.12***	10.40***
	(2.37)	(1.66)	(2.02)
% with tertiary qualifications	0.90*	0.60	0.27
	(0.44)	(0.33)	(0.33)
Teacher shortage	−10.53	−3.31	−18.95**
	(10.96)	(7.19)	(6.92)
Climate			
Teacher behavior	2.04	0.96	−2.54
	(6.51)	(4.63)	(5.31)
Student behavior	3.13	2.53	2.42
	(4.84)	(3.45)	(4.16)
Pressure from parents	5.14	4.92	14.02
	(11.34)	(9.23)	(9.24)
Resources			
Educational resources	0.39	2.77	0.08
	(5.09)	(4.21)	(4.27)
Extracurricular activities	−2.88	−2.86	0.40
	(4.44)	(2.68)	(2.89)
Accountability			
To parents	13.00	18.01	8.45
	(11.87)	(10.03)	(10.90)
Achievement tracked	−8.18	−7.71	−18.28
	(16.58)	(12.10)	(14.33)
Achievement used to evaluate principal	−21.31*	−17.89**	−18.85**
	(8.32)	(6.53)	(6.21)
Governance			
Autonomy over resource allocation	7.16	2.32	3.16
	(4.62)	(3.32)	(4.04)
Autonomy over curriculum	−8.54	−6.18	−10.82**
	(5.51)	(3.45)	(3.79)
School leadership	−2.55	−2.55	−3.66
	(8.46)	(3.92)	(4.75)

table continues next page

Table 7.3 **Characteristics and Performance of Middle Schools** (continued)

	Math	Reading	Science
Background controls			
Female	−11.25*	28.97***	−10.81**
	(4.30)	(3.44)	(3.36)
Wealth	−4.40	−3.26	−4.08*
	(2.29)	(2.05)	(1.94)
Home education resources	8.34**	8.74***	9.66***
	(2.48)	(2.12)	(2.27)
Home cultural possessions	12.26***	8.63***	10.39***
	(2.39)	(1.84)	(1.83)
Parental education	3.11**	2.67***	2.34**
	(0.98)	(0.72)	(0.77)
Preschool for at least one year	36.54***	25.65***	22.95***
	(6.90)	(5.54)	(5.67)
Remedial	−29.69***	−12.00**	−16.29*
	(5.13)	(3.85)	(6.35)
Enrichment	17.63***	1.52	9.11
	(4.16)	(4.45)	(7.39)
R^2	0.36	0.36	0.35
Number of observations	2,041	2,041	2,041

Source: OECD 2010b.
Note: Standard errors in parentheses. All models control for grade level, student background characteristics, and participation in enrichment and remedial classes. *** $p < 0.001$, ** $p < 0.01$, * $p < 0.05$.

science scored 19 points lower than those that did not. Interestingly, schools whose principals are evaluated based on student achievement tend to be lower-performing schools. Finally, middle schools with more autonomy over curriculum seem to be lower performing; in particular, the association is significant for science.

Among background control variables, preschool attendance is associated with as much as 23- to 37-point higher PISA scores, and the association is statistically significant across all three subjects. Family background, including educational resources, cultural possessions and parental education, also matter for middle school students' performance. In addition, girls perform significantly better than boys in reading but worse in mathematics and science. These results hold cross-nationally in the PISA sample.

General High Schools

Similar analysis using the high school student sample generates interesting results (table 7.4). The most important finding is that school resources are significantly related to performance: higher quality educational resources, as well as provision of extracurricular activities, is related to higher performance in all three subjects even after controlling for other individual and school-level factors. As is true for middle schools, better student-teacher relations are correlated with higher scores. Better performing schools also tend to have a higher level of teacher participation in school governance. Although in our initial comparison, experimental and

Table 7.4 Characteristics and Performance of General High Schools

	Math	Reading	Science
School characteristics			
Organizational			
Student-teacher ratio	2.04	4.23**	4.89*
	(1.92)	(1.45)	(1.90)
Public	86.68**	81.52**	78.01***
	(29.58)	(25.42)	(19.74)
Competition from other schools	0.79	−12.16	−20.35*
	(13.24)	(8.93)	(8.93)
Policy			
Tracking	−8.2	5.64	−4.8
	(8.28)	(6.86)	(6.66)
Teachers			
Student-teacher relations	5.24*	3.48	1.96
	(2.43)	(1.99)	(2.08)
% with tertiary qualifications	−5.8*	−6.25***	−6.59***
	(2.11)	(1.63)	(1.57)
Teacher shortage	−6.72	−15.24	−2.37
	(9.29)	(10.86)	(8.62)
Climate			
Teacher behavior	−22.1***	−14.9*	−14.17*
	(6.23)	(5.83)	(5.68)
Student behavior	5.56	0.2	1
	(5.19)	(3.79)	(4.65)
Pressure from parents	18.43	14.11	5.98
	(11.74)	(10.10)	(9.57)
Resources			
Educational resources	17.58**	12.57***	13.9**
	(5.18)	(3.37)	(3.90)
Extracurricular activities	10.41	10.07**	14.91***
	(5.34)	(3.45)	(3.40)
Accountability			
To parents	3.15	−2.67	5.95
	(8.72)	(10.09)	(9.22)
Achievement tracked	11.22	−2.01	−7.26
	(12.15)	(11.58)	(13.44)
Achievement used to evaluate principal	−5.06	1.81	1.92
	(8.81)	(7.45)	(6.99)
Governance			
Autonomy over resource allocation	−5.08	0.74	3.48
	(4.68)	(3.96)	(3.81)
Autonomy over curriculum	5.47	1.01	5.67
	(4.97)	(3.43)	(4.21)
School leadership	−17.21	−15.72	−14.05
	(12.89)	(8.94)	(9.36)
Teacher participation	7.91*	3.47	5.03*
	(3.00)	(2.29)	(1.90)

table continues on next page

Table 7.4 Characteristics and Performance of General High Schools *(continued)*

	Math	Reading	Science
Background controls			
Female	−11.43**	23.89***	−14.06***
	(3.28)	(2.45)	(3.09)
Wealth	−0.98	−1.69	−2.19
	(2.14)	(1.88)	(1.95)
Home education resources	−0.85	2.88	2.25
	(2.93)	(2.32)	(2.29)
Home cultural possessions	7.07**	4.31	3.80
	(2.51)	(2.52)	(2.20)
Parental education	0.32	0.96	−0.15
	(0.89)	(0.74)	(0.75)
Preschool for at least one year	9.96	2.40	5.25
	(8.07)	(5.31)	(6.45)
Remedial	−23.76***	−18.84**	−3.96
	(3.63)	(5.66)	(5.43)
Enrichment	0.41	−2.53	12.93*
	(5.34)	(5.88)	(5.61)
R^2	0.25	0.28	0.26
Number of observations	1,376	1,376	1,376

Source: OECD 2010b.
Note: Standard errors in parentheses. All models control for grade level, student background characteristics, and participation in enrichment and remedial classes. *** $p < 0.001$, ** $p < 0.01$, * $p < 0.05$.

model schools are more likely to have their principals evaluated using achievement data, this accountability policy does not seem to be related to student performance after controlling for other factors. Our analysis also reveals several interesting findings unique to high schools. For example, higher performing students tend to go to schools with higher student-teacher ratios. Although tracking within schools mattered for middle schools, it does not have a significant correlation with high school students' performance. Despite the overall high percentage of teachers with tertiary qualifications among high schools, schools at the higher end of the range actually perform slightly worse than those with lower percentages of teachers with tertiary qualifications. Teacher behavior issues reported by principals is negatively linked to performance, possibly because principals in better performing schools might be more aware of and thus more likely to report problematic teacher behavior.

Unlike middle school students, among students who have gotten into general high schools, family background is not significantly associated with performance, except that family cultural possessions appear to be associated with higher math scores. Preschool attendance does not seem to be correlated with high school students' PISA performance.

Vocational High Schools

Results from the vocational school sample are relatively less consistent across subjects, most likely because vocational schools often offer specialized curriculums and have specific admissions criteria that either do not necessarily take into account academic performance or consider only some subjects (table 7.5). Our results confirm that vocational schools that admit students based on academic performance score higher on PISA in all three subjects. Nonetheless, the data generate several interesting findings. For example, lower-performing vocational schools face constant pressure from parents. Principals of better-performing vocational schools are more likely to report disruptive teacher behavior, but less likely to report problematic student behavior. Schools that have higher performance in mathematics tend to have higher quality educational resources and higher levels of autonomy over resource allocation. Their performance data are more likely to be tracked. There is also evidence that teacher participation in school governance might be related to better performance.

Among background characteristics, the presence of home educational resources and cultural possessions correlate with higher scores among vocational school students, but family wealth, interestingly, is associated with lower performance. Preschool attendance is positively correlated with students' performance in vocational school, and the association is statistically significant for reading scores.

Lessons from Shanghai

Shanghai's experience demonstrates that schools play an important role in developing youth cognitive skills. Most importantly, the quality of the educational resources at a school appears to be the key characteristic that distinguishes

Table 7.5 Characteristics and Performance of Vocational Schools

	Math	Reading	Science
School characteristics			
Organizational			
Student-teacher ratio	0.22	0.02	0.44
	(0.35)	(0.22)	(0.36)
Competition from other schools	1.38	23.63*	15.83
	(11.41)	(9.91)	(14.99)
Policy			
Academic admissions criteria	26.28***	22.39**	11.02
	(7.28)	(6.72)	(9.14)
Tracking	−3.2	−1.79	−4.77
	(7.24)	(6.76)	(8.68)
Teachers			
Student-teacher relations	1.77	0.81	−0.62
	(2.91)	(1.87)	(2.45)
% with tertiary qualifications	−0.01	0.14	0.37
	(0.49)	(0.30)	(0.60)
Teacher shortage	49.65***	12.68	17.82
	(8.65)	(10.21)	(9.91)

table continues on next page

Table 7.5 Characteristics and Performance of Vocational Schools *(continued)*

	Math	Reading	Science
Climate			
Teacher behavior	−9.43*	−3.78	−2.32
	(4.01)	(3.57)	(4.85)
Student behavior	7.75*	0.89	2.62
	(3.28)	(2.54)	(3.01)
Pressure from parents	−66.39***	−43.48**	−40.41**
	(12.04)	(13.29)	(13.11)
Resources			
Educational resources	11**	1.67	−2.74
	(3.60)	(2.72)	(3.75)
Extracurricular activities	4.53	0.96	−1.97
	(3.11)	(3.29)	(3.43)
Accountability			
To parents	−2.15	−4.29	8.52
	(7.69)	(5.36)	(6.09)
Achievement tracked	19.25**	6.12	3.32
	(5.98)	(8.49)	(8.80)
Achievement used to evaluate principal	2.37	−6.4	−5.69
	(9.84)	(10.16)	(9.99)
Governance			
Autonomy over resource allocation	10.28*	0.98	−0.85
	(4.41)	(2.77)	(5.49)
Autonomy over curriculum	3.9	3.39	−0.21
	(3.15)	(2.50)	(3.84)
School leadership	5.63	7.54	3.86
	(4.32)	(4.12)	(3.71)
Teacher participation	0.11	3.64	5.12*
	(2.35)	(2.21)	(2.12)
Background controls			
Female	−17.51***	31.33***	−7.25
	(5.09)	(4.68)	(4.11)
Wealth	−9.70**	−8.04**	−9.93***
	(2.95)	(2.36)	(2.52)
Home education resources	7.24*	9.71***	12.78***
	(2.67)	(2.03)	(2.29)
Home cultural possessions	9.99***	8.55***	8.64***
	(2.76)	(2.39)	(2.42)
Parental education	−0.09	0.65	0.74
	(1.20)	(0.78)	(1.11)
Preschool for at least one year	12.21	9.28*	8.45
	(6.50)	(4.61)	(6.11)
Remedial	−22.06*	−21.98*	−12.60
	(8.17)	(8.92)	(15.99)
Enrichment	12.05	−18.54	−12.06
	(9.70)	(12.91)	(13.28)
R^2	0.18	0.27	0.15
Number of observations	1,063	1,063	1,063

Source: OECD 2010b.
Note: Standard errors in parentheses. All models control for grade level, student background characteristics, and participation in enrichment and remedial classes. *** $p < 0.001$, ** $p < 0.01$, * $p < 0.05$.

higher-performing schools from lower-performing schools, especially at the upper secondary level. The experience of Shanghai has not only demonstrated the importance of abundant investment in educational resources in schools, but more importantly, it has pinpointed the specific areas in which resources can most efficiently be put into use. Resources could be invested in quality instructional resources and facilities, such as laboratories, teaching materials, computers and the Internet, and libraries. Additional investments could be made in organizing extracurricular activities, ranging from student choirs and volunteering activities to arts and sports.

Other critical elements of school resources include abundant teacher resources, high teacher qualifications, and supportive student-teacher relations. Resources could be invested in hiring qualified teachers and in providing teacher training. In addition, Shanghai's experience also suggests that teacher involvement in decision-making about school governance, including resource allocation and curriculum, might be beneficial for both general high schools and vocational schools.

Privatization could be an option to mobilize resources and improve quality even at the middle school level. Private middle school students in Shanghai perform better on PISA than public middle school students, even after controlling for family background and school admission criteria. The better performance measured near the end of middle school suggests the better quality of private middle schools in Shanghai, rather than the competencies of students prior to entering middle school.

PISA Shanghai also suggests the benefits of pre-primary education on students' later academic paths and cognitive skills development. The positive effects of preschool attendance remain significant even after accounting for school-level characteristics. In particular, middle school students who have attended pre-primary school for at least one year do consistently better in all subjects than those who have not. As middle school performance predicts student stratification into the general or vocational track and into the higher-or lower-performing high schools, early childhood development is critical in providing an important foundation for cognitive skill development.

In light of lessons from Shanghai PISA, the low levels of resource input and limited coverage of pre-primary education in Yunnan might put Yunnan's children at a disadvantage for the later development of important skills. In 2009, the 3,790 kindergartens in Yunnan provided pre-primary education to nearly 1 million children, more than double the enrollment in Shanghai of 400,000. However, with a per student expenditure of Y2,031, Yunnan has the lowest level of spending on pre-primary education after Guangxi, Hebei, and Anhui (figure 7.4). Although Shanghai has popularized pre-primary education for children aged three to six, enrollment rates in pre-primary schools remain low and vary greatly within Yunnan. Half of the 16 cities and prefectures have enrollment rates lower than the provincial average of 60 percent (figure 7.5). Kunming has the highest enrollment with nearly 88 percent.

Figure 7.4 Per Student Expenditure at the Pre-Primary Level, Yunnan

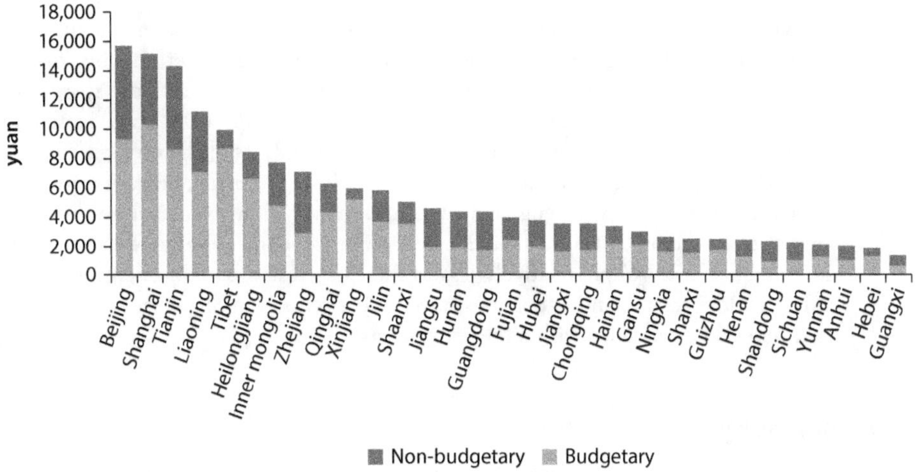

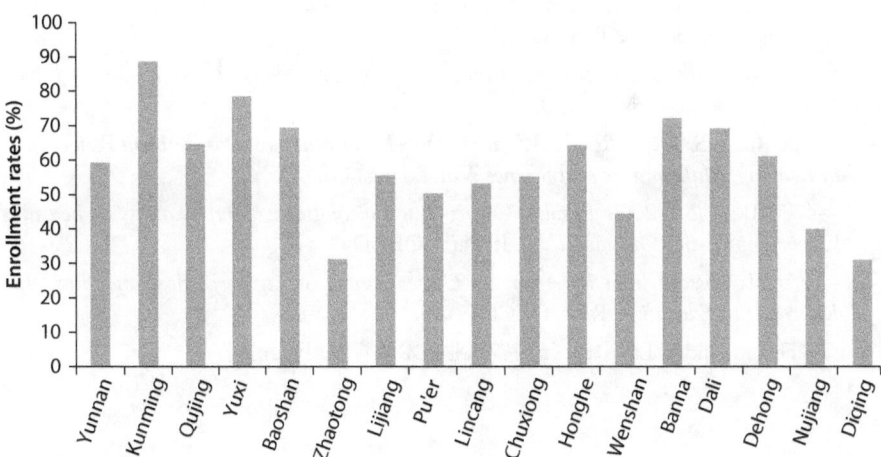

Source: China Education Expenditure Statistical Yearbook 2010.

Figure 7.5 Enrollment Rates in Pre-Primary Schools, Yunnan

Source: Yun, Liu, and Li 2011.

Notes

1. A student is classified as resilient if he or she is in the bottom quarter of the PISA index of economic, social, and cultural status (ESCS) in the country of assessment and performs in the top quarter across students from all countries after accounting for socio-economic background.
2. A student is classified as a disadvantaged low achiever if he or she is in the bottom quarter of the PISA index of ESCS in the country of assessment and performs in the bottom quarter across students from all countries after accounting for socio-economic background.

http://dx.doi.org/10.1596/978-1-4648-0079-5

3. As measured by the slope and strength of the socio-economic gradient. See OECD 2010c.
4. A major limitation in using the PISA data is the selection bias. Because students were stratified into different upper secondary schools based on their performance on the high school entrance examination before the PISA was administered, the score variance we observe in PISA on the upper secondary level is more likely an indication of the students' prior performance than the result of the effects of the upper secondary schools that the students attend. Nonetheless, because, in general, higher performing schools admit better performing students, our data still allow us to analyze the more competitive schools that attract higher performing students. The same issue affects the middle school sample relatively less as the PISA test was administered near the end of middle school, and admissions into middle schools in Shanghai are based on neighborhood attendance with a few exceptions.

Bibliography

Bertschy, K., M. A. Cattaneo, and S. C. Wolter. 2009. "PISA and the Transition into the Labour Market." *LABOUR* 23 (s1): 111–37.

National Bureau of Statistics of China. 2010. *China Education Expenditure Statistical Yearbook*. Beijing: China Statistics Press.

OECD (Organisation for Economic Co-operation and Development). 2009. *PISA 2009 Assessment Framework*. Paris: OECD.

———. 2010a. *Pathways to Success: How Knowledge and Skills at Age 15 Shape Future Lives in Canada*. Paris: OECD.

———. 2010b. *PISA 2009 Results: What Students Know and Can Do—Student Performance in Reading, Mathematics and Science*. Vol. I. Paris: OECD.

———. 2010c. *PISA 2009 Results: Overcoming Social Background—Equity in Learning Opportunities and Outcomes*. Vol. II. Paris: OECD.

———. 2011. *Lessons from PISA for the United States, Strong Performers and Successful Reformers in Education*. Paris: OECD.

Yun, B., H. Liu, and Y. Li. 2011. 云南省职业技术教育发展研究报告.

CHAPTER 8

Conclusions and Policy Implications

As in many parts of the world, the economy and labor market of Yunnan, China, exhibit an increasing demand for both strong, high-level technical skills and noncognitive skills, such as communication, problem solving, and teamwork. Upper secondary and tertiary level education are critical to ensuring that Yunnan's workers gain these skills.

The demand is driven by various factors. First, the human development stock in Yunnan is relatively weaker in these skills than in the rest of China. The relatively short supply of well-educated and high-skilled labor is creating pent-up demand, in particular in the context of the rapid economic development and increasing globalization of the last three decades.

At the same time—and unique to China—the central and provincial economic development strategies and their associated investments in key economic sectors have become strong drivers for the acquisition of more and better worker skills. China is determined to transform itself from a "world-factory" into a "high-tech, high-quality" producer of goods and services. As such, it recognizes the importance of upgrading worker skills in ensuring a better-skilled labor force. Yunnan, as a strategic border province, benefitted from the central government's Bridgehead Strategy and related investments. Strong demand for higher skills is also driven by technological changes associated with the modern production process and the expanding service sector.

In addition to the skills shortage, albeit to a lesser degree, Yunnan also exhibits skills mismatches, as evidenced by unfilled job vacancies in the midst of unemployment, as well as by feedback from employer surveys. It is important to keep in mind that skills gaps and mismatches result from an imbalance in the demand and supply of skills and are indeed normal. Skills gaps and mismatches tend to exist in almost all countries, developing and developed. What is most important is to recognize is the need to reform education and training systems so that they are responsive to the ever-changing demands from the economy and society at large.

This report does not attempt to analyze factors that cause bottlenecks in the labor market itself, such as *hukou* (household registration), minimum wage policy, and pension portability, all of which may contribute to the mismatch of skills. Rather, the report closely examines Yunnan's education and training system and its capacity to be responsive to the labor market and supply sufficient quantity and quality of skilled labor.

Both the Chinese government and the provincial government of Yunnan demonstrate a strong commitment to education and training. Our analysis reveals the remarkable progress Yunnan has made in the last three decades in improving various aspects of its education and training system, including formal TVET education, non-formal training, work-based training, and general education. A relatively higher proportion of gross domestic product and the government budget has been spent on education and training in Yunnan than in most other provinces.

Technical and Vocational Education and Training (TVET) is one of the most important means of providing sought-after skills to Yunnan's workforce. The most recent vision and policy direction outlined in the national and provincial Medium- and Long-Term Education Development Plan calls for; establishing closer partnerships between industry and TVET; improving teacher quality; creating pathways that allow students more flexibility to move between TVET and general education—thus improving the attractiveness of TVET; and emphasizing rural skills development. These are all important steps that will help create a more conducive environment for effective TVET.

Our analyses reveal certain policy gaps that may have hampered Yunnan's system from operating at its full potential. Admittedly the Chinese education and training system is vast and complicated. Any reform effort, such as curriculum reform and teacher training, will have enormous resource implications. Developing and implementing a set of centralized policies poses enormous challenges, especially for a resource-constrained province like Yunnan.

Globally, nations and sub-national governments (regions, provinces, and so on) are responding to the skills demands and challenges in various ways, both within and beyond the education and training sector. Drawing on global trends, we offer the following policy suggestions to help Yunnan strengthen its current efforts in skills development and achieve a demand-driven, high-quality education and training system.

Basic cognitive skills are the foundation for higher-level technical skills and socially important values. For many, particularly those in lower-income countries with limited access to primary education, the key to strengthening skills development may lie in improving the quality of basic education. In the Chinese context, however, we take for granted that there has been near 100 percent enrollment in nine-year basic education. Although there continues to be great variation in quality, in general the Chinese system has achieved marvelous results in basic education. Internationally, Shanghai is recognized as the number one system, producing the highest average Programme for International Student Assessment (PISA) score with the least variation. Our recommendations for strengthening the skills supply system therefore focus more on improving the skills development system beyond basic education, specifically formal TVET, non-formal education, and work-based training.

We also identify pre-primary education as another area worthy of policy attention for Yunnan, not only because it is currently not yet part of compulsory education, but, more importantly, because evidence suggests that investment in pre-primary education has a significant payoff in cognitive skills later in life, as our analysis of Shanghai PISA demonstrates.

Some policy areas, such as governance and coordination, industry participation, financing, and quality assurance cut across sectors. They pertain not just to the formal TVET system, but also to non-formal education, and even to work-based training. Sector-specific recommendations for non-formal training, work-based training—especially for small and medium-sized enterprises—and pre-primary education follow.

Implications for Cross-Subsector Issues

Governance and Coordination

The effective functioning of all subsectors could be improved by greater coordination among the relevant stakeholders in government, education, and industry.

In the short and medium term, it is feasible to develop and strengthen the role of existing coordination mechanisms, such as the Interdepartmental TVET Coordination Committees. Areas such as policy development, planning, and service delivery at both the provincial and local levels should be addressed. It is important to revitalize Yunnan's committee and regularize its operations.

In the long term, Yunnan might consider consolidating policymaking, planning, financing, and service delivery of TVET into a central government agency, such as a new Skills Development Authority, or into one of the existing ministries. This would eliminate the distinction between schools governed by the Department of Education and those governed by the Department of Human Resources and Social Security, as Shanghai has already done for its secondary TVET institutions.

Consolidated governance and management may be even more pertinent for non-formal training, which currently appears even more fragmented and less structured. The strongly vested interests of various stakeholders in this sector may mean that consolidation will be a long-term effort.

Industry Participation

Industry and employer involvement can play a key role in ensuring that the educational and training system, especially at the TVET level, is responsive to the demand side of the skills equation. Though industry participation is still emerging, it has yet to be systematically incorporated into the governance structure of any of the education and training sectors. Industry involvement should be further institutionalized and expanded to include a diverse range of issues related to skills development, including setting skills development priorities, developing competency standards for skills certification, allocating resources, and making policies regarding work-based training. In many countries, employer- or industry-based bodies participate at different levels, providing advice, taking part in setting development strategies, voicing the needs and demands of the industry, and even exerting decision-making power.

At the school level, Yunnan could introduce a legal framework and implementation guidelines to promote school–industry collaboration. The framework and regulations should establish the rights and obligations of employers, schools, teachers, students, and all relevant stakeholders in the school–industry partnership.

Similar principles are applicable in the context of non-formal education and work-based training. For example, industry and employers could be more involved in managing work-based training funds, designing training programs, and assessing training participants.

Quality Assurance

Under an effective qualifications framework, skills certifications are demanded by employers and sought by students and employees. Certifications are accepted measures of competency and substantive learning. A well-developed framework could address both accreditation of providers and certification of learners.

The existing qualifications framework needs to be updated with standards and competencies that reflect the demands of the labor market. Competency standards should be based on input from industry, employers, education and training providers, and other stakeholders. An updated qualifications framework can also facilitate recognition of non-formal learning, integrating different kinds of non-formal education and training and improving their quality and efficiency. The qualifications framework should respect all forms of learning. It should assess learners based on competencies rather than credentials, and should not disadvantage one type of learning against another.

At the operational level, Yunnan must consider several important parameters as it develops its qualifications framework. For example, to what extent will Yunnan rely on the existing national framework in developing one specific to its provincial context? How will the coordinating entity be chosen and how will industry input be systematically incorporated into the development of the framework and each of the underlying standards? To what extent should the framework take into consideration regional and even international standards? It might be most feasible to develop a framework first in key industries with a mature, organized private sector before extending it to all sectors and occupations. Good examples can be found in Turkey, Australia, New Zealand, Hong Kong SAR, China, Singapore, and the European Union. Ultimately what is most important is the development of a consensus specific to the needs of Yunnan on the scope and depth of the framework and on the operational details.

Financing TVET

The targeted and efficient use of both public and private resources is critical in financing TVET. School resources appear insufficient in the current system, especially for secondary TVET—even though public expenditures are high when measured as a percentage of Yunnan's provincial gross domestic product and total government spending. Yunnan should explore ways to use its existing public resources more efficiently.

Returns to private financing of upper secondary and tertiary education are high, however, and continue to increase. Yunnan could mobilize more private resources to increase the level of investment in education and training, leading to even greater returns. Yunnan should be able to increase the relatively low level of private financing and provision in the current system, letting high-income households share the cost of education and training, while further diversifying and freeing up other sources of revenue for education and training. The Yunnan government's recent announcement of regulations and establishment standards for private TVET institutions is an important first step.

At the same time, more public resources could be directed toward promoting equity of financing and bridging gaps between rural and urban areas and between schools. With the current resource allocation, huge disparities exist in secondary TVET across cities and prefectures, and between urban and rural areas within Yunnan. Special funds for TVET tend to disproportionally benefit already stronger schools. Public finance should be targeted at helping TVET schools in disadvantaged localities, low-income families, and poor-performing schools with more resource constraints.

Monitoring and Evaluation

Monitoring and evaluation provide feedback on the extent to which policies have been implemented across the system, what outcomes have been achieved, and what interventions have been effective or ineffective in achieving the expected outcomes. The very fact that the monitoring system exists and works creates an incentive for local authorities and schools to implement required policies and adhere to standards. Evaluation findings can also be used to promote good practices within the system and replicate them on a wider scale.

Although our analyses identify certain policy gaps in Yunnan's skills development system and propose broad policy suggestions, to a large extent, many of the challenges and issues arise not from a lack of central policies but from a lack of consistent and full implementation of these policies, particularly in rural and disadvantaged areas. This suggests the need to invest further in the monitoring and evaluation of existing policies and programs. Commissioned special studies and ad hoc impact evaluations currently exist, but conducting routine monitoring and evaluation in a more systematic manner and with more sophisticated methodologies would be a big step forward.

In addition, the use of pilot and experimental programs, and an analysis of their results, is critical to ensuring the long-term health of the education and training system. China has been learning from other TVET systems around the world, but its unique social, cultural, and economic context makes the adoption of any imported good practice a challenge. Even within China, practices differ greatly among provinces. Policies and practices that are effective in Shanghai cannot be easily transplanted to Yunnan. Developing a Yunnan-style TVET system is the only choice, and the willingness to experiment and evaluate is key.

Implications for Subsector-Specific Issues

Non-Formal Training

China's industrial sector growth and economic development strategies have led to the need to retrain large numbers of rural workers outside the formal educational system for transfer to the secondary and tertiary sectors. In Yunnan, rural surplus labor amounts to a third of the total rural labor force. Yunnan's rural working-age population averages only seven years of education, and more than 85 percent of rural workers have received no training. Those who remain in the agricultural sector also need training in both higher-value-added agricultural activities and in technology to improve their productivity. Non-formal training is a critical means of implementing the necessary rural training.

Yunnan faces challenges in improving both the delivery and content of, and access to, non-formal training. *The design and implementation of non-formal training needs to be better informed by a needs assessment and demand analysis.* The forms of delivery and the content of training should be tailored to the specific needs and circumstances of training participants, such as rural laborers with relatively low levels of education and literacy, and the employers in the industrial sectors in which they may ultimately work.

An improved qualifications framework would provide a mechanism that enables non-formal training programs to lead to skills certification. Participation in non-formal training is hampered by barriers, such as the requirement of a minimum education level, a lack of awareness of the value of training, and the quality and relevance of the training itself. Encouraging both enterprises and workers to value skills certifications, and adding flexibility that accounts for prior work and life experience, can help overcome these barriers.

Public, private, and industry funding for non-formal training could be consolidated into a single fund. A set of transparent funding criteria for the disbursement of training funds would be necessary. To assure quality of training, the funding criteria should be outcome-based rather than input-based. Training vouchers would be another option, creating a competitive market for non-formal training while giving participants more choices.

Incentives and Technical Assistance for Work-Based Training

China's ambitious economic goals require a well-educated and highly-skilled labor force. Work-based training will be the means by which enterprises improve the skills and performance of their existing employees.

Employers are currently required to dedicate 1.5–2.5 percent of their wage bill to training, and Yunnan must ensure the effective implementation of this requirement. Other mechanisms that provide more incentives and quality assurance for work-based training should also be considered. Korea's Employment Insurance Scheme is a good example.

In addition to financial assistance, the government should provide technical and institutional assistance to facilitate the provision of work-based training, especially by small and medium-sized enterprises. Technical assistance is particularly needed in the areas of needs assessment, training design and implementation, and monitoring and evaluation. Institutional support might include organizing groups of small and medium-sized enterprises to reduce the cost of training design and delivery. Government can also systematically help firms build partnerships with training providers.

Pre-Primary Education
Yunnan could invest more heavily in and help popularize pre-primary education. Ample research demonstrates that early childhood development programs, such as nutrition and health services, parenting interventions, and center-based programs, can improve children's physical and cognitive development, as well as their social and emotional wellbeing. Data from the Shanghai PISA and other cross-national evidence show the benefits of early childhood education for children's later cognitive development. Currently, government investment and enrollment rates in pre-primary school and early childhood development programs in Yunnan are low. Investing in pre-primary education might be a relatively cost-effective way to improve the skill levels of a young generation.

APPENDIX A

Returns to Education and Skills

Table A.1 Estimates of Rates of Return to Education in Urban China

	1998	1995	2002	2007
Years of education	0.0324***	0.0432***	0.0705***	0.0610***
	(0.00132)	(0.00190)	(0.00287)	(0.00318)
Education level (reference group = junior secondary school)				
Less than primary school	−0.161***		−0.286**	0.156
	(0.0248)		(0.0942)	(0.222)
Primary school	−0.0836***		−0.130***	−0.0627
	(0.0114)		(0.0240)	(0.0580)
High school	0.0707***		0.0987***	0.111***
	(0.00812)		(0.0130)	(0.0237)
Secondary TVET	0.117***		0.211***	0.280***
	(0.0105)		(0.0148)	(0.0303)
Tertiary, non-university	0.172***		0.283***	0.455***
	(0.0129)		(0.0158)	(0.0263)
College and above	0.263***		0.361***	0.676***
	(0.0140)		(0.0201)	(0.0298)
Potential experience	0.0299***	0.0492***	0.0482***	0.0179***
	(0.00107)	(0.00170)	(0.00173)	(0.00269)
			−0.330*	
			(0.158)	
			0.000552	
			(0.0440)	
			0.116***	
			(0.0179)	
			0.260***	
			(0.0218)	
			0.422***	
			(0.0203)	
			0.574***	
			(0.0255)	
			0.0596***	0.0161***
			(0.00235)	(0.00273)
Potential experience squared	−0.000222***	−0.000724***	−0.00100***	−0.000274***
	(2.39e−05)	(3.81e−05)	(5.13e−05)	(6.00e−05)
			−0.00114***	−0.000295***
			(5.28e−05)	(6.00e−05)
Female	−0.0641***	−0.131***	−0.185***	−0.226***
	(0.00626)	(0.00954)	(0.0124)	(0.0157)
		−0.130***	−0.183***	−0.224***
		(0.00953)	(0.0124)	(0.0153)
Minority	0.0142	−0.0391	0.00177	−0.0565
	(0.0165)	(0.0241)	(0.0334)	(0.0740)
		−0.0247	−0.00429	−0.0675
		(0.0240)	(0.0333)	(0.0722)

table continues next page

Table A.1 Estimates of Rates of Return to Education in Urban China *(continued)*

	1998	1995	2002	2007
Ownership				
State-owned enterprise	−0.0644*	−0.0152	−0.0161	0.0248	0.0260	0.0607*	0.0633*
	(0.0313)	(0.0252)	(0.0251)	(0.0151)	(0.0151)	(0.0299)	(0.0292)
Urban collective	−0.142***	−0.263***	−0.252***	−0.180***	−0.180***	−0.0443	−0.0481
	(0.0320)	(0.0273)	(0.0273)	(0.0247)	(0.0245)	(0.0518)	(0.0506)
Government							0.228***
							(0.0324)
Institution							0.0451*
							(0.0207)
Constant	6.008***	6.663***	7.456***	7.787***	7.751***	8.334***	9.265***	10.02***
	(0.215)	(0.214)	(0.143)	(0.141)	(0.0741)	(0.0644)	(0.0994)	(0.320)
Observations	6,788	6,788	11,137	11,137	9,147	9,147	5,695	5,694
R^2	0.503	0.505	0.261	0.265	0.327	0.335	0.286	0.321
Number of provinces	17	17	11	11	12	12	9	9

Sources: CHIP 1988, 1995, 2002; RUMiC 2007.
Note: All models include fixed effects for sectors, cities, and provinces. Standard errors in parentheses. TVET = Technical and Vocational Education and Training. *** $p < 0.001$, ** $p < 0.01$, * $p < 0.05$.

Table A.2 Estimates of Rates of Return to Education in Urban Yunnan

	1988	1995	2002
Years of education	0.0337*** (0.00302)	0.0399*** (0.00535)	0.0717*** (0.00784)
Education level (reference group = junior secondary school)			
Less than primary school	−0.192** (0.0623)	−0.188 (0.294)	−0.948* (0.446)
Primary school	−0.0778** (0.0241)	−0.0915 (0.0566)	−0.0348 (0.0880)
High school	0.0462* (0.0227)	0.0876* (0.0398)	0.174** (0.0531)
Secondary TVET	0.137*** (0.0229)	0.171*** (0.0381)	0.224*** (0.0521)
Tertiary, non-university	0.202*** (0.0323)	0.213*** (0.0446)	0.430*** (0.0560)
College and above	0.265*** (0.0311)	0.320*** (0.0590)	0.584*** (0.0670)
Potential experience	0.0143*** (0.00243)	0.0570*** (0.00521)	0.0641*** (0.00742)	0.0549*** (0.00538)	0.0668*** (0.00755)
Potential experience squared	0.000147** (5.36e−05)	−0.000868*** (0.000117)	−0.000827*** (0.000124)	−0.00108*** (0.000164)	−0.00115*** (0.000168)
Female	−0.0373* (0.0156)	−0.0883*** (0.0261)	−0.0853** (0.0265)	−0.0624 (0.0318)	−0.0610 (0.0319)
Minority	0.0260 (0.0307)	−0.0454 (0.0371)	−0.0416 (0.0373)	0.0730 (0.0440)	0.0711 (0.0441)

table continues next page

Table A.2 Estimates of Rates of Return to Education in Urban Yunnan *(continued)*

	1988		*1995*		*2002*	
Ownership						
State-owned enterprise	0.0777	0.0596	−0.0750	−0.0865	−0.0866*	−0.0926*
	(0.130)	(0.130)	(0.0807)	(0.0813)	(0.0386)	(0.0386)
Urban collective	−0.0609	−0.0748	−0.247**	−0.258**	−0.336***	−0.339***
	(0.133)	(0.132)	(0.0894)	(0.0900)	(0.0643)	(0.0645)
Constant	6.106***	6.449***	7.467***	7.809***	7.713***	8.349***
	(0.259)	(0.255)	(0.145)	(0.128)	(0.281)	(0.266)
Observations	893	893	1,082	1,082	833	833
R^2	0.471	0.481	0.262	0.257	0.376	0.384

Source: CHIP 1988, 1995, and 2002.
Note: All models include fixed effect for sector and city. Standard errors in parentheses. TVET = Technical and Vocational Education and Training. *** $p < 0.001$, ** $p < 0.01$, * $p < 0.05$.

Table A.3 Description of the Weighted Analytic Sample from STEP Household Survey, Kunming, 2012

	Proportion (%)	Standard errors
Gender		
Male	51.99	0.0186951
Female	48.01	0.0186951
Level of education		
Less than primary school	0.37	0.0021799
Primary school	6.55	0.0105317
Middle school	27.73	0.0236402
High school	16.47	0.0145356
Secondary TVET	14.16	0.0121012
Tertiary, non-university	19.15	0.0168621
College and above	15.58	0.0191622
Sector		
Primary	1.26	0.0044776
Secondary	18.79	0.0218992
Tertiary	79.95	0.0223624
Occupation		
Managers	3.61	0.0064444
Professionals	16.38	0.0171537
Technicians and associate professionals	7.35	0.0131564
Clerical support workers	20.89	0.0148527
Service workers	24.99	0.0173865
Skilled agricultural, forestry, and fishery workers	0.61	0.0025663
Craft and related trades workers	7.07	0.0101211
Plant and machine operators, assemblers, and drivers	7.09	0.0100183
Elementary occupation	12.02	0.0154774

Source: STEP Household Survey 2012.
Note: TVET = Technical and Vocational Education and Training.

Table A.4 Estimates of Rates of Return to Education, Kunming, 2012

	Years of education	Level of education
Years of education	0.0802***	
	(0.00793)	
Less than primary		−0.0903
		(0.0958)
Primary		−0.0349
		(0.0737)
Upper secondary (general)		0.181***
		(0.0463)
Upper secondary (TVET)		0.222***
		(0.0551)
Tertiary, associate degree		0.457***
		(0.0582)
Tertiary, bachelor's and above		0.754***
		(0.0538)

table continues next page

Table A.4 Estimates of Rates of Return to Education, Kunming, 2012 *(continued)*

	Years of education	Level of education
Potential experience	0.00733	0.0161**
	(0.00463)	(0.00499)
Potential experience squared	–0.000187	–0.000398***
	(0.000102)	(0.000109)
Female	–0.107**	–0.0145
	(0.0319)	(0.0410)
Government agencies	0.182***	0.172***
	(0.0471)	(0.0461)
State-owned enterprises	0.153***	0.144***
	(0.0392)	(0.0390)
Constant	8.880***	9.522***
	(0.108)	(0.0638)
Observations	1,026	1,026
R^2	0.279	0.306

Source: STEP Household Survey 2012.
Note: All models control for sector-level fixed effect. Data are weighted. Standard errors in parentheses. TVET = Technical and Vocational Education and Training. *** $p < 0.001$, ** $p < 0.01$, * $p < 0.05$.

Table A.5 Rates of Return to Education by Gender, Ownership, and Ethnicity

China	1988	1995	2002	2007
Female × year	0.00855***	0.0200***	0.0286***	0.0104*
	(0.00)	(0.00)	(0.00)	(0.00)
Minority × year	–0.00318	0.00650	–0.00123	0.00868
	(0.01)	(0.01)	(0.01)	(0.03)
Ownership (reference group = other)				
SOE × year	–1.81%	–0.0407***	–0.0157**	–0.0404***
	(0.01)	(0.01)	(0.01)	(0.01)
Collective × year	–0.0188	–0.0332***	–0.0251*	–0.00286
	(0.01)	(0.01)	(0.01)	(0.02)
Government × year	n.a.	n.a.	n.a.	–0.0246**
				(0.01)
Institution × year	n.a.	n.a.	n.a.	–0.0185**
				(0.01)
Yunnan	**1988**	**1995**	**2002**	**2012[a]**
Female × year	–0.00317	0.0208*	0.0182	0.00220
	(0.01)	(0.01)	(0.01)	(0.00945)
Minority × year	0.00734	0.0147	–0.0253	n.a.
	(0.01)	(0.01)	(0.01)	

table continues next page

Table A.5 Rates of Return to Education by Gender, Ownership, and Ethnicity *(continued)*

China	1988	1995	2002	2007
Ownership (reference group = other)				
SOE × year	0.0541	−0.0238	−0.00626	−0.0130
	(0.05)	(0.03)	(0.02)	(0.0153)
Collective × year	0.0437	−0.00448	−0.0318	n.a.
	(0.05)	(0.03)	(0.03)	
Government × year	n.a.	n.a.	n.a.	0.0316*
				(0.0137)

Sources: Author's calculations using CHIP 1988, 1995, 2002; RUMiC 2007; STEP Household Survey 2012.
Note: Standard errors in parentheses. SOE = state-owned enterprise; n.a. = not applicable. *** $p < 0.001$, ** $p < 0.01$, * $p < 0.05$.
a. STEP Household Survey 2012 was administered only in Kunming.

Table A.6 Definitions of Variables Used in the Analysis, STEP Household Survey 2012

Variable	Definition
Cognitive skills	
Lengths of reading	Size of the longest document normally read at work
Never read at work	
2–10 pages	
11–25 pages	
More than 25 pages	
Numeracy	Level of numeracy skills used at work
Never use	
Easy	Measure or estimate, calculate prices, multiplication, division
Intermediate	Fractions, decimals, or percentages
Advanced	Algebra, geometry, trigonometry
Lengths of writing	Size of the longest document normally written at work
Never write	
2–10 pages	
11–25 pages	
More than 25 pages	
Think	Frequency of undertaking tasks that require at least 30 minutes of thinking at work
Never	
Less than once a month	
Less than everyday	
Everyday	
Technical skills	
Contact	Contact with people other than co-workers as part of the work
	1 = yes 0 = no

table continues next page

Table A.6 Definitions of Variables Used in the Analysis, STEP Household Survey 2012 *(continued)*

Variable	Definition
Computer	Use computer at work
	1 = yes 0 = no
Repair	Repair/maintain electronic equipment as part of the work
	1 = yes 0 = no
Operate	Operate or work with any heavy machines or industrial equipment
	1 = yes 0 = no
Freedom	On a scale of 1 to 10, how much freedom to decide how to do your work in your own way
	0 if self-rating is equal to or less than 2; 1 if greater than 2
Fluent in a foreign language	yes = 1 no = 0
Non-cognitive skills	Average of the items listed on the scale: 1 = almost never, 2 = some of the time, 3 = most of the time, 4 = almost always
Extraversion	Are you talkative?
	Do you like to keep your opinions to yourself? Do you prefer to keep quiet when you have an opinion? (reversed)
	Are you outgoing and sociable, for example, do you make friends very easily?
Conscientiousness	When doing a task, are you very careful?
	Do you prefer relaxation more than hard work? (reversed)
	Do you work very well and quickly?
Openness	Do you come up with ideas other people haven't thought of before?
	Are you very interested in learning new things?
	Do you enjoy beautiful things, like nature, art, and music?
Emotional stability	Are you relaxed during stressful situations? (reversed)
	Do you tend to worry? (reversed)
	Do you get nervous easily? (reversed)
Agreeableness	Do you forgive other people easily?
	Are you very polite to other people?
	Are you generous to other people with your time or money?

Source: STEP Household Survey 2012.

Table A.7 Estimates of Wage Returns to Cognitive and Technical Skills, Kunming, 2012

	Model 1	Model 2	Model 3	Model 4	Model 5
Cognitive skills					
Lengths of reading (reference = never read at work)					
2–10 pages	0.0898*	0.0972*	0.0949*	0.103*	0.0843
	(0.0449)	(0.0435)	(0.0426)	(0.0436)	(0.0431)
11–25 pages	0.127*	0.126*	0.138*	0.132*	0.124*
	(0.0565)	(0.0563)	(0.0540)	(0.0563)	(0.0547)
More than 25 pages	0.140*	0.103	0.105	0.103	0.0919
	(0.0651)	(0.0634)	(0.0615)	(0.0626)	(0.0619)
Numeracy (reference = do not use at work)					
Easy	0.0804	0.103*	0.0742	0.0989*	0.0768
	(0.0457)	(0.0449)	(0.0446)	(0.0445)	(0.0451)
Intermediate	0.0175	0.0162	0.0193	0.0112	0.0149
	(0.0488)	(0.0461)	(0.0440)	(0.0462)	(0.0449)
Advanced	0.114	0.0671	0.0602	0.0361	0.0297
	(0.0649)	(0.0594)	(0.0574)	(0.0603)	(0.0575)
Lengths of writing (reference group = do not write at work)					
2–10 pages	0.0518	−0.00738	−0.0269	−0.0126	−0.0292
	(0.0456)	(0.0449)	(0.0423)	(0.0442)	(0.0408)
11–25 pages	0.0776	−0.0220	−0.0327	−0.0258	−0.0356
	(0.0676)	(0.0650)	(0.0611)	(0.0640)	(0.0596)
More than 25 pages	0.355***	0.219*	0.181*	0.209*	0.173*
	(0.0934)	(0.0839)	(0.0810)	(0.0840)	(0.0777)
Think (reference = never)					
Less than once a month	0.0384	0.0106	0.0105	0.00328	0.0122
	(0.0371)	(0.0360)	(0.0354)	(0.0358)	(0.0353)
Less than everyday	0.104*	0.0722	0.0559	0.0592	0.0518
	(0.0443)	(0.0418)	(0.0416)	(0.0410)	(0.0405)
Everyday	0.254**	0.217**	0.180*	0.217**	0.199**
	(0.0883)	(0.0751)	(0.0702)	(0.0762)	(0.0741)
Technical skills					
Contact	−0.202***	−0.181***	−0.197***	−0.161**	−0.184**
	(0.0568)	(0.0509)	(0.0517)	(0.0525)	(0.0551)
Computer	0.212***	0.0973*	0.158***	0.108**	0.160***
	(0.0466)	(0.0413)	(0.0409)	(0.0412)	(0.0404)
Repair	0.00967	0.00345	−0.0192	0.0124	−0.00890
	(0.0444)	(0.0406)	(0.0396)	(0.0408)	(0.0412)
Operate	0.120	0.123	0.0890	0.0754	0.0620
	(0.0654)	(0.0634)	(0.0705)	(0.0623)	(0.0672)
Freedom	0.0313***	0.0280***	0.0244***	0.0287***	0.0226***
	(0.00623)	(0.00575)	(0.00549)	(0.00571)	(0.00542)
Foreign language	0.185***	0.107*	0.101*	0.115*	0.0917
	(0.0535)	(0.0482)	(0.0484)	(0.0491)	(0.0481)

table continues next page

Table A.7 Estimates of Wage Returns to Cognitive and Technical Skills, Kunming, 2012 *(continued)*

	Model 1	Model 2	Model 3	Model 4	Model 5
Controls					
Level of education		Yes	Yes	Yes	Yes
Sector				Yes	Yes
Occupations			Yes		Yes
Non-cognitive skills					Yes
Potential experience	Yes	Yes	Yes	Yes	Yes
Potential experience squared	Yes	Yes	Yes	Yes	Yes
Female	Yes	Yes	Yes	Yes	Yes
Observations	1,007	1,007	1,007	1,007	1,007
R^2	0.287	0.362	0.408	0.368	0.420

Source: Author's calculations using STEP Household Survey 2012.
Note: Standard errors in parentheses. *** $p < 0.001$, ** $p < 0.01$, * $p < 0.05$.

Table A.8 Estimates of Wage Returns to Non-Cognitive Skills, Kunming, 2012

Variables	Model 1	Model 2	Model 3	Model 4	Model 5
Non-cognitive skills					
Extraversion	−0.017	0.0192	0.0294	0.026	0.0175
	−0.0358	−0.0319	−0.0309	−0.0311	−0.0283
Conscientiousness	0.0827	0.0719	0.0473	0.069	0.0515
	−0.0502	−0.0445	−0.0395	−0.0442	−0.0404
Openness	0.174***	0.0805*	0.0810*	0.0843*	0.0666*
	−0.038	−0.0327	−0.0324	−0.0325	−0.0306
Emotional stability	−0.00502	0.0193	0.0139	0.0222	0.00809
	−0.0504	−0.0416	−0.0385	−0.0422	−0.0363
Agreeableness	0.0377	−0.0162	−0.00803	−0.0185	−0.0133
	−0.042	−0.0367	−0.0339	−0.0359	−0.0322
Controls					
Level of education		Yes	Yes	Yes	Yes
Sector				Yes	Yes
Occupations			Yes		Yes
Cognitive and technical skills					Yes
Potential experience	Yes	Yes	Yes	Yes	Yes
Potential experience squared	Yes	Yes	Yes	Yes	Yes
Female	Yes	Yes	Yes	Yes	Yes
Observations	1,007	1,007	1,007	1,007	1,007
R^2	0.13	0.3	0.355	0.311	0.42

Source: Author's calculations using STEP Household Survey 2012.
Note: Standard errors in parentheses.

References

CHIP (Chinese Household Income Project Series) [database]. ICPSR03012-v2. Inter-university Consortium for Political and Social Research [distributor], Ann Arbor, MI. http://www.icpsr.umich.edu/icpsrweb/DSDR/series/00243.

RUMiC (Longitudinal Survey on Rural Urban Migration in China) [database]. Institute for the Study of Labor, Bonn, Germany. http://idsc.iza.org/?page=27&id=58.

STEP (Skills Toward Employment and Productivity) Employer Survey. 2012. World Bank, Washington, DC.

APPENDIX B

Education and Training System in Yunnan

Table B.1 Number of Students Admitted, Enrolled, and Graduated in Yunnan, 2010

Type of school	Admissions	Enrollment	Graduates
Kindergarten	—	986,900	—
Primary school	669,300	4,352,084	736,946
General middle school	706,567	2,073,500	641,624
Vocational middle school	1,517	6,908	2,875
General high school	228,997	632,812	184,415
Specialized and vocational high school[a]	169,557	575,301	128,904
Secondary skilled-worker school	38,215	93,835	28,908
Regular higher education institution	140,966	439,042	95,379
Bachelor's degree	77,755	255,788	46,727
Associate degree	63,211	183,254	48,652

Sources: National Bureau of Statistics 2011; Yunnan Statistical Bureau 2011.
Note: — = not available.
a. Specialized schools and vocational high schools open admissions not only to middle school graduates of the current year, but also to anyone who has a middle school diploma or equivalent. Admissions here include only middle school graduates of the current year. Admissions of all students totaled 279,015.

Table B.2 Training Duration, Certification Rates, and Employment Rates by Training Providers in Yunnan, 2009

	Skilled-worker schools		Employment training centers		Non-public training agencies	
Number of agencies	36		94		676	
Total number of trainees	106,570[a]		143,231		477,188	
	Number	Percent	Number	Percent	Number	Percent
Duration of training						
Less than 6 months	—	—	110,735	77	39,355	8
6–12 months	—	—	3,456	2	9,594	2
Over 12 months	—	—	6,990	5	10,751	2

table continues next page

Table B.2 Training Duration, Certification Rates, and Employment Rates by Training Providers in Yunnan, 2009 *(continued)*

	Skilled-worker schools		Employment training centers		Non-public training agencies	
	Number	Percent	Number	Percent	Number	Percent
Graduates	69,645	100	121,181	100	427,415	100
Total certified	69,645	100	98,542	81	386,772	90
Junior (level 5)	38,140	55	90,265	74	204,196	48
Medium (level 4)	20,916	30	6,211	5	149,748	35
Senior (level 3)	8,358	12	1,936	2	27,113	6
Technician and senior technician (Levels 1 and 2)	2,231	3	130	0.11	5,715	1
Employment	—	—	91,757	76	325,662	76

Source: Yunnan Statistical Bureau 2010.
Note: — = not available.
a. Does not include students advancing from middle school.

Table B.3 Formal Technical and Vocational Education and Training Provision in Yunnan, 2010

Level of education	Number of institutions	Enrollment
Lower secondary		
Junior vocational	14	6,900
Upper secondary school		
Specialized secondary	91	290,000
Skilled-worker school	36	93,800
Vocational high school	184	279,600
Tertiary		
Tertiary specialized college	35	
Tertiary technical and vocational college	26	
Total tertiary		183,300

Source: Yun, Liu, and Li 2011.

Table B.4 Sources of Financing for Education in Yunnan and China, 2009

	China		Yunnan	
	Y, millions	Percent	Y, millions	Percent
Total	1,650,271	100	44,132	100
Fiscal allocation for education	1,223,109	74.12	37,283	84
Percent of gross domestic product		4		6
Budgetary allocation	1,141,930	69	36,012	82
Central	117,169	7	47	0.11
Local	1,024,762	62	35,965	82
Education surcharges at all levels of local government	73,738	4	1,116	3
Education surcharges	55,567	3	1,023	2
Local education surcharges	13,506	1	93	0.21
Local education fund	4,664	0.28	..	..

table continues next page

Table B.4 Sources of Financing for Education in Yunnan and China, 2009 *(continued)*

	China		Yunnan	
	Y, millions	Percent	Y, millions	Percent
Allocation by enterprise for enterprise-run schools	4,413	0.27	46	0.11
School-generated funds	3,028	0.18	110	0.25
Investment from sponsors of private schools	7,498	0.45	174	0.39
External donations	12,550	0.76	169	0.38
Income from undertakings	352,759	21.00	5,641	13.00
Miscellaneous fees portion	251,560	15.00	4,296	10.00
Other income	54,354	3.00	864	2.00

Source: National Bureau of Statistics 2010.
Note: .. = negligible.

Table B.5 Recurrent Budgetary Expenditures per Student by Level of Education, 2010

	Primary school	General middle school	General high school	Secondary TVET[a]	Regular higher education institution
China					
Personnel	3,083	3,800	3,438	3,374	5,227
Public	930	1,414	1,072	1,468	4,363
Total	4,012	5,214	4,510	48,420	9,590
Yunnan					
Personnel	2,484	3,187	3,289	2,875	3,909
Public	803	1,162	1,027	1,854	46,064
Total	3,286	4,349	4,316	4,728	8,515

Source: National Bureau of Statistics 2010.
Note: TVET = Technical and Vocational Education and Training.
a. Includes secondary specialized schools, vocational high schools, and skilled-worker schools.

Table B.6 Total and Rural Budgetary Expenditure per Student in Yunnan, 2009

	Primary school	General middle school	General high school	Vocational high school
Rural				
Recurrent	2,780	3,599	3,626	2,334
Public	587	9,256	800	398
Personnel	2,193	2,673	2,826	1,936
Infrastructure	160	558	78	n.a.
Total	2,940	4,157	3,704	2,334
Yunnan				
Recurrent	2,773	3,716	3,898	3,770
Public	585	995	877	1,097
Personnel	2,189	2,721	3,021	2,673
Infrastructure	154	595	96	190
Total	2,928	4,311	3,994	3,960

Source: National Bureau of Statistics 2010.
Note: n.a. = not applicable.

Table B.7 Per Student Expenditure in Yunnan and China, 2009

	Pre-primary		Primary school		Middle school		General high school		Secondary TVET		Bachelor's degree		Associate degree	
	Yuan	Percent	Yuan	Percent	Yuan	Percent	Yuan	Percent	Yuan	Percent	Yuan	Percent	Yuan	Percent
Yunnan														
Budgetary	1,208	60	2,928	81	4,311	89	3,993	64	4,438	61	9,859	58	5606	55
Nonbudgetary	823	40	688	19	554	11	2,227	36	2,871	39	7,123	42	4,519	45
Total	2,031	100	3,616	100	4,865	100	6,220	100	7,309	100	16,982	100	10,125	100
China														
Budgetary	2,240	57	3,425	82	4,538	82	3,912	55	4,548	57	10,561	50	5,411	45
Nonbudgetary	1,662	43	747	18	1,026	18	3,148	45	3,440	43	10,709	50	6,498	55
Total	3,902	100	4,172	100	5,564	100	7,060	100	7,988	100	21,270	100	11,909	100

Source: National Bureau of Statistics 2010.
Note: TVET = Technical and Vocational Education and Training.

Bibliography

National Bureau of Statistics. 2010. *China Education Finance Statistical Yearbook 2010*. Beijing: China Statistics Press.

———. 2011. *China Statistical Yearbook 2011*. Beijing: China Statistics Press.

Yun, B., H. Liu, and Y. Li. 2011. "云南省职业技术教育发展研究报告."

Yunnan Statistical Bureau. 2010. *Yunnan Labor Statistical Yearbook 2010*. Beijing: China Statistics Press.

———. 2011. *Yunnan Statistical Yearbook 2011*. Beijing: China Statistics Press.

APPENDIX C

Honghe Rural Labor Training Impact Evaluation

Table C.1 Tracing Households with and without Training in 2006

		2006		2007		2008		2009		2010	
		Number	Percent	Number	Percent	Number	Percent	Number	Percent	Number	Percent
Total number of households	Training	571	100	571	100	571	100	571	100	571	100
	No training	1,452	100	1,452	100	1,452	100	1,452	100	1,452	100
Households with transferred laborer	Training	79	14	72	13	98	17	128	22	95	17
	No training	101	7	111	8	147	10	160	11	151	10
To secondary sector	Training	18	3	10	2	24	4	25	4	16	3
	No training	37	3	29	2	52	4	59	4	59	4
To tertiary sector	Training	60	11	44	8	60	11	68	12	38	7
	No training	55	4	35	2	52	4	67	5	46	3
Inter-provincial	Training	1	0	2	0	3	1	6	1	1	0
	No training	1	0	4	0	5	0	6	0	9	1
Intra-provincial	Training	9	2	19	3	20	4	38	7	41	7
	No training	14	1	54	4	54	4	47	3	48	3

Source: Honghe Rural Household Survey 2006–10.

Technical Notes on Propensity Score Matching

Households with one or more members participating in training and those with none might differ in various ways that affect their income. Therefore, simply comparing the outcomes of the two groups might yield biased estimates of the training effect. In order to account for the nonrandom selection into training of participating households, we use propensity score matching estimators to control for the observable characteristics that might confound the relationship between training participation and income.

To implement propensity score matching, we first fit a logit model to estimate the propensity score for each household. The model includes all of the pretreatment covariates listed in appendix table C.2, as well as quadratic term

Table C.2 Selected Characteristics of Households with and without Training

	No training (percent)	Training (percent)	Chi^2
Ethnic minority village			***
No	16	51	
Yes	84	49	
Village distance to county town			***
Less than 2 km	1	0	
2–5 km	4	4	
5–10 km	4	16	
10–20 km	11	23	
More than 20 km	81	57	
Village geographic features			***
Plain	8	30	
Hilly	7	26	
Mountainous	85	43	
Highest education attainment of household members			***
Illiterate	7	1	
Primary	34	16	
Junior secondary	46	56	
Senior secondary	12	24	
Tertiary and above	1	2	
Having household members who are village cadre			***
No	91.39	83.01	
Yes	8.61	16.99	
	No training (mean)	Training (mean)	t-Test
Proportion of households in the village participating in training	0.05	0.83	***
2006 net income per person in the household (Y)	3061.15	4293.59	***
2006 household monthly agricultural net income (Y)	208.71	284.61	***
Proportion of young labor (aged 21–40) in the household	0.56	0.50	**
N	1,452	571	

Source: Honghe Rural Household Survey, 2006–10.
Note: *** $p < 0.001$, ** $p < 0.01$, * $p < 0.05$.

incomes, interaction terms of incomes with variables indicating whether the household is in a minority village, distance to county town, whether the household has a cadre member, and the highest educational attainment of the household, and interaction terms of the proportion of young laborers with variables indicating whether the household is in a minority village, distance to county town, whether the household has a cadre member, and highest educational attainment.

Then we perform one-to-one matching with replacement using *Matching*, a package in R (Sekhon 2011). We find matches for all 571 households in the treatment group, indicating a wide and representative common region of support. Results from balance check after matching is available upon request.

Matching then produces estimates for (1) average treatment effect for the treated (ATT)—the average training effect among the households who attend training; (2) average treatment effect (ATE)—the average training effect over the total population represented by the analytic sample; and (3) average treatment effect for the controls (ATC)—the extent of benefit that households with no training would have experienced had they attended training.

Bibliography

Honghe Rural Household Survey (database). Honghe Statistics Bureau and the Statistical and Mathematical College at the Yunnan University of Finance and Economics, Kunming, China.

Sekhon, J. S. 2011. "Multivariate and Propensity Score Matching Software with Automated Balance Optimization: The Matching Package for R." *Journal of Statistical Software* 42(7): 1–52.

APPENDIX D

PISA Shanghai

Table D.1 PISA Shanghai 2009 Sample Description

Program	Total
Middle school	
Middle school	1,716
Mixed secondary school	448
Upper secondary/general	4[a]
Middle school program total	2,168
Upper secondary general	
Upper secondary school	1,380
Vocational school	22[b]
Mixed secondary school	475
Upper secondary general total	1,877
Upper secondary vocational school	1,070
Total	5,115

Source: OECD 2010.
Note: a. Students attend lower secondary programs in an upper secondary school.
b. Students attend general upper secondary program in a vocational school.

Table D.2 Variables and Definitions Used in the PISA Analysis

Variables	Definitions
School characteristics	
Organizational	
Student-teacher ratio	Student-teacher ratio
Public	1 = public 0 = private
Competition from other schools	1 = at least one other school in this area that competes for students
Policy	
Academic admissions criteria	1 = always consider academic performance or feeder-school recommendation
Tracking	1 = ability grouping in all or some subjects
Teachers	
Student-teacher relations	Scale[a]
Tertiary qualifications	Percent of teachers with tertiary qualification
Teacher shortage	1 = teacher shortage in the designated subject
Climate	
Teacher behavior	Scale
Student behavior	Scale
Pressure from parents	1 = school faces constant pressure from parents
Resources	
Educational resources	Scale
Extracurricular activities	Scale
Accountability	
To parents	1 = school provides information to parents on their child's academic performance relative to other students in school, relative to national or regional benchmarks, or relative to students in the same grade in other schools
Achievement tracked	1 = achievement data tracked over time by an administrative authority
Achievement used to evaluate principal	1 = achievement data used in evaluation of principal's performance
Governance	
Autonomy on resource allocation	Scale
Autonomy on curriculum	Scale
School leadership	Scale
Teacher participation	Scale
Background controls	
Female	1 = female
Wealth	Scale
Home education resources	Scale
Home cultural possessions	Scale
Parental education	Scale
Preschool for at least one year	1 = attended pre school for at least one year
Remedial	1 = attended remedial classes in the designated subject
Enrichment	1 = attended enrichment classes in the designated subject

Source: OECD 2010.
Note: School characteristics are reported by school principals, except for student-teacher relations, which is reported by students. Background controls are reported by students.
a. The scale of choices that was constructed for each variable can be found in OECD 2012.

Table D.3 Comparison of Student Backgrounds by Type of School

Background characteristics	Middle school		High school		Vocational school		t-Test
	Mean	SE	Mean	SE	Mean	SE	
Female	0.47	0.01	0.55	0.01	0.48	0.03	***
Wealth	−1.33	0.06	−1.11	0.04	−1.45	0.04	***
Home education resources	−0.32	0.06	0.00	0.03	−0.30	0.05	***
Home cultural possessions	0.35	0.04	0.52	0.02	−0.03	0.05	***
Parental education	12.47	0.17	13.23	0.10	11.67	0.15	***
Preschool for at least one year	0.86	0.02	0.91	0.01	0.82	0.02	***
Enrichment in math	0.36	0.02	0.28	0.01	0.12	0.01	***
Enrichment in reading	0.19	0.01	0.08	0.01	0.07	0.01	***
Enrichment in science	0.09	0.01	0.11	0.01	0.06	0.01	**
Remedial math	0.50	0.02	0.35	0.02	0.16	0.02	***
Remedial reading	0.30	0.01	0.08	0.01	0.08	0.01	***
Remedial science	0.08	0.01	0.07	0.01	0.03	0.01	**

Source: OECD 2010.
Note: SE, standard error. *** $p < 0.001$, ** $p < 0.01$, * $p < 0.05$.

Table D.4 Comparison of Student Backgrounds in Model and Experimental High Schools and General High Schools

Background characteristics	Model and experimental		General		t-Test
	Mean	SE	Mean	SE	
Female	0.58	0.02	0.54	0.01	*
Wealth	−0.92	0.07	−1.32	0.07	***
Home education resources	0.18	0.03	−0.19	0.08	***
Home cultural possessions	0.69	0.04	0.38	0.04	***
Parental education	14.13	0.17	12.41	0.17	***
Preschool for at least one year	0.91	0.01	0.91	0.01	
Enrichment in math	0.31	0.03	0.22	0.02	
Enrichment in reading	0.07	0.01	0.07	0.02	
Enrichment in science	0.17	0.03	0.08	0.02	*
Remedial math	0.29	0.02	0.37	0.03	*
Remedial reading	0.06	0.01	0.08	0.02	
Remedial science	0.08	0.01	0.06	0.02	

Source: OECD 2010.
Note: SE, standard error. *** $p < 0.001$, ** $p < 0.01$, * $p < 0.05$.

Table D.5 Comparison of School Characteristics

	Middle school		High school		Vocational school		t-Test
	Mean	SE	Mean	SE	Mean	SE	
Organizational							
Student-teacher ratio	11.62	0.36	11.23	0.26	23.33	1.84	***
Public	0.81	0.02	0.93	0.01	1.00	0.00	***
Competition from other schools	0.83	0.05	0.82	0.06	0.92	0.04	
Policy							
Academic admissions criteria	0.29	0.05	0.90	0.03	0.59	0.08	***
Tracking	0.56	0.07	0.69	0.06	0.65	0.08	
Teachers							
Student-teacher relations	0.19	0.03	0.30	0.02	0.09	0.03	***
Tertiary qualifications (%)	86.35	0.02	97.47	0.01	92.71	0.01	***
Science teacher shortage	0.48	0.06	0.29	0.05	0.19	0.04	***
Math teacher shortage	0.43	0.06	0.27	0.05	0.23	0.06	*
Reading teacher shortage	0.37	0.06	0.26	0.06	0.31	0.08	
Climate							
Teacher behavior	−0.65	0.18	−0.49	0.19	−0.70	0.14	
Student behavior	0.30	0.23	0.51	0.20	−0.89	0.12	***
Pressure from parents	0.21	0.05	0.21	0.05	0.05	0.04	*
Resources							
Educational resources	0.04	0.17	0.21	0.13	0.27	0.18	
Extracurricular activities	0.39	0.10	1.53	0.11	1.02	0.16	***
Accountability							
To parents	0.87	0.04	0.86	0.04	0.52	0.07	***
Achievement tracked	0.84	0.05	0.76	0.06	0.26	0.09	***
Achievement used to evaluate principal	0.49	0.07	0.51	0.06	0.25	0.09	
Governance							
Autonomy over resource allocation	0.81	0.09	0.63	0.13	1.26	0.14	**
Autonomy over curriculum	−0.16	0.13	−0.46	0.11	0.59	0.17	***
School leadership	0.16	0.11	−0.02	0.07	−0.17	0.12	
Teacher participation	0.91	0.22	0.87	0.18	0.84	0.31	

Source: OECD 2010.
Note: SE, standard error. *** $p < 0.001$, ** $p < 0.01$, * $p < 0.05$.

Table D.6 Comparison of School-Level Characteristics of Model and Experimental vs. General High Schools

	Model and experimental		Ordinary		
	Mean	SE	Mean	SE	t-Test
Organizational					
Student-teacher ratio	11.05	0.31	10.68	0.56	
Public	1.00	0.00	0.91	0.01	***
Competition from other schools	0.80	0.10	0.74	0.12	
Policy					
Academic admissions criteria	1.00	0.00	1.00	0.00	
Tracking	0.85	0.09	0.50	0.13	*
Teachers					
Student-teacher relations	0.42	0.44	0.18	0.04	***
Tertiary qualifications (%)	99.62	0.16	98.81	0.68	
Science teacher shortage	0.15	0.09	0.35	0.09	
Math teacher shortage	0.10	0.07	0.35	0.11	
Reading teacher shortage	0.15	0.09	0.29	0.10	
Climate					
Teacher behavior	0.77	0.40	0.31	0.34	
Student behavior	−0.28	0.39	−0.57	0.29	
Pressure from parents	0.25	0.09	0.14	0.08	
Resources					
Educational resources	0.93	0.25	−0.33	0.17	***
Extracurricular activities	2.14	0.20	1.06	0.15	***
Accountability					
To parents	0.90	0.07	0.79	0.07	
Achievement tracked	0.70	0.12	0.83	0.09	
Achievement used to evaluate principal	0.70	0.23	0.47	0.24	*
Governance					
Autonomy over resource allocation	−0.28	0.18	−0.58	0.20	
Autonomy over curriculum	−0.15	0.11	−0.05	0.12	
School leadership	0.40	0.12	0.73	0.09	
Teacher participation	1.42	0.35	0.28	0.26	*

Source: OECD 2010.
Note: SE, standard error. *** $p < 0.001$, ** $p < 0.01$, * $p < 0.05$.

References

OECD (Organisation for Economic Co-operation and Development). 2010. PISA 2009 Results: What Students Know and Can Do—Student Performance in Reading, Mathematics and Science. Vol. I. Paris: OECD.

———. 2012. PISA 2009 Technical Report. Paris: OECD.

Environmental Benefits Statement

The World Bank is committed to reducing its environmental footprint. In support of this commitment, the Publishing and Knowledge Division leverages electronic publishing options and print-on-demand technology, which is located in regional hubs worldwide. Together, these initiatives enable print runs to be lowered and shipping distances decreased, resulting in reduced paper consumption, chemical use, greenhouse gas emissions, and waste.

The Publishing and Knowledge Division follows the recommended standards for paper use set by the Green Press Initiative. Whenever possible, books are printed on 50% to 100% postconsumer recycled paper, and at least 50% of the fiber in our book paper is either unbleached or bleached using Totally Chlorine Free (TCF), Processed Chlorine Free (PCF), or Enhanced Elemental Chlorine Free (EECF) processes.

More information about the Bank's environmental philosophy can be found at http://crinfo.worldbank.org/crinfo/environmental_responsibility/index.html.

www.ingramcontent.com/pod-product-compliance
Lightning Source LLC
Chambersburg PA
CBHW082120230426
43671CB00015B/2757